D0154361

Pre-Publication Reviews of

THE BIBLE *AS* THEATRE

by Shimon Levy

Shimon Levy, who teaches theatre at Tel Aviv University, has found a highly original new approach to the Bible: to treat the narrative portions of the Old Testament as dramatic texts that can by analyzed in terms of dialogue, stage directions, scenic design, gesture, plotline, dramatic tension, characterization, and all the other viewpoints applicable to dramatic texts.

Parts of the Bible, such as the Book of Job, have long been regarded as dramatic texts on a par with a Greek tragedy. But Shimon Levy's approach opens up a vast field of analysis. That is not to say that he thinks these texts can be performed without adaptation, he merely shows that, looked at as dramatic texts – and he deliberately refers to the authors of such texts as "the playwright" – they open up fascinating and very unusual perspectives on the role of women, both when depicted as despised pictures and as proto-feminist models, the prophets as performers, the nature of political leadership and, above all, the figure of God as the protagonist, on-stage and off-stage of all these dramas.

To these fascinating disquisitions Shimon Levy brings what must be a truly unique combination of total mastery of stagecraft and the vocabulary of dramatic criticism with an astonishing knowledge of the Bible and its Hebrew language.

This is a book to be read with the Bible at one's side: by treating these texts on a strictly factual, down-to-earth basis, with due reverence but without uncritical devotion, it not only deepens one's understanding of a multitude of cultural, social and historical aspects of its contents, but also re-tells these tremendous stories with riveting detail, emotion and suspense.

Martin Esslin

Shimon Levy's study *The Bible AS Theatre* is a fascinating study. Its consideration of a wide variety of Biblical materials from a dramaturgical point of view adds a rich new dimension to many familiar stories and brings fresh prominence and fresh perspectives to an even greater number of less familiar ones. Character relationships and motivations are explored in striking and memorable detail and the attention to the physical settings and symbolic properties that frame these actions provides illuminating contextualization. The consideration of how women are granted or denied a dramaturgical voice in these narratives produced in a masculine-dominated literary and cultural tradition is particularly interesting and well presented.

The dramatic potential of the stories of Job and Esther, and occasionally Daniel and a few other figures have been considered by previous scholars, with interesting and worthwhile results, but no previous study has considered so wide a range of Biblical material from a dramaturgical perspective, nor considered it so thoroughly and profitably as this. The book will be an important contribution both to Biblical and theatre studies.

Marvin Carlson, Sidney E. Cohn Professor of Theatre and Comparative Literature, CUNY Graduate Center, New York University

THE BIBLE *AS* THEATRE

And the Lord routed Sisera, and all his chariots, and all his host, with the edge of the sword before Barak, so that Sisera alighted from his chariot, and fled away on his feet.

But Barak pursued after the chariots, and after the host, unto Harosheth of the nations: and all the host of Sisera fell upon the edge of the sword; and there was not a man left.

Howbeit Sisera fled away on his feet to the tent of Jael, the wife of Heber, the Kenite; for there was peace between Jabin, the king of Hazor, and the house of Heber, the Kenite.

And Jael went out to meet Sisera, and said unto him, Turn in, my lord, turn in to me; fear not. And when he had turned in unto her into the tent, she covered him with a mantle.

And he said unto her, Give me, I pray thee, a little water to drink; for I am thirsty. And she opened a skin of milk, and gave him drink, and covered him.

Again he said unto her, Stand in the door of the tent, and it shall be, when any man doth come and inquire of thee, and say, Is there any man here? that thou shalt say, No.

Then Yael, Heber's wife, took a nail of the tent, and took a hammer in her hand, and went softly unto him, and smote the nail into his temples, and fastened it into the ground; for he was fast asleep and weary. So he died.

And behold, as Barak pursued Sisera, Jael came out to meet him, and said unto him, Come, and I will show thee the man whom thou seekest. And when he came into her tent, Sisera lay dead, and the nail was in his temples
(*Judges* 4:15–21)

The Bible as Theatre

SHIMON LEVY

sussex
ACADEMIC
PRESS

BRIGHTON • PORTLAND

2 4 6 8 10 9 7 5 3 1
First published 2000 in Great Britain by
SUSSEX ACADEMIC PRESS
PO Box 2950
Brighton BN2 5SP

and in the United States of America by
SUSSEX ACADEMIC PRESS
5804 N.E. Hassalo St.
Portland, Oregon 97213-3644

British Library Cataloguing in Publication Data
A CIP catalogue record for this book is available from the British Library.

Library of Congress Cataloging-in-Publication Data
Levy, Shimon, 1943–
The Bible as theatre / Shimon Levy.
p.   cm.
Includes bibliographical references and index.
ISBN 1–898723–50–8 (hc : alk. paper)
1. Bible as literature. 2. Theater—Religious aspects. 3. Narration in the Bible.
4.   Religion and drama.   5. Religion in drama. I. Title.
PN1650.B3 L48 2000
809'.93522—dc21   99–048949

Printed on acid-free paper
Printed by Bookcraft, Midsomer Norton, Bath

Contents

———

Preface *vii*
Introduction *1*

Contents

Preface

———

'Bible and Theatre' was originally the title for a seminar given at the Tel Aviv University Theatre Department in 1995, with the assumption that Israeli students of drama find it relatively easy to read the Old Testament. The differences between the language of the Old Testament and modern Hebrew are smaller than between Classical and modern Greek, or between medieval and modern English. But even native speakers of modern Hebrew (often called 'Israeli') are frequently confused by the original, ancient meaning of the apparently recognizable words. We often think we have understood the 'inner form' of biblical Hebrew, whereas what we have really grasped is only the 'external form'. This partial misunderstanding, however, does not prevent Israelis from both conceiving and experiencing the Old Testament text as 'theirs': a quaintly familiar cultural affinity, even for the secular theatre students, who are in the majority.

Israeli students are exposed to the cultural background necessary for the understanding of Classical Greek plays, of English (Shakespeare), French (Moliere), Spanish (Lorca) or German (Brecht) plays, mostly in Hebrew translation. In the 'Bible and Theatre' course, however, we went from culture to theatricality rather than the other way round, examining our own cultural background and exploring its theatrical potential. We were obliged to ignore the text's own warning against the idolatry of theatricality: "Thou shall not make any graven image . . ." – a disregard that did not pose a difficult task for the majority of non-religious students.

Whereas the impact of the Old Testament on world and Hebrew drama has been given a fair amount of critical attention, the core problem has hardly ever been researched: What is theatrical – not only 'dramatic' – in the Old Testament itself? Consequently, the title of the seminar was changed to 'The Bible AS Theatre'. The predominantly theatrical approach illuminated certain obscure points, and exposed hidden layers in the texts. Among others, we learned that some biblical narratives and poetry do not lend themselves as easily as others (or at all) to the same theatrical method-

———

ological treatment. We also discovered that a number of current method-
ologies (e.g. Marxist, psychoanalytical, semiotic, structuralist etc. and
their derivatives) of theatre research demand dusting, change and renewal,
at least in regard to biblical texts.

A theatrical dialogue with the Bible was initiated, in the course of which
we studied theatricality itself through the book, and vice versa. Trying out
a number of verses, excerpts and stories, using voice, movement and some
basic *mise-en-scène*, proved helpful in supporting the mainly theoretical
approach with some practical aspects. In fact, we discussed and tried out
many more biblical scenes than this book is able to include. Among the
numerous excerpts not dealt with here, are the highly theatrical relationships between Jacob and his four wives; the Dinah story in *Genesis* 34;
Jeremiah's initiation (1:4-10); the initially explosive dramatic situation of
Job (regarded by sixteenth-century Hebrew playwright Leone Di Sommi
as 'the first Hebrew drama'); the story of David and Goliath; Lot and his
daughters, who bore their own father's children in the fear that they are
the very last people on Earth – and even some of the laws, such as *Leviticus*
12:1-8; the creation of Man/Woman stories, etc. I am truly grateful to my
students for their enthusiastic participation and invaluable contribution
to this book.

In June 1996 the FIRT (IFTR: International Federation of Theatre
Research) World conference was hosted by the Tel Aviv University
Theatre Department, under the title 'Holy Script and Theatre', which I
suggested as a fitting tribute to the hosting Holy Land. As a pre-confer-
ence project, theatre scholars were invited to participate in a 'Bible *As*
Theatre' workshop, and to examine whether and how biblical texts can
actually be performed 'as written', without any distortion or adaptation.
Twenty-five academics, including theatre practitioners, signed up for the
adventure. The area chosen was an arid, rocky landscape, located 900
meters above sea level at the upper edge of the Ramon Crater in the Israeli
Negev desert. Having recovered from the initial shock of the encounter
with the silence of the desert, which practically erased all the anticipatory,
pre-conceived 'how-do-we-do-it' notions, we began to work with an
astounding degree of openness, modesty and enthusiasm. The 'empty'
space, the wind and the unique light offered themselves as a vast inspiring
stage. The result was not only the expected (under the unique circumstances of nature and group dynamics) emotional experience for these
academics, most of whom did not even know one another, but an exhil-
arating intellectual experience as well.

The 'Holy Script and Theatre' participants came from fifteen different
countries, ranging from Korea and China through Europe to the United
States. They brought their own favorite Bible excerpts, which were treated

in the desert (texts and participants alike) according to three main aspects. The first was to make an as objective as possible linguistic, literary, dramatic and finally theatrical analysis of the verses, based on their original Hebrew, because all Bible translations are imprecise by definition. The second aspect was a deliberately subjective-personal dialogical attempt to communicate with the chosen text, using 'Playback-theatre' technique, and asking questions like: how do I interpret myself through the (ancient, religious, emotional, relevant, mythical, etc.) text; how does the text interpret itself through me? The third stage was the actual acting-out of the piece, as a monologue, dialogue or group work, in different natural-theatrical environments such as a hill-top, a plateau; at sun-rise, sunset or at night. Various modes of movement and voice production were experimented with, as well as some shawls as improvised costumes.

After three days of theatricalizing the Bible, the unique circumstances caused all of the resulting exercises, to be, at the very least, 'interesting'. Some of these little shows, moreover, had a genuinely powerful impact, and it was felt that the desert had truly inspired the performers. None of the under-rehearsed performances suffered from the mutually complementary 'kitsch or pathos' syndrome, so typical to holy shows, real or pseudo. Back in Tel Aviv and ready for the large, and purely academic conference, a number of question marks still hovered restlessly in the air: What might happen to such biblical texts if they were to be performed on a traditional indoor stage, rather than in the kitsch-resistent desert? Would the desert-workshop be as effective if we had tried out works by Beckett or Shakespeare instead of biblical texts?

In the two years that followed I have conducted about a dozen further workshops in Israel, Germany and Holland with professional actors, teachers and theatre students. Some of these workshops, like that held at the University of Groningen, resulted in a modest production. In the summer of 1997 a small international group was formed in Basel, Switzerland, to work on *Meine Schwester, Meine Braut* ('My Sister, My Bride'), concentrating on female characters in the Old Testament, like the story of Tamar and Judah in *Genesis* 38, the killing of Sisera by Jael in *Judges* 4–5, and some of the complex links between Leah, Rachel, Silpah and Bilha – Jacob's wives (*Genesis* 29). The show traveled successfully in Germany and Switzerland.

To conclude these brief personal notes of introduction, it should be borne in mind that the Old Testament was not intended only for silent reading, but also to be read aloud in public. In this respect it can easily be regarded as 'dramatic', or 'theatrical', and certainly performative, concerning communication with an audience, for example. Ezekiel's oral prophesies or Deborah's Song were actually performed in the old days, and as such are clearly theatrical. Moreover, the Hebrew Bible has been read aloud in synagogues for hundreds of years, indeed as a holy ritual and an educational weekly event. Casting a modern look at the theatricality of the Bible is, consequently, not intended to deprive it of its holiness, but to focus on its theatrical expressive means. Some chapters and stories are evidently more 'theatrical' than others, but theatricality, I believe, ensues from modes of presentation rather than from content.

Without arguing that there was a direct Classical Greek influence on Old Testament theatricality, I do use a number of theatrical terms such as *hubris* and *anagnorisis*, because they are familiar dramatic terminology, and universally applicable even outside their indigenous environment. This book focuses on the theoretical aspects of the intrinsic potential of biblical theatricality, and explores the 'stage directions' that are often built into biblical texts. It is important to add, however, that an extensive practical artistic experience has indicated that certain biblical texts really work on a modern stage, without being changed, adapted or distorted. In addition to casting a contemporary look at ancient texts, I also discovered that a theatrical perspective in reading the Old Testament may contribute a healing effect, of which modern theatre is in dire need.

To
Lucia

Introduction

"Not the Mandate is our Bible, but the Bible is our Mandate", declared Zionist leader and Israel's first Prime Minister David Ben-Gurion, who appeared before the British Peel committee in 1937. After the British Mandate ended and the State of Israel was established in 1948, the Ministry of Education attempted to present the Old Testament indeed as a historical Mandate, a secular-national text, an ancient promise now fulfilled. As an important aftermath of the Holocaust, "the Bible is our Mandate" declaration gained an extra power of conviction. As a predominantly secular movement, the Zionist attitude toward the Old Testament had been problematically ambivalent long before 1948. Until the nineteenth century, traditional Jewish scholarship interpreted the Hebrew Bible primarily as a religious text, in which God, and His unique relations with the People of Israel, is the main protagonist. Since the beginning of this century, and following Wellhausen's critical approach in his *Prolegomena zur Geschichte Israels* (1876), Zionist ideology too has presented the Old Testament indeed as a Jewish text, re-appropriated however to the secular national ethos.[1] The young Israeli generation was taught to read the Old Testament in the country about and in which it had been written; to learn the linguistic sources and various layers of biblical Hebrew; and to internalize the moral, rather than religious values of the "Book of Books", in order to succeed to the cultural right over the country together with its geography and politics. The Old Testament was understandably conceived as the ultimate proof of belonging – culturally, nationally, linguistically and geographically, though not religiously – in the traditional Jewish sense. In the footsteps of the Jewish nineteenth-century Enlightenment movement, the Hebrew Bible was read in the context of a new and hopeful interpretation for social and political changes in the twentieth century.

As long as most Jews were dispersed in their many places of Exile, namely 'not *here* in the desired space', the biblical 'place' too was imagined from 'there'. Once back home, the 2000-year yearned-for space of the Old

Testament itself became a physical reality. At the same time, it was also conceived as a retrieved map to be superimposed on the geographical landscape, indeed a practical guidebook for finding hidden cultural treasures and overt indications of Israeli (rather than 'Jewish') identity. If, regretfully, many ancient biblical remnants are covered by layer upon layer of other cultures that have also left their mark in the Land of *Our* Fathers, we shall dig as deep as necessary, and expose 'ourselves' and the signs of our identity signs in the profundity of 'here'. In modern Israeli myths, Time sometimes reveals the tendency to replace Space. As a tiny country inhabited by a highly heterogeneous people, the Israeli collective consciousness is burdened – or blessed – with an immense historical perspective. Israeli archeology is hence an understandably unique local quest for identity, in which time is transposed into space, squeezed into small and immensely significant pieces of land, 'soil', 'dust' and 'earth'. Moreover, early Israeli biblical archeology has shown a tendency to replace the 'Jewish' spiritual quest of the long years in the Diaspora with an Israeli, local and material 'hard-proof'. Political Zionism has explored, read, and imposed the 'facts', rather than their traditional metaphysical and religious justifications.[2]

Like the Old Testament and its 'space', which was rediscovered and interpreted in the first years of Jewish settlement in the country, theatre too needs a 'space' in which to exist. Halachic religious Judaism had long held a theatre-hating and theatre-phobic tradition, and theatre was practically a non-existent medium of art for the majority of tradition abiding Jews throughout the ages. Many free-thinking Jews, nevertheless, began to be active theatre practitioners, especially in Europe, from the beginning of the nineteenth century. Reinstated in 'Our Land', mainly as a result of non- or even anti-religious motivations, theatre, like the Bible, was discovered and intensively (re-)introduced into the newly developing culture. It was not only treated as an art, but employed as an ideological vehicle to educate native Sabras, new immigrants and the young generation alike.

Other than the re-appropriation (or relocation), common to the employment of both theatre and the Hebrew Bible in the Zionist ethos, the Old Testament has beyond doubt strongly influenced innumerable plays in world as well as Hebrew drama, written and performed in the footsteps of the infinitely rich Old Testament figures and situations. Rather than dealing with the direct and indirect influence of the Old Testament on drama, however, this book explores the Old Testament *from a theatrical perspective*, with the intention of illuminating the intrinsic theatrical qualities in the biblical texts themselves. The approach offered is predominantly medium oriented and 'theatrical', rather than genre oriented and 'dramatic'.

While the Greeks celebrated their three-day drama festivals in the fifth century BCE, the Jews, back from their Babylonian Exile, were busy rebuilding the ruins of the Temple in Jerusalem under the leadership of Ezra and Nehemiah. The differences between the Greek culture that produced drama and the equally dramatic Hebrew myths that did not, have indeed occupied Israeli scholars. Leibowitz argues that Job – an amazingly dramatic figure – fears God "for its own sake" (a Rabbinic expression), because for Job the meaning of Creation is incomprehensible, since Creation is divine.[3] Kurtzweil answers the question unambiguously: "The dramatic description of biblical themes can be legitimate only for those who believe in a sacred reality, as described in the Holy Scriptures."[4] The problem, he rightly adds, is that those people who do hold such a belief would not be interested in a mere dramatization or stage imitation of the sacred reality. Jewish 'sacral' reality thus found its expression in traditional rituals, never on a secular stage. Interestingly, the Hebrew word 'bamah' means 'an altar' (usually for idolatrous purposes) in biblical Hebrew, but translates as 'a stage' in modern Hebrew. While this study is not performed from a traditional Jewish perspective, it does take the inherent biblical religious belief very seriously.

Judaism has opposed theatre not so much because of its alleged (and real) 'lasciviousness', but because theatre at its best may present an alternative reality to the Sacred itself. If words and gestures, as in the Samuel initiation scene, are conceived as performative (i.e., neither true nor false), they *create* a reality rather than *describe* one. According to Jewish tradition, however, there is only one Creator. In Schechner's terms, Judaism can be said to dread the efficacious aspects of theatricality much more than its entertaining functions.[5] This observation separates Judaism (and the theatricality of the Hebrew Bible) not only from the Classical Greek world of drama, because the Greeks treated performatives in a different way,[6] but from Christianity as well. "A Christian Redemption contradicts the idea of tragedy", says Jaspers,[7] but even if Christian tragedy does not exist, Christian drama has been with us for hundreds of years. Transubstantiation appears in Christian theatre as endless metamorphoses of matter into spirit, spirit into matter. For biblical texts in their traditional Jewish interpretations (at least after Christianity became stronger and much more hostile towards Judaism), – this is hardly possible. For Judaism, the implicit or overt Christian aspirations to enlist the corporeality of the theatre stage for spiritual purposes or even to allow the stage to create 'new realities', are equally unacceptable. It should nevertheless be added that the more mystical trends in Judaism were less harshly opposed to theatricality.

A theatrical analysis of Old Testament stories, chapters and excerpts requires a number of methodological clarifications with regard to the two main disciplines, violently yoked together here by this study's very title, as well as by the country's space and language. In his introduction to *The Cambridge Companion to Biblical Interpretation*, John Barton rightly specifies: "Almost everyone who writes about biblical studies today talks in terms of 'a new paradigm' for reading the text . . ."[8] He also maps some of the varied approaches to biblical studies in the 1990s, among them the historical-critical, literary, social, political, linguistic, feminist and post-modern. In this context, at least, a theatrical approach requires no special apologetics other than that already offered. The theatrical lion will not devour the biblical sheep (or vice versa), since neither Theatre nor the Bible, as presented in this study, claim any mutually exclusive rights to the interpretation of the other. I do, however, try to explore the performability of biblical excerpts and analyze their theatrical potential.

While maintaining that the book offers a radical approach and a rarely treated disciplinary conjunction, I also rely on a number of adjacent areas in biblical research that have greatly contributed to the study. One of these areas is the anthropological perspective on theatre, especially as concerned with 'performatives'. This was helpful in connecting biblical myths and rituals with theatre rituals. Notwithstanding, sometimes during the process of writing I caught myself wondering whether the biblical characters I was trying to scrutinize would not treat me like the Balinese people treated Clifford Geertz at the beginning of his research on cock-fights: like thin air, totally ignoring my theatrically invasive attitude.[9] Victor Turner, however, has supplied the invaluable and well-known distinction between 'Dramatic Ritual' and 'Ritual Drama'.[10] Some of the scenes and 'plays' presented here are situated half-way between these two notions, which were also developed by Richard Schechner,[11] David Cole,[12] Christopher Innes[13] and others in the 1970s and early 1980s. The application of some of these insights to biblical theatricality, is my responsibility. I find the intrinsic links between ritual and drama to be sufficiently explicated as well as supportive of the basic argument in this study, even without resorting to the problem of whether drama really ensued from ritual. Even Eli Rozik, who strongly doubts the origins of theatre in ritual, says: "Drama is umbilically connected to the holy scriptures through their sharing the mythical system."[14]

Moreover, some of the most innovative contemporary directors, such as Peter Brook, have looked for a Holy Theatre: "The Theatre of the Invisible-Made-Visible: the notion that the stage is a place where the invisible can appear has a deep hold on our thoughts."[15] Mnouchkine, Barba and the late Grotowski, to name but a few, have all searched for variations of 'The Holy' experience in their respective theatrical quests, using holy scriptures from many cultures. Major theatre scholars in the 1980s and 1990s, such as Erika Fischer-Lichte[16] and Marvin Carlson,[17] have also noted this major trend of resorting to holy scriptures in modern theatre, and noticed the richness of critical approaches in theatre studies – the 'Holy' one included.

Among the literary approaches to the Old Testament, Meir Sternberg's *The Poetics of Biblical Narrative*[18] is a major breakthrough in the field, as well as Robert Alter's insightful *The Art of Biblical Narrative*[19] and Uriel Simon's *Reading Prophetic Narratives*.[20] However, whereas the term 'dramatic' is used in most literary-oriented works mainly to indicate particular structural elements, as well as the prevalence of conflict, dialogue, modes of characterization, and other drama-as-genre elements, this book shifts the focus from a literary genre-oriented discussion to a medium-oriented one. It could, moreover, be argued that the entire traditional genre division of Epics, Lyrics and Drama is a convenient late imposition on early classical texts, the Old Testament included, which may – and do – comprise elements of all three literary genres in a much less neatly organized way. In analyzing biblical excerpts as theatrical, I contend that some of them can be performed verbatim, since the biblical 'stage-instructions' pertaining to time, space, movement, costumes, props, lighting and other theatrical components, are often built-in. Though completely verbal in a written text, notions of costumes and props, for instance, serve as non-verbal 'biblical stage-directions' when performed.

The space in I *Samuel* 3:1–10, for instance, is uniquely 'theatrical,' and so are many of the spaces, real, dreamed, metaphoric and visionary in *Daniel*. As a prop, Samuel's coat is given a particularly interesting interpretation in the book itself: Hanna, the young prophet's mother, makes him a little coat before handing him over, as promised, to Eli the priest. After Samuel's death, King Saul recognizes Samuel by his coat – obviously not the same one, yet a coat nevertheless, which becomes Samuel's dead giveaway. Tamar's shawl, and the way she puts on (and off again) her widow's clothes, is a sophisticated means of theatrical characterization. Props like Yael's tent-peg and hammer and Ezekiel's brick substitute for many spoken words. Stage gestures such as the concubine of Gibeah's outstretched hand on the threshold, or Ruth touching Boaz's legs (or feet), are exquisite moments of theatre. Even 'stage'-lighting can easily be read into scenes of David watching Bathsheba on top of the roof, or the lighting at Belshazzar's feast when the hand writes the famous 'Mene Mene' (Daniel 5:25).

Nisan Ararat is the only Israeli (and one of the only scholars at large) to have treated the Old Testament from a predominantly dramatic perspective, convinced that there are 'dramas' interspersed in the Bible, though they are "principally meant to be read aloud rather than be performed".[21] Perhaps because of his religious conviction, he is extremely careful in avoiding the actual performative aspects.

The exploration of the Bible *As* Theatre is an invitation for a dialogue between the two fields. The conjunction and "stands for dialogue, for two equals speaking to one another, listening to one another, in an attempt to learn something from the encounter: to change".[22] I do not believe the Bible will (or should) change due to its encounter with Theatricality. But the latter might, and so may those who participate as an active audience to the dialogue. Such an encounter between the Old Testament and Theatre not only exposes theatrical qualities and potentials in the Bible, but also enriches our understanding of theatre.

Since examination of the Old Testament as theatre can be a life-long (and very rewarding) occupation, it has been necessary to structure the book along certain guidelines, and to use a 'dialogical' methodology; this structure ensues partly from selected criteria of (potential!) performance analysis, and partly from the discussed biblical scene itself.

Part I, "Samuel's Initiation and the Possibility of Biblical Theatre", is an analysis of the boy Samuel's truly inspiring initiation, in which the problematic issue of biblical theatricality itself is analyzed and problematized: how far can we imagine a theatre performance of I *Samuel* 3:1–10, in which God 'came and stood and called' (3:8) without falling into the trap of hollow pathos on the one hand, and melodramatic kitsch on the other? An actual, 'realistic' or symbolic depiction of God onstage is definitely one of the major difficulties, both from the religious viewpoint of the Old Testament, and from a purely practical perspective, in the realm of biblical or any other theatricality. While medieval European theatre coped with the problem of re/presenting God with a certain (albeit alleged and reconstructed) degree of success, the very notion of presenting the Almighty in a corporeal fashion is strongly opposed to the second commandment: "Thou shalt not make unto thee any graven image, nor any manner of likeness . . ." (Exodus 20:4). In stage-oriented language this means that the closer we get to the core of 'The Holy', the more impossible it is to theatricalize it, at least in biblical terms. On the other hand, the wish to be in touch with 'The Holy' through the theatre constitutes one of the irresistible temptations of this research. Furthermore, God's 'position' in the Old Testament may be perceived as a contradiction in terms in 'reality', but it is nevertheless a highly creative theatrical metaphor: He is presented as sensually and physically unimaginable, yet He is spiritually very much 'there', a constantly present Offstage persona, with varying degrees of 'presentness', to follow Jack Miles's distinctions in his *God, A Biography*.[23]

Part II, "Female Presentations: Oppressed and Liberated", offers a close theatrical reading of five female oriented biblical stories. The field of feminist biblical interpretations has been greatly enriched in the last few years by scholars such as Mieke Bal, Athalya Brenner, Cheryl Exum and Alice Bach,[24] to name but a few from whom I have learned a great deal. The respective analyses provided indicate that the 'female' images produced in many of the stories fall somewhere between the two main biblical perceptions of women. One perception follows the more egalitarian approach of the mythical tradition "And God created man in His own image . . . male and female created He them" (*Genesis* 1:27). The other follows the alternative (or complementary) tradition according to which "the rib, which the Lord God had taken from the man, made He a woman, and brought her unto the man" (2:22). The five discussion chapters in Part II portray events as (most probably) described by men, in a male-dominated society which, nevertheless, exposes through the carefully designed dramatic narrative, a highly critical attitude toward its own moral as well as emotional standards. Prior to supplying a summary of the individual female-oriented chapters, a number of introductory notes within this introduction concerning women images in the Old Testament are necessary as a background.

The Old Testament has shaped many historical, social, moral, religious and psychological modes through which Judeo-Christian civilization has seen itself.[25] Within these complex modes, women have often been forced to accept and internalize a male-oriented discourse – albeit 'artistic,' 'favorable,' or 'considerate' – in which the depiction of women was more characteristic of the male-describers than of the described women.

The Old Testament has bequeathed western culture about 150 names of women, ranging from sporadic mysterious notes on Mehitabel daughter of Matred daughter of Mei-Zahav, wife of Hadar, the Edomite king of Pa'u (*Genesis* 36:39) for example, to a comprehensive description of personality, such as Sarah, Deborah, Esther or Queen Jezebel. The very act of naming, especially since it is a performative rather than merely descriptive act, must be regarded as a typical paternalistic trait in the Bible. The Old Testament includes by far more names of men than women, and it is useful to remember that it is often customary for the biblical father to name the first-born son, while mothers give names to the next, 'less important' offspring.

Many of the Old Testament women are simply referred to through their husbands (in Hebrew the term *Ba'al* means both 'owner' and 'husband', as well as being the name of Ba'al, the god of fertility). Potifar's wife receives no private name, like Job's wife and Moses's black wife. Women are also referred to through their sons: mother of Sisera, mother of

Abimelech; through their fathers: daughter of Pharaoh, daughters of Lot and daughters of Jethro, the priest of Midian. Some women are called after their place of origin and dwelling: the woman from Thebetz, the prostitute from Gaza, the widow from Tzarefat, the Queen of Sheba and the 'woman who divineth by ghosts'. Yet other women are named by both their names and their professions: Pu'a the midwife, Rahav the prostitute, the 'women who sew gloves' and the keeners for the god Tamuz, another god and symbol of pagan virility and fertility, which clearly suggests that the women 'belong' to the men. Some women appear with more complete names, such as Bath-Sheba, Daughter of Eliam, wife of Uriah the Hittite or Yael, wife of Hever the Kenite.

Since biblical male names often carry a formative as well as performative meaning, women's names and other modes of referring to them should also be given special attention. Biblical figures are often characterized through a variety of ways in which other people refer to them. Ruth, for instance, is called 'bride', 'the Moabite', 'girl', 'the foreigner', 'servant', 'slave', 'daughter' and 'woman' – depending on the particular image that the author wishes to endow her with, according to the 'naming-gaze' of the woman's partners in any given scene, narrative context, social class or degree of emotional proximity.

A further consideration indicates the violence inherent in certain female-oriented metaphors. The People of Israel were often compared to a faithful woman, a prostitute, a lover, a little girl, a bride, a virgin, a widow, a mother, an orphan, and an old hag: way beyond the usage made of male-name metaphors. In the book of *Ezekiel* (chs. 16 and 23) the detailed anatomical descriptions of how Samaria (Israel) and Jerusalem (Judea), named Ohola and Oholiva, expose intimate parts of their bodies to strangers, are the metaphoric whereby the prophet expresses his attitude toward the religious-erotic disloyalty of the people to the one and only jealous – Owner and Husband – God. The prophet Hosea was required to perform not just a process of metaphorization, but an actual realization of a metaphor, by marrying the prostitute Gomer daughter of Divlaiim. One may wonder what she thought about that marriage. The very use of female images relating to their family, social status, age, body and mental situation, is often an artistic and rhetorical rape. In this kind of treatment, which was certainly effective for the market-place audiences of those times, womanhood is abused as a free-for-all image, a bereft-of-individuality literary object.

While recognizing the patriarchal character of ancient Hebrew society, one must nonetheless distinguish between the overtly metaphorical uses of female-*images*, often explicitly sexist; and the actual, by far more egalitarian and realistic descriptions dedicated to many of the *individual* women in the Bible. Between the more egalitarian mode and the 'oppressive' one, many biblical texts tell gruesome stories of women exploited, raped and abused, of social deprivation and emotional oppression. While men too were also exposed to horrors (such as wars, in which women usually did not take an active part), men were nevertheless not placed *a priori* in an inferior status.

In "Female Presentations, Oppressed and Liberated", the focus is on five of the more 'dramatic' biblical female-characters. A close theatrical reading of the texts reveals a double standard. Whereas the dialogue text conforms to the paternalistic social standards, the biblical playwright nevertheless gives vent to a pro-feminist attitude, which is expressed in and through the 'stage-directions'. This, I believe, has so far gone unnoticed by most readers. "The Concubine in Gibeah" (CHAPTER 1) could easily have become a Classical Greek tragedy in the hands of Euripedes, for example; but even in *Judges* it is extremely theatrical. The female body features as a mere stage-property, while the playwright clearly displays a profoundly moral attitude toward the rape, killing and dismembering of the concubine, and the later abuse of many other women.

In contradistinction, "Deborah: Anti-feminism in Text and Stage Directions" (CHAPTER 2) deals with the discrepancy between the prosaic *Judges* 4 and the poetic *Judges* 5 in the depiction of the prophetess. This chapter also pays attention to Yael's uniquely dramatic role in a feat that was supposed to be exclusively Deborah's. In "Tamar: Acting out a Role Imposed" (CHAPTER 3) one of the more 'liberated' women in the Old Testament takes her destiny into her own hands and plays a 'judo-exercise', in fact within the framework of a play-within-a-play, in her confrontation with male sexual dominance. Special attention is paid in this chapter to props like Tamar's shawl and Judah's staff. Ruth, traditionally perceived as the innocent good-soul of Moab, is discovered, under a theatrical scrutiny, to be far more sophisticated than previously believed. *Ruth* is one of the most dialogical books in the entire Old Testament, and could easily be performed as such ("Ruth: the Shrew-ing of the Tame" [CHAPTER 4]). Esther, thoroughly massaged into her queenly role at Ahasueros's court, is treated in "Esther and the Head of the Sceptre" (CHAPTER 5) as an exceptionally courageous lady, who is first manipulated by others, but later turns herself from a sex-doll into a highly responsible person. The book of *Esther* also includes a play-within-a-play device.

Part III, "Women and Men, Participants and Spectators" is dedicated to two dramatically opposed 'dramatic' confrontations between men and women. In "The Voice of my beloved knocketh" (CHAPTER 6), *Song of Songs* 4–5 focuses on one of the most refined erotic dialogues in world literature, and one which may have really been acted out in ancient times. The entire book is related more from the feminine point of view than from the masculine, and CHAPTER 5 is indeed a wonderful example of a woman's gaze at her distant lover. It is, among others, a response to his sensual communication with her. In "The Educational Theatre of Proverbs" (CHAPTER 7), *Proverbs* 7 (leaving aside the final accolade to the Good Woman) represents a totally male-oriented perspective, especially within the structural framework of a play-within-a-play – an explicitly negative, though humorous attitude toward 'bad' women, offering a good example of how the Old Testament employs 'educational' theatre.

Part IV, "Prophets as Performers", deals with four very different biblical prophets: Elisha, Jonah, Ezekiel and Daniel. Biblical prophets are performers by the nature of their vocation, and the theatrical gaze cast in the direction of Elisha (in "Elisha: Religion, Sex and Miracles" (CHAPTER 8), reveals his unique relationships with the Shunamite woman. His sanctity is not doubted; rather, it is illuminated with something more than sheer spiritual motives, in regard to the lady who hosted him, and her child, whom Elisha resurrects. CHAPTER 8 is intended to clarify some of the sub-textual elements through an analysis of movement and ('stage') locations in the dramatic spaces in which the protagonists are placed. In "Jonah: a Quest Play" (CHAPTER 9), the only real dramatic conflict in *Jonah*, perhaps the most 'universal' of all Old Testament prophets, is this man's singular, perhaps ridiculous but nevertheless utterly anthropocentric argument with an omnipotent and omnipresent God. CHAPTER 9 analyzes the story as a Quest play structured along 'stations,' leading the human hero toward his deliberately avoided *anagnorisis*. Ezekiel, I believe, is the most theatrical prophet, and the holiest of actors. In "Ezekiel: the Holy Actor" (CHAPTER 10) the notion of 'Holy Theatre' is taken-up again in order to delineate yet another limit in the potential presentation of biblical theatre. A note on the unique spaces in the book of *Daniel* is included in chapter 10, dedicated to biblical inner and outer spaces, as portrayed through Daniel's dreams, the holy vessels and the unique visionary spaces. The main part of the chapter deals with Ezekiel as an actor. Whereas theatre has been described as a willing suspension of disbelief, biblical prophecy in this case is an unwilling acceptance of belief.

Part V, "Leaders: A Theatrical Gaze", casts a theatrical look at three leaders, two of whom, Moses and David, are among the most popular and familiar personalities in the Old Testament. "Moses in Flesh and Spirit" (CHAPTER 11) is a discussion of yet another holy scene mainly under the theatrical terms of space, and the potential harnessing of the Spiritual to the Material element. Flesh and Wind (or 'Spirit', in Hebrew) is dealt with both literally and as a political metaphor. CHAPTERS 12 and 13, because the divine intervention in their plot is more indirect, provide exemplary dramatic materials. "Jehu's Bloody Show" (CHAPTER 12) a 'Jacobean' biblical drama, describes in theatrical structure the rise of King Jehu to power, and the many corpses upon which his way was paved – with the help of the prophet Elisha. CHAPTER 13 offers a complete theatrical treatment of the David and Bathsheba story, bringing together all the various theatrical components that previously dealt with separately or in various combinations. The divine intervention here is mediated through the prophet Nathan, who designs the sophisticated biblical 'Mouse- (or Sheep) trap' for David.

Having begun this book with the theatrically problematic initiation scene of Samuel, I end with the David and Bathsheba play, presented as a superbly designed five-act drama, indeed a model for the immense theatrical potential of Old Testament.

Part I

Samuel's Initiation:
On the Possibility of
Biblical Theatre

Introduction to Part I

Potential Theatre

Chapter 3 of the first *Book of Samuel* displays many characteristics common to theatre and ritual. These characteristics constitute the basis of the dialogical situation, which mediates between the Here and the Beyond, between the then and the now. As this is an initiation passage, it is akin to the materials from which theatre sprung. The idea of theatricality can be used to uncover qualities and meanings in the passage that a strictly literary analysis might miss; so theatricality will be both the method and the object of the analysis.

The passage clearly reveals a belief in the creative word, a conviction that language not only describes reality but also creates it. This quality of language constitutes a link between theatre, whether secular or religious, and the Bible, both of which understand language as action. The first ten verses describe the initiation ritual by which the boy Samuel becomes a prophet.

The author of the *Book of Samuel* presumably understood the narrative as not only a literary text but also as an historically accurate account, or, at least, a story which follows the description of a hero.[1] Consequently, and also due to the author's literary knowledge and skill, the way the message is conveyed is less prominent than the message itself.[2]

The passage may therefore be regarded as *potential* theatre, as something that constituted a 'scene' when it occurred and that can be reconstructed as theatre. The reconstruction offered here relies not only on the language of the biblical text itself, but also on other, theatrical languages that may contribute to our understanding of the passage – the 'sub-textual' grammar of props, set design, lighting, movement, and other theatrical modes of expression.

In initiation rites not only words but also the accompanying gestures carry considerable meaning. Being three-dimensional, theatre provides an analytic framework which is sensitive to these multiple communication devices. The following analysis covers the initiation itself, which in this case is centered around the revelation of God and can be seen as the boy Samuel's 'bar mitzvah' or confirmation, in which he assumes responsibility as a partner worthy of dialogue with God. Also examined are the events that precede the revelation, the theatrical elements present in Chapters 1 and 2, and the operation of time in the passage.

Time

The account of Samuel's life begins with a description of events which had occurred prior to his birth and ends with events which took place after his death, namely the raising of Samuel from the dead in En-Dor (I *Samuel* 28). Thus the life of Samuel extends beyond his physical existence.[3] The entire account emphasizes the miraculous, the prophetic, and Samuel's closeness to God. Samuel did many other things too, but his actions were always dictated by his persistent and uncompromising religious attitude.

In the first two chapters of *Samuel* a series of scenes of increasing intensity builds up to the dramatic climax at the beginning of Chapter 3, which is followed by scenes of lessening intensity. The passages cover about twenty years – from Hannah's inability to conceive to Samuel's coming of age (3:19) – and include many references to time. Cyclical time[4] appears in the phrases 'every year' (1:3), 'year after year' (1:7), 'at the turn of the year' (1:20), and the 'annual sacrifice' (1:21), which attest to the recurrence of ritual events connected to religious traditions and festivals. Participants in these ceremonies are consciously integrated into the encompassing cyclical pattern, although the focus is more on making obeisance and sacrificing to God than on the seasons of the year, perhaps to emphasize man's free will in the face of the automatic cyclicality of nature.

Cyclical time serves as a sort of *ostinato* in the first three chapters of *Samuel*; it provides an underlying rhythm to events and recalls the divine order to which the world is subject. Within this cycle, moments of particular importance to the plot are made to stand out through the use of techniques such as simultaneity and slowing the pace of the action, as in "after they had eaten and drunk at Shiloh, Hannah rose" (1:9), "early next morning" (1:19), and of course "one such day" (1:4) and "one day" (3:2). In this way, moments in time and somewhat longer periods of time are brought into contact with cyclical time. Hannah's suffering as an infertile woman is attributed not just to Peninnah's taunts, but also to the accumulation and repetition of taunts "year after year" (1:7).

In some verses, time is measured by biological clocks – Hannah's pregnancy, the period of Samuel's weaning, Samuel growing up in the House of God. At the same time, Eli begins to age. The contrast here suggests that the same time passes differently for people of different ages, particularly in light of the imminent decline of the House of Eli, which the man of God reveals will have no elders. Three generations are seen here in sequence: the generation of Samuel, his brothers, sisters, and half-brother;

the generation of Elkanah, Hophni, Phinehas, Peninnah; and the generation of Eli's daughter-in-law, who dies giving birth to Ichabod. This then is linear time, with a beginning, a middle and an end.

There is yet another type of time which appears as the story unfolds – the 'futurized present', which is the time of prophecies and requests for oneself or others. These represent an attempt to influence future events, to control the future from the present. They are expressions of desire, an intention *toward* something; this desire is a basic property of drama without which there can be no action. In the first three chapters of Samuel, the future determines the present retroactively, for the events of the present belong to a divine plan and represent the gradual realization of a teleological process. Samuel must do that which it is incumbent upon him to do. The time between the prophecy and its fulfillment (and most prophecies are eventually fulfilled) is taut with tension, threatening and dramatic. Thus the children Hannah bears after Samuel, who are outside the focus of the dramatic action, are born in a single verse; their births together occupy less time than the period between the prophecy of Samuel's birth and its fulfillment.

The fulfillment of favorable prophecies creates the expectation that unfavorable prophecies will also be fulfilled. There are a number of such prophecies at the beginning of *Samuel*, made by the man of Benjamin, the man of God, God himself, and the narrator.

An essentially different type of time can be found in prayers, curses and thanksgiving: the time of the 'presentized future' in which the speech act is conditioned by the future. Here, words aim to accomplish their own fulfillment and speech becomes an act. The speaker turns toward the future, but in fact the power of the word brings the future into the present and what is to come is already underway in the speech act. The element of prophecy – in the man of God's words, Hannah's wish for a child, Eli's assurance that her wish would be fulfilled, and his subsequent blessing for more children – all belong to the category of 'futurized present'; on the other hand, the naming of Samuel, the element of curse in the man of God's words, and the words of God in Chapter 3, are speech acts proper and belong to the category of 'presentized future'.

Eli links Hannah's request for a child with the giving of Samuel to God through a play on the word *sha'al*, (lend) which connects past, present and future. This fusion is also suggested by the name of God, YHWH, which contains the three tenses: he was (*haya*), he is (*hove*), he will be (*yihye*). The fulfillment of prophecy is like the clapping of the past left hand against the future right hand, like audience applause for the event to come.

Hannah's prayer of thanksgiving occurs in this type of suspended time.

It is not a description of feeling but a speech act which gives thanks (even if Hannah's prayer is understood as a product of the culture that also produced the *Book of Psalms* and is read in that context). This type of externalization of the present is an expansion of time beyond temporality. A temporal time appears explicitly in Hannah's promise to give Samuel to God "for good" (1:22) and in God's words about the terrible things which would befall Eli (2:27–36).

Dramatic time can be described as 'the correlation between the time of the performance and the time of the action'.[5] The dialogues in the text under consideration contain a one-to-one correspondence between the time of the description and the time of the action. Such a correlation can be expected to increase the spectator's sense of involvement and interest in the events as 'happening now', especially as the dialogues contain divine revelation.

'Loops' of time also occur at several junctions in the text. While the narrative generally progresses chronologically, small leaps forward in time sometimes intervene, as when the births of Hannah's other children are reported before they occur, as a future event. Similarly, Elkanah's second ascent to Shiloh to offer the annual sacrifice is interrupted by the information that Hannah will stay home to nurse Samuel. But this is perhaps not so much a leap forward in time as an explanation of Hannah's reason for staying behind, for she knows that her son, when weaned, will be brought to the House of God, and she is motivated by her desire to spend as much time as possible with him until that time. Thus far, Chapters 1 and 2 of I *Samuel* prepare us for the encounter between divine time and human time that occurs in CHAPTER 3.

Space

A theatrical event must occur in a space. Biblical descriptions of space are economical, except when the space is an arena for action or is itself an agent of action.[6] From Elkanah's place of habitation, described at the beginning, Samuel *ascends* to Shiloh, to the House of God, to the House of Eli, and to the altar found there or nearby. Elkanah ascends each year when he makes his pilgrimage, but the text describes only four of these ascents.

The first description (1:4–19) begins by focusing on the place where Elkanah distributes the sacrifice portions and speaks to Hannah. Hannah then rises from this unspecified site and goes to a place to pray. This is near to or in the presence of Eli, who is seated "on the seat near the door-post of the temple of the Lord" (1:9). Thus the movement of the text brings us progressively closer to the temple itself. During the second visit it becomes clear that the House of Elkanah refers not only to a literal house but also to Elkanah's lineage. The Biblical use of the word for 'house' often departs from the literal meaning and transforms the house into an organic and personal temporal–spatial entity which functions as a metaphor for the situation of its inhabitants.[7]

During the third visit Hannah brings Samuel to the House of God in Shiloh while Elkanah returns to his own house in Ramah (2:11). As the narrative progresses, houses assume an increasingly central position and their metaphorical function takes precedence over the literal meaning: finally it is Samuel and his 'house' that takes over Eli's dynasty of priests to officiate in the house of the Lord.

Between the third and fourth visits the text describes the desecration of the altar by the transactions performed there by the sons of Eli. We later learn that this desecration is the reason why the House of Samuel will supplant the House of Eli (the names of the sons of Eli appear at the very beginning of the text [1:3], for the omniscient narrator knows their subsequent importance to the narrative). The movement of ascent to the House of God provides a contrast with the moral descent of Hophni and Phinehas. Indeed, the verb *alla* (rise, ascend) appears in a number of senses and is emphasized throughout the text, as for instance during the fourth visit when Hannah 'brings up' a robe for Samuel (2:19). Here too, space is not only a physical or geographic reality (the fact that Shiloh is situated atop a hill) but also assumes a spiritual meaning.

The 'entrance of the Tent of Meeting' (2:22) is another *threshold*, but quite different from 'the doorpost of the temple of the Lord', for in the first the sons of Eli lay with women. The parallel between the two locations, both of which are thresholds of a Temple, emphasizes the contrast between the activities taking place there. Subsequently, the word for house assumes its full meaning and functions as the key word in the man of God's speech (2:27–36), appearing in the phrases 'your father's house' (4), 'the house of the Pharaoh', 'your house' (5), and 'an *enduring* house', which of course represents the desired goal.

The 'place' of god may refer to the temple, the House of God or the altar. The most important of the words for 'place' is *makom*. The word for 'in his (or its) place' (*bimkomo*) appears three times, sometimes in contexts which exploit the potential ambiguity of meaning. For example, after Eli blesses Elkanah and Hannah, the text reads *vehalchu Limkomo* – "and they went to his place" (2:20) – and there seems to be an intentional ambiguity here. It is unclear who went, and to what place. Elkanah, Hannah and possibly Eli may have gone to Elkanah's place, or Eli's place, or God's place. The words immediately following, "*for* the Lord took note of Hannah," seem to suggest that they went to the place of God, but the passage is somewhat elusive. As will be seen, Eli will later lie in *his* place (3:2) and Samuel will lie in his (whose?) place (3:9).

It is necessary, also, to consider the movements between these places. Elkanah and members of his household often travel between Ramah and Shiloh for the purpose of performing the ritual ceremonies. This back-and-forth movement reappears as a motif in Chapter 3, in which Samuel runs from his place to Eli's and back, reproducing in miniature the previous movement between Ramah and Shiloh, between the secular and the sacred. Moreover, Samuel has to raise his head toward the Ark of God, to ascend to a higher level, a slight yet very significant additional movement.

Physical movements effect both changes of scene and dramatic transitions. When, for example, Elkanah leaves to return to his place and Samuel remains, the movement is emphasized as a dramatic opposition, making the effect of the parting stronger but without sentimentality. There is also an implicit contrast between Samuel's quiet and restrained movements and the wild, almost grotesque lifting of the fork by Eli's sons and the priest's servant.

The word for 'there' (*sham*) appears four times. While it has a literal meaning defined in opposition to 'here', it is also used in a broader sense. When Hannah says of Samuel "he must stay there for good" (1:22), her words resonate with the grief of parting, creating a tension between two locations. The reader is aware that 'there' also means where the wicked sons of Eli reside. In some lines, *sham* indicates perspective: "This was the practice at Shiloh with all the Israelites who came there" (2:14). The narrator may be alluding to the fact that Shiloh will not remain a spiritual center forever; Samuel will be a judge in Bethel, in Gilgal, in Mitzpeh, and when he is established as a judge he will move the spiritual center to Ramah, "for his home was there, and there too he would judge Israel. He built an altar there to the Lord" (7:17). 'There' is used three times in this passage to emphasize Samuel's return home, which adds a psychological dimension to the narrative.

Set Design, Costumes and Props

These are other spatial elements used to transmit meaning. Eli is first seen in his chair. The narrator prepared his entrance by naming him. Phinehas and Hophni are introduced as his sons, indicating their dependence on their father. Eli will sit in the same chair when he receives the bitter news of the death of these two sons, as well as the defeat of the people in the war and, most important, the capture of the Ark of God; he will fall from this very chair, literally and metaphorically, and die (4:18). The economic use of theatrical props focuses attention on the dramatic figure Eli and his chair, emphasizing honor and grandeur in the beginning, and great misfortune in the end.

The prop with which Elkanah is most closely associated is the sacrifice. Elkanah's offering has a specifically religious function, and its division also indicates his love for his family in general and Hannah in particular. After he has divided the offering the text uses the word for 'portion' rather than the word for 'meat' (1:4–5), in this way emphasizing its function. It is shared as a sign of love for God and for the family. Later, Elkanah and Hannah bring an offering for the redemption of the son, which is specifically identified as three bulls. Evidently, yet subtly, Samuel himself is 'the offering' his father brings.

Food appears as a prop when Hannah initially refuses to eat and then agrees to eat after Eli's promise. In a religious ceremony, eating has great importance for it symbolizes the internalization and integration of a divine gift. In contrast, in the desecration of the altar scene, the meat is emphasized rather than its function: "The priest's boy would come along with a three-pronged fork while the meat was boiling and he would thrust it into the cauldron, or the kettle, or the great pot, or the small cooking pot and whatever the fork brought up, the priest would take away on it" (2:13–14). The description of Elkanah's offering focuses on the *idea* of offering, while the description of Hophni's and Phinehas' offering emphasizes the *technique* of offering. In the first case the focus is on quality; in the second, on quantity. The redundant naming of the pots provides an ironic comment on the situation, verging on the grotesque. Similarly, the mechanics of thrusting the three-pronged fork into the pot is in keeping with the religious desecration and moral corruption of the ritual.

Samuel's coat can also be considered as a prop, especially when set against the holy ephod he usually wears in Shiloh (2:18). The coat was a gift of love from Hannah; Hannah brings it to him when she ascends with her husband to make the annual offering, and the coat is a sort of private offering made in consideration of Hannah's sorrow on parting from her son. The coat reappears as a characterizing prop when Saul grips the edge of Samuel's coat in his distress, causing it to tear. After Samuel's death, Saul identifies him from the witch of Ein Dor's description of him as "an old man who is rising and he wears a coat". The abrupt scenic transition from the desecration of the altar scene to the bringing of the coat produces a sharp contrast between the corruption of Eli's sons and the sanctity of the boy Samuel, which is expressed in theatrical terms by the semiotic difference between the fork and the coat.

Dialogue

The dramatic quality of a text derives from the dialogues it contains. Analysis of the dialogues in the first three chapters of *Samuel* reveals the following:

(a) who takes part in the dialogue and how;
(b) whether the dialogue is verbal or action-centered (i.e., a non-verbal encounter);
(c) whether the dialogue is reported through direct or indirect speech; and
(d) the modes of presence of the participants.

A more or less traditional division of the three chapters might be as follows:

1 *The opening* (1:1–3). Exposition: presentation of space, time, the characters, and part of the conflict.
2 *The offering* (1:4–18). Development: the offering, the taunts, an attempt at reconciliation, the prayer, the promise.
3 *Birth* (1:19–23). Intercourse, pregnancy, birth, nursing, weaning.
4 *Renunciation* (1:24–28). The boy is "lent" to God.
5 *Thanksgiving* (2:1–10). The prayer to God.
6 *Separation* (2:11). Separation from family and service to God in the House of Eli.
7 *The fork* (2:12–18). Corruption at the altar in the House of God at Shiloh.
8 *The visit* (2:19–21). The coat, the blessing, more children; the cycle of the House of Elkanah is concluded.
9 *The report* (2:22–26). The rift between Eli and his sons.
10 *The words of the man of God* (2:26–36). External intervention by the representative of God.

A more theatrical '*mise-en-scène*'-oriented division would, however, be organized around entrances and exits. In most scenes, three characters appear:

1 Elkanah, Hannah, Peninnah
2 Eli, Hophni, Phinehas
3 Hannah, God, Eli
4 Elkanah, Hannah, God

5 Elkanah, Hannah, Samuel
6 Hannah, Samuel, Eli
7 The priest's boy, the 'young men', the man bringing the offering
8 Hannah, Elkanah, Eli
9 Eli, Hophni, Pinehas
10 The man of God, Eli

This triangular pattern builds up to the climactic encounter between God, Eli and Samuel in Chapter 3. The opening scene shows Elkanah and the conflicts between his two wives. Elkanah prefers Hannah to Peninnah; the latter disappears from the stage after receiving 'her portion'. The unstable relationship might have been repaired by the birth of Samuel, but from that point on the narrator is no longer interested in Peninnah.

The triangular relationship between Eli and his two sons is also introduced at the beginning. Just as the 'gun hanging on the wall' in the first scene had better go off in the third, this relationship is introduced here to indicate an impending confrontation. The inevitable explosion does indeed occur and the antagonists to divine order are dismissed, although not before a substitute is found. Eli's misplaced loyalty to his sons provides a contrast to Elkanah's justified loyalty to Hannah, and the attempt to reform Eli's sons parallels Elkanah's attempt to appease Hannah; both attempts ultimately fail and the divine plan is fulfilled. The two triangles represent two future alternatives – service to God against failure to serve God. The parallels between them can be seen as a foreshadowing effect: the present is regarded as a retrospective phase of the future.

It is clear that among these triangles God prefers the House of Elkanah over the House of Eli. The matter is complicated because of sources of conflict and stability within and between the two triangles, for the divine choice considers human psychology as a motivating factor.

In the first two chapters (64 verses) of *Samuel*, there are 18 encounters among characters (some of which are closer in time and space than others).

1 One-way non-verbal communication, reported [8]
Elkanah divides the offering between Peninnah and Hannah, giving Hannah a double portion. God is an unseen participant here, insofar as the offering is made to Him. The action consists primarily of the division of the meat. It is non-verbal and is reported to the reader.

2 One-way verbal communication, reported
Peninnah's taunt of Hannah is related through indirect quotation in the

third person: "Moreover, her rival, to make her miserable, would taunt her that the Lord has closed her womb" (1:6). God is thus presented as the one who had closed Hannah's womb. The verb for 'to make angry' appears three times in the dialogue and once when Hannah explains herself to Eli. So too is the word for 'to cry' used four times to characterize Hannah and her reactions. This encounter of crying and taunting is repeated yearly.

3 One-way verbal communication, reported and direct

Elkanah tries to appease Hannah and the narrator at first seems almost to go out of his way to emphasize the gentleness of his approach. There follows a direct quote beginning with the word 'Hannah', when Elkanah asks her three questions to which he presumably receives no answer. The last of these is "Am I not more devoted to you than ten sons?" The reason Hannah doesn't answer is that Elkanah's well-intentioned but tactless remark has increased her sorrow. Her silence in response to Elkanah's speech is indicated by the sentence 'Hannah rose', which ends the dialogue. Dialogue between a talking man and a silent woman is, primarily, a dialogue between verbal language and non-verbal (theatrical) language. Hannah's silence, coupled with her crying, refusal to eat and 'wretchedness' communicates her state of mind and contributes to making her a dramatic and well-rounded character in a superbly theatrical scene:

> ELKANAH: Hannah . . .
> HANNAH: (doesn't answer)
> ELKANAH: Why are you crying?
> HANNAH: (doesn't answer)
> ELKANAH: And why aren't you eating?
> HANNAH: (doesn't answer)
> ELKANAH: Why are you so sad?
> HANNAH: (doesn't answer)
> ELKANAH: Am I not more devoted to you than ten sons?
> HANNAH: (rises)

This dialogue is comparable in its dramatic effectiveness to the best of modern psychological, realistic and poetic drama, from Ibsen to Lorca.

Hannah now leaves this triangle and a new triangle consisting of Hannah, Eli and God is formed. Hannah's silent appeal to God occurs while Eli 'watches her mouth', only then does he intervene. The misunderstanding is soon clarified.

4 One-way 'silent' verbal communication, reported and direct

In her prayer to God, Hannah speaks from the heart. God is a silent participant here and Eli, sitting on his chair, a passive participant. The motif of misunderstanding, which first appeared in Elkanah's failure to appease Hannah, now reappears in sharper form when Eli thinks Hannah is drunk, and in still sharper form when Eli fails to reform his sons. The motif thus grows steadily in intensity, building up to a climax in the initiation scene.

5 Two-way verbal communication, reported and direct

Eli reprimands Hannah as though she were just another of the many women who come to his door step. He does so because of his age, his dulled senses, because of natural misunderstanding or perhaps because Hannah is indeed unique. Hannah's silent prayer is a kind of pantomime that emphasizes the difference between spoken words and 'words from the soul', between interpersonal communication and an appeal to God. God can be considered present in this dialogue, for "man sees only what is visible but the Lord sees into the heart" (I *Sam.* 16:7). Hannah finally revives, and there is sad dramatic irony in Eli's question, "How long will you make a drunken spectacle of yourself?," for Hannah is actually fasting in sorrow while all others are celebrating, eating, drinking and feasting. After the conversation with Eli, Hannah 'ate and was no longer downcast'. This, the first full dialogue in the narrative, focuses on the future of Samuel. After Hannah's silences and evasions, her speech is impressive, dramatically effective, and repays the reader for the wait.

6 One-way non-verbal communication, reported

The following morning Elkanah and Hannah bow to God before returning home. The characters are seen for only a moment in this dramatic flash, but it has a more important function than simply effecting the transition between scenes. Elkanah, Hannah and God are now the participants, and God is the main 'character'. The triangle then shifts from Elkanah, Hannah and God to Elkanah, Hannah and Samuel; God remaining present.

7 One-way non-verbal communication, reported

The concept of Samuel is now reported: "Elkanah knew his wife." This can be considered a dialogue insofar as the verb 'to know' has a spiritual/communicative sense as well as a carnal meaning. Furthermore, the verb is used only when conception results, not for mere physical contact. God can be said to be present here, for He has 'remembered' Hannah.

8 One-way verbal communication, reported and direct

Hannah names Samuel; the name includes the theophoric ending *el.*

Names perform an important function in the Bible. This is especially true here, for the name refers to Samuel's past, present and future: He was lent to his mother and will be returned to the lender. God is actively present and the dialogue is notable in that speech becomes an *action* here, in the 'performative' sense.[9]

9 Two-way verbal communication, reported and direct

Hannah and Elkanah conduct a complete direct dialogue in the presence of the baby Samuel. Elkanah is about to depart for Shiloh and Hannah tells him she will remain behind. The narrator chooses to pick up the dialogue in progress, gradually gliding into direct speech. Hannah did not go up, but speaks to her husband:

> HANNAH: When the child is weaned I will bring him. For when he has appeared before the Lord he must remain there for good.
> ELKANAH: Do as you think best. Stay home until you have weaned him. May the Lord fulfill His word.
> HANNAH: (so the woman stayed at home [immediately] and nursed her son [soon after] until she weaned him. [until the end of that period])

Ending the scene reflects the same technique of shifting from the specifically individual to the more expansive time needed to wean Samuel physically and mentally from his mother.

10 One-way verbal and non-verbal communication, reported and direct

God, Elkanah, Hannah, Eli and Samuel are present in the scene of handing Samuel over to Eli. The name of God appears five times! Hannah's speech is recorded verbatim: "It was this boy I prayed for." They worship God again at the end of the scene. Two dialogues occur here. In the first Hannah and Eli speak to God about Samuel in the presence of Elkanah. The second dialogue exists between the non-verbal offering of the bull, and the former speech act. The bringing of Samuel to Eli is connected with the slaughter of the bull, creating a powerful theatrical metaphor: "after slaughtering the bull, they brought the boy to Eli." The text establishes a connection between the sacrifice, Hannah's vow and the boy Samuel, especially in the gap between the spoken text and the reported action. Samuel's passivity is emphasized, setting the stage for the dramatic scene in which God calls upon Samuel to act.

The narrator skillfully includes Elkanah in the scene in which Hannah speaks and delivers Samuel to Eli and God. Although the separation of Samuel from his family is gradual and gentle, it is also difficult, in contrast to the abrupt and casual exit of the less sympathetic figure Peninnah. The scene in which Hannah brings Samuel a coat and is offered more children testifies to God's mercy. It also draws attention to Hannah's sorrow in separating from Samuel and her need for 'compensation'.

11 One-way verbal communication, direct
Chapter 2 opens with Hannah's prayer of thanksgiving. There are no witnesses now other than God, and the text specifies that Hannah speaks aloud. Like the naming of Samuel, the prayer of thanksgiving is also a speech act rather than a description. No further reply is necessary, for the prayer has already been answered.

12 One-way non-verbal communication, reported
The following verse returns to the narrative. We are told through reported speech of Elkanah's return home and Samuel's service to God under Eli. There is allusion to the separation of Samuel from his family. Three times it is said that Samuel grew up in the service of Eli (2:11, 18, 21), indicating that a certain dialogue is developing between Samuel and God.

13 Two-way verbal and non-verbal communication, reported and direct
A full explicit dialogue occurs between the priest's boy and the man who has come to make an offering. The boy is probably a servant like Samuel. God is present, as are Eli's sons. But while Samuel serves God faithfully, the sons of Eli blaspheme and desecrate God's name. The narrative descends from the sacred and noble to the corrupt and sacrilegious. A holy event is debased; that which should be given is taken:

> PRIEST'S BOY: Hand over some meat to roast for the priest, for he won't accept boiled meat from you, only raw.
> MAN BRINGING OFFERING: Let them first turn the suet into smoke, and then take as much as you want.
> PRIEST'S BOY: No, hand it over at once, or I'll take it by force.

14 One and two-way verbal and non-verbal communication, reported and direct
Eli blesses Elkanah and Hannah in a one-way direct verbal dialogue. The juxtaposition of this dialogue, which includes the offering and the small coat, with the immediate preceding desecration scene, sharpens the contrast between quality and quantity, between Eli and his sons, between the House of Elkanah and the House of Eli. The tension surrounding the fate of Eli's sons, who have been previously referred to as scoundrels, increases here.

15 Two-way non-verbal communication, reported
In this encounter, similar to the preceding one, Eli's blessing is fulfilled,

and God gives Hannah three sons and two daughters. Here Elkanah is of course an implied participant and a period of at least five times nine months is compressed into one verse, making the whole passage problematic as dialogue. Still, God's earlier speech act of promise is fulfilled.

16 One-way non-verbal communication, reported

Hannah prays by the temple while the sons of Eli compound the sin of desecration through sins of unchastity (2:22). Eli hears of this in a reported encounter; the word for 'hear' functions as a leitmotif.

17 One-way verbal communication, direct

Eli lectures his sons in a direct dialogue of which we hear one side only, but they do not obey their father, "for the Lord was resolved that they should die". Eli is punished for the sins of his sons, whom he had failed to control. (Later his eyes darken, and the Hebrew verb *kaha* (dark) is used to describe both Eli's crime in not seeing what his sons were doing, and his punishment!) Eli speaks softly to his sons, telling them "it is no favorable report I hear the people of the Lord spreading about", when he ought instead to reprimand them severely, and this is held against him. His inaction when he learns of his sons' sin is not only immoral from a religious point of view but also represents a failure on his part to carry out his responsibilities as a father. Communication between Eli and his sons is flawed from the start, as is made clear by the way the sons are presented; they first appear without their father, then as 'scoundrels' and are then seen disregarding Eli's warnings.

18 One-way verbal communication, direct

The final encounter of Chapter 2 presents the relationship between Eli, his sons and God in a clear and pitiless light. The words of the man of God are rendered directly and harshly: "You have honored your sons more than Me." This may have been an unconscious choice on Eli's part, for he is devoutly religious and dies when he learns that the Ark of God has been captured, not when he learns of the death of his sons. However, as a priest, Eli should have acted correctly, not just *felt* correctly. By making the wrong choice in *deed*, Eli neglected his duties to an uncompromising God. Eli's subdued reaction to the death of his sons also indicates that he has developed a double relationship with Samuel, at once religious and paternal.

The role of God is notable in all these 'dialogical' encounters; God is present to varying degrees of involvement and intensity, and even his *absence* is significant, as when Hannah's womb is closed. The name of

God appears fifty times in these two chapters; indicating that God is both in and above the narrative, directing all that happens and occupying a central position in the drama. In Chapter 1 the term 'Lord of Hosts' appears for the first time in the Bible, emphasizing God's potentially aggressive role, especially in what follows. In this text, which is inhabited by the presence of God, the idea of words as speech acts is important, for the words of God are deeds. Naming a son, giving thanks, blessing and cursing – all have a powerful theatrical effect.[10]

The grouping of characters in these chapters is governed by a triangular principle, a pattern that reaches its completion in Chapter 3, when only three characters remain. The events of the first two chapters have winnowed out the other *dramatis personae* and focused the choice between the House of Eli and the House of Elkanah on two characters. Peninnah disappears from the Hannah–Elkanah–Peninnah triangle; Hannah and Elkanah disappear from the Hannah–Elkanah–Peninnah triangle; and Hophni and Phinehas disappear from the Eli–Hophni–Phinehas triangle (as the man of God prophesies, saying "And I will raise for Myself a faitherful priest"), finally leaving only Samuel, Eli and God.

The traditional division of the text answers the demands of a literary reading, whereas the division into eighteen encounters offered here, as previously noted, is better suited to a theatrical approach organized around entrances and exits. The traditional division considers the material it does not incorporate into any unit as merely transitional, but in fact these passages can be seen to constitute legitimate scenes in their own right.

The Characters and Their Names

The first ten verses of Chapter 3 contain the following names:

1	Samuel	Adonai	Eli	Adonai	
2	Eli				
3	Elohim	Samuel	Adonai	Adonai	
4	Adonai	Samuel			
5	Eli				
6	Adonai	Samuel	Samuel	Eli	
7	Samuel	Adonai	Adonai		
8	Adonai	Samuel	Eli	Eli	Adonai
9	Eli	Samuel	Adonai	Adonai	Samuel
10	Adonai	Samuel	Samuel	Samuel	Samuel

In the first ten verses Eli's name appears seven times and Samuel's name appears twelve times; Samuel is twice referred to as 'the boy' and once, by Eli, as 'my son'.[11] The name of God appears eleven times as 'Adonai' and twice as 'Elohim'.

The names serve to characterize the *dramatis personae* and the relationships among them. Samuel's name is discussed (1:20, 27) and a number of interpretations of the verb *sha'ol* (lend) are presented. Samuel's name foreshadows the events that occur in Chapter 3: his name (*Shemuel*) contains the name of God (*el*) and suggests that Samuel must eventually incorporate God into his life in a conscious way. He must recognize and know God, and confirm the promise contained in his conception: he must be worthy of his name. *Anagnorisis*, which is crucial to Greek drama, here takes the form of a duty to know, whereby knowledge effects a revolutionary change. The divine revelation entails a dialogue between God and Samuel, and Samuel will come to know God in and through himself. In this sense, his name reveals his essence.

Verse 1. Samuel appears first center 'stage' and is summoned by God. Eli is the third character present. The name of God appears again at the end of the verse, with greater dramatic significance.

Verse 2. Eli appears alone 'in the darkness of his eyes'. He will soon be dismissed by God and his mission will be passed on to Samuel.

Verse 3. Now the focus shifts to the sacred props with which Samuel is surrounded: the lamp of God, the Ark and the shrine.

Verse 4. Only the names of God and Samuel appear; there is an attempted movement toward an exclusive intercourse between them.

Verse 5. Eli's loneliness is emphasized as it was in verse 2: Samuel addresses him only in error. In verse 2, Eli appeared alone to highlight his solitude; here, the same effect is achieved through Eli's participation in a conversation in which he was not intended to take part.

Verse 6. Here Samuel is torn between his relationship with Eli, which is both religiously insufficient and in a stage of 'no-more', and a relationship with God, which does 'not-yet' exist. His spiritual umbilical cord is still tied to Eli, his adoptive parent, priest, and teacher.

Verse 7. The events related in verse 6 are explained. Although Samuel is immersed in divinity and surrounded by sacred objects, he has not directly experienced revelation and does not yet *know* divinity. The fact that Samuel runs back and forth is significant; his eyes have yet to be opened.

Verse 8. God calls Samuel again. The focus then moves to Eli, who has 'understood' and will relinquish the priesthood to Samuel of his own will.

Verse 9. Samuel's name appears twice. It appeared once in the preceding verse and will appear three times in the following verse. The dramatic focus thus returns to Samuel.

Verse 10. The focus is on the power and growing frequency of the call.

Of the 145 words in these ten verses, 32 are names. They have great importance, and reading only the names could still elicit an accurate understanding of the meaning of the text. The 'hide and seek' quality of such a reading of names alone will – numerically and from the point of view of distribution – lead to the final encounter between Samuel and God.

Verbs

Verbs are the driving force of drama. The following chart shows the verbs used in the first ten verses of Chapter 3. In our passage, the word has a performative function, so verbs indicating speech must be considered descriptions of deeds and have the same status as action verbs.

	God	**Samuel**	**Eli**
1	serves		
2			lies
			begun to darken
			could not see
3	was not yet extinct	lies	
4	called	said	
5		ran, said	
		(have you called?)	
		went, lay	
6	added, called	rose, went, said	
		(have you called?)	said, I have not called
7		not yet knew	
		not yet revealed	
		(to him)	
8	added, called	rose, went, said	understood
		(have you called)	
9		went, lay	said, go lie
			if He calls . . . say,
			speak
10	came,		
	presented Himself	say, (speak, hear)	

The chart can be analyzed according to various criteria. The verbs indicate negation ('I didn't call'), the conditional ('if you are called'), command ('go back, lie'), interrogation ('did you call?'), time ('did not yet know'), etc. The particular sense of the present tense of Biblical Hebrew verbs is also significant in some cases.

The number and frequency of distribution of the verbs (rather than Martin Buber's well-known observation regarding the 'leitwort' in the Old Testament) can be used to measure the dramatic density of the scene as it develops, from the beginning to the denouement. In these ten verses, over one-third of the words are verbs, endowing the revelation scene with dramatic intensity and dynamism. The frequency of verbs indicates that the action reaches a peak in the middle of the scene. The middle verses (vv. 5 and 6) contain 9 and 10 verbs respectively. By contrast, the scene begins slowly; the first four verses contain fewer action verbs and more negations, indicating an inability to act. Similarly, the tone of verse 7 is calm, allowing a pause in the tension, before the scene ends with a return to more intense action. There are also various verb sequences and patterns of repetition – for example, "rose and went . . . and said" (3:6) or "The Lord came and stood there and He called" (3:10).

Another important criterion is that of the speaker and the modes of his characterization through the verbs used by him or about him. Most verbs of which Eli is the subject are either negations, in the conditional, or express inability: "His eyes had begun to fail and he could barely see," 'I didn't call you', "if you are called". The only decidedly positive verb associated with Eli is the word for 'to understand', a quality typically associated with Eli. Ironically, his understanding too is passive. Eli is weak, dull and dim-sighted, a priest who can no longer officiate. As Samuel's teacher, however, Eli is in a position to *understand* God's meaning and to instruct Samuel: "Go lie down. If you are called again, say, Speak Lord, for Your servant is listening."

Samuel is the subject of very different types of verbs, which express activity. He is first seen lying, but soon rises, runs and goes. Only at the end of the scene, when Eli instructs him to receive the word of God, does his activity subside into the quiet readiness of "speak . . . for I hear". Samuel's activity must be seen in contrast with Eli's passivity and weakness.

The first reference to God in the scene appears in the phrase, "the lamp of God had not yet gone out", both literally and metaphorically. Subsequently, God is the subject of the verb 'to call' and then of verbs that indicate His gradual approach (3:10). God moves from a position of relative remoteness, typical of the previous two chapters, to one of proximity; it is one of the most intimate encounters in the Bible. He calls Samuel until He receives an answer.

The verb 'to call' has a different resonance when associated with different characters. God's call is clear; it grows stronger and more frequent. Samuel's call is a question, and Eli's a negation or a condition. The verb appears in every mode and in descriptions of past, present and future actions.

The revelation scene employs theatrical modes of expression. Spatial, temporal and plot elements combine with precise and economic use of movement, voice and visual features to create a dramatic masterpiece. The scene may also serve as a paradigm for analyzing the relationship between mysticism and theatre. The description of the revelation begins with the word for 'boy', which has already been used in the preceding chapters in reference to Samuel, as well as to the sons of Eli and the priest's boy. After a painful 'no-children' situation (and also 'seed', 'son') Samuel's name appears first in 2:18 and then in 2:22, 26. As 'boy' he appears ten times, with the comment that he is 'constantly improving' – *holech vegadel vatov*. In this episode Samuel's 'service to God' is placed in a new context. The text has told us four times previously that Samuel was in the service of God: after Samuel's separation from his parents, after the description of the sins of desecration, after the birth of his siblings and after God's intention to kill the sons of Eli is revealed.

Each of these references has a distinct function. The first, like the first verse of Chapter 3, presents the three main characters. The second omits Eli's name, perhaps foreshadowing Eli's eventual expulsion; by contrast Samuel's coat is emphasized. The third makes clear that Samuel, unlike his brothers, grew up in the House of God. The fourth establishes a sharp contrast between Samuel and the sons of Eli. The movement through these four verses is towards an ever closer relationship between God and his servant.

At the beginning of the revelation scene Samuel's service to God is noted yet again. It is followed by the statement, "In those days the word of the Lord was rare." The word 'rare' here has been interpreted to mean infrequent and therefore 'expensive' (*yakar*) by Rashi. Kimhi explains that the verse means "there were no prophets in Israel" and he interprets it as an introduction to what ensues, for a new prophet is about to be initiated.

'The word of God' can be understood as both a thing and a deed, for 'word' in Hebrew (*davar*) is used in both scenes. The word of God, there-fore, has the power of action but is also intended to be heard. (Eli, however, cannot hear what Samuel hears.) The revelation thus has an explicitly auditory element, not just a visual one. The distinction between eye and ear is initially maintained, but the two modes of perception are joined in the verse "the word of the Lord had not yet been revealed (*gala*) to him", since *gala* can refer to both visual and auditory revelation.

After telling us that the word of God was rare 'on that day' as part of 'those days', the text proceeds to the initiation of Samuel, which is introduced by the words 'one day'. The revelation is presented as an event that occurs at a specific point in time. These two modes of time both fall into the realm of the 'not yet': something that will happen, but has not yet happened.

The great dramatic impact here is derived from the tension between the knowledge of destiny and the observation of its unfolding. For example, the text tells us that Eli's sons "did not know God" while Samuel "did not yet know God". The revelation is situated in time at the point of intersection between what is *not yet* and what is *already not* – Samuel's destiny to know God. For God does not allow "the sun of one righteous man to fall before making the sun of another righteous man rise". A compression of events occurs in this encounter and time becomes charged with activity: there is *yet* something to be seen, and, to a certain extent, actual 'seeing' depends not only on God but also on the person's (in this case Samuel's) readiness to *see*.

The most important place names in the previous chapters are Shiloh, where the House of Elkanah is located, and Ramah, where the House of God is located. In the climactic scene of revelation the spatial focus is condensed, very specific and precise. The site is dark and enclosed; Samuel opens the doors of the house only in the morning (3:15). The event presumably occurs very deep inside the temple. (Rashi interprets "in his [Eli's] place" as a location which is deeper inside the temple than the place of the Levites.) Samuel lies "in the temple of the Lord where the Ark of God was". Kimhi states that Samuel did not actually sleep by the Ark and Rashi agrees that Samuel slept in the chamber of the Levites; whereas Ralbag interprets the text to mean that Samuel did in fact sleep by the Ark.

These locations characterize the participants in the scene. Eli lies in his 'usual' place, tired and blind. His blindness has metaphorical significance: he has lost the power of prophecy. Samuel, on the other hand, is close to the Ark, and therefore to God. When Eli realizes that God is calling Samuel, he tells him to go lie down and answer God should he call again. The text then reads, "Samuel went *to his place* and lay down", possibly suggesting that Samuel would take Eli's place. The set design is minimal but precise.

GOD'S
ARK
(God's "place")

Eli's "place"   Samuel's "place"

The scene is lit by the lamp of God; it is certainly night. Eli is surrounded by darkness; he can see neither the objects around him nor the vision. The lamp of God serves a metaphoric function and is linked with the word of God and with the revelation. The small light stands out against the surrounding darkness, an image of confusion and loss of direction, and represents the end of Eli's journey.

The word for 'not yet' (*terem*) appears three times, in connection with light, voice and knowledge. The revelation is not merely an audio-visual experience in the modern sense, but rather a paving of routes of initiation through the senses into knowledge of God, in a way that Samuel is likely to receive as well as accept.

The first three verses of Chapter 3 as an exposition contain the dramatic elements of space, time, character and conflict, which will be developed in what follows. There is a vision to be perceived but it requires a person fit to perceive it. The opening of this chapter provides a parallel to the opening of the book of *Samuel* as a whole, but raised to a higher level of expectation. The movements of the characters mediate between space and time and provide a dynamic expression of dramatic tension. Eli's passivity is all the more intense in contrast to Samuel's active role and his growing closeness to God. A stage chart would look like this:

God's communication with Samuel is one-way, exclusive and particular. Communication between Samuel and Eli is two-way; they have grown progressively closer and the revelation scene brings them closer still. The intimacy between Samuel and Eli is emphasized both visually and verbally: when Eli calls Samuel 'my son', his words are not only reassurance but also a confirmation of Eli's recognition that Samuel, rather than Phinehas or Hophni, is his spiritual heir.

Eli becomes aware that Samuel may be hearing the voice of God before the narrator tells us that 'Eli understood'. But Samuel and Eli are both hesitant to identify the voice of God, for one does not yet know God and the other no longer knows him. The reader's superior knowledge produces irony and intensifies the dramatic tension. It must be remembered, however, that while the reader knows *about* God, Samuel comes to know God Himself.

The triple repetition of the exchange between Eli and Samuel clarifies the nature of their relationship, which is intimate and based on emotional and intellectual rapport. But God is absent from the relationship, and the intimacy between Eli and Samuel renders God's renunciation of Eli and his exclusive address to Samuel all the more poignant.

When God chooses Samuel over Eli, the series of triangular relationships that structures the beginning of the *Book of Samuel* is finally resolved into a single dialogical relationship between God and Samuel.

Samuel says, "Speak, for Your servant is listening", thus establishing the two-way dialogic relationships with God for which he had been destined. The preceding triangular relationships and the actions of the characters can now be seen as stages in the fulfillment of God's plan.

Thus the positions of the characters fall into a pattern: Eli and God have *no* relationship, Samuel and Eli have a close *emotional* relationship, and God and Samuel are about to develop a *spiritual* relationship. Samuel heard God's call but did not understand it; Eli understood the call but did not hear it. Eli directs Samuel toward God: the deep relationship Samuel has with Eli serves as a preparation for the relationship he will have with God and which will persist for the rest of his life.

When we are told that "Eli understood that the Lord was calling the boy", there may be a suggestion that Eli also understands that he has reached the end of his own journey. As in Greek drama, the question is not what will happen, for we are familiar with the plot. Instead, the focus is on how destiny unfolds and the characters react. In this encounter between the divine–absolute and the human–relative, it is the 'relative' which provides the greatest dramatic interest. Samuel's mistakes in identifying God's voice must be seen as important stages of his initiation. Yet once the divine revelation has taken place, the ladder toward it can be cast away.

A true revelation requires no proof; it is its own confirmation. Samuel is powerfully affected by the revelation and experiences, like many other later prophets. This is Kierkegaardian 'fear and trembling': "Samuel was afraid to report the vision to Eli." Samuel is also afraid for another reason: he does not wish to reveal to Eli the dreadful prophecy against him. While the prophecy concerns Eli, the fact that it is revealed to Samuel is significant primarily for the relationship between Samuel and God.

God's role is now more pronounced: "The Lord came and stood there (*vayityatzav*) and He called as before." God needs a respondent, a partner in dialogue, in order to effect the act of revelation. The image of the lamp of God is relevant here, for the lamp too gives light only when there is someone to witness it. The physicist Wheeler suggests that the existence of creation itself depends on active viewers,[12] and this principle certainly holds true for the exclusive religious context of this passage. Samuel's reply is subject to free will; in this scene he exercises free will by choosing to receive God's word. Immediately after the revelation the text tells us, "Samuel grew up." The significance of this statement extends of course to Samuel's new spiritual link with God and the choice he makes in accepting his role.

Samuel's revelation is unique in the Bible (cf. *Exod.* 3:5–6, 20; 20:19; *Deut.* 5:23–25; *Isaiah* 6:5, etc.) in that it raises the potential of theatricality. By employing the medium oriented categories of theatre to analyze the scene we can cast light on the various languages used by the biblical text and the multi-sensuous modes of expression implicit therein. Different levels of awareness can thus be aroused in the reader. A secular performance would not do justice to the story of Samuel's initiation for it would desecrate the intentions of the author. But as rituals of initiation were presumably the forerunners of theatre, and theatre only subsequently became secular and mimetic, the staging of the initiation would not in itself be sacrilegious.

In the initiation ritual, relative immediately-present reality confronts the absolute. This encounter between the human and the divine can be understood in theatrical terms as a representation of *off-stage*.[13] God hovers above the stage; in the story of Samuel He intervenes and enters the arena. This is not an 'artistic' fictitious drama that recreates extratheatrical reality for the sake of entertainment, but rather a multi-sensual presentation of trans-sensual events that operates on many levels of consciousness and is described by means of theatrical tools. Modern theatre that seeks to return to its sacred sources – as in the case of the works by Mnushkin, Grotowski and Brook – does so by the methods examined here. Through this process, theatre ceases to be a substitute for life and becomes a profound and intense experience.

Part II

FEMALE PRESENTATIONS: OPPRESSED AND LIBERATED

1

The Concubine in Gibea:
the Female Body as a Stage-prop

───────

Within the rapidly developing discourse between The Bible, Women and Theatre, I have concentrated in Part II on certain ways in which the Old Testament treats women. I propose a theatrical rather than merely dramatic reading of the story of the *Concubine in Gibeah* (*Judges* 19–21), as a masterfully designed pro-feminist play.

A close reading of this gruesome, highly dramatic story, indicates that the group-rape and killing of the one woman, followed by the killing of thousands more, constituted events that fall somewhere between the two general main perceptions of women, according to the author[s] of *Judges*. The proposed theatrical reading of *The Concubine in Gibeah* supports the more egalitarian approach between the two creation stories of *Genesis* (1:27; 2:22).

Between the more egalitarian mode and that which treats women as second-class human beings, a great number of biblical stories tell about women exploited and abused by sexual violence, social deprivation and emotional oppression. While men too were exposed to similar and other horrors (mostly wars in which women usually did not take an active part), men were nevertheless not placed *a priori* in an inferior status. The story of the Concubine in Gibeah is the last and perhaps most effective story in *Judges*, which begins with the typical opening "And it came to pass in those days, when there was no king in Israel . . ." Both this particular story and the book itself end with the same words and with another typical phrase: "every man did that which was right in his own eyes" and in this particular context it must be emphasized: 'in *His* own eyes', not Hers. Cheryl Exum assumes that "women in the biblical narrative are male constructs, and, as such, tells us more about the men who produce them than about actual women".[1] The following analysis certainly supports this contention, favorable as it is from the author's point of view. Between the beginning and the end, the narrative strategies in rendering the plot suggest that the author used the formulaic phrasing in order equally to enhance the non-formulaic meaning of the words: was the lack of a king, as an expression of the need for law and order, the only explanation for the unusually cruel events depicted even in a book notorious for its explicitness in describing cruelties; or was a more radical solution required even then?

The specific exposition (19:1) of this 'play' states "that there was a certain Levite sojourning on the farther side of the hill-country of Ephraim, who took to him a concubine out of Bethlehem in Judah". The mention of three names of tribes (Levi, Judea, Ephraim) anticipates the inter-tribal aspect of the entire story, preparing the ground for the war against the tribe of Benjamin.[2]

Act I, Scene i (19:2)   Quarrel

"And his concubine played the harlot against him and went away from him unto her father's house to Bethlehem in Judah and was there the space of four months." The original Hebrew usage of the verb 'and she prostituted against him' (rather than the translation 'played the harlot . . . ') – literally translated 'on him' – does not make it sufficiently clear whether the very act of the woman leaving her husband (perhaps having been mistreated by him if she ran back home to her father?), was in itself considered 'playing the harlot' or perhaps she had indeed betrayed him sexually.[3] As often in the Old Testament, such vagueness can easily be considered both intentional and dramatically effective in terms of drawing the reader's more intensive attention. On the surface the story may seem to follow the 'Crime and Punishment' formula: since the woman whored, although her punishment is indeed exceedingly hard, it is still 'understandable' under the cultural circumstances, the laws and ethical codes of the period, etc. However, the (deliberate?) textual vagueness relating to the concubine's actions whatever they may have been, serves to unbalance this simplistic equation of 'since she sinned, she deserved due punishment'. It is the playwright's theatrical way of portraying her that indicates his profound sympathy and shock.[4]

Act I, Scene ii (19:3)   Reconciliation

Change of scene takes place with shifts in time, space or entrances and exits of the characters. The husband follows his concubine to her father's house in a narrative style that suggests a mixture of possessiveness and warmth. In this second scene, however, the drama has already shifted its point of view and moves from him to her and back to him again: "And her husband arose, and went after her, to speak kindly unto her (literally in Hebrew – 'to talk to her heart' *ledaber al libba*) to bring her back, having his servant with him, and a couple of asses." Theatrically, though only 'stage directions' and no dialogue have been used up to this point, the implied spectator has so far been invited to see the Levite's 'broken home', the house of the concubine's father, and thirdly, to join the Levite out on the road, between two indoor spaces. The next scene shift is a smooth letting-in of the husband, over a threshold that will shortly prove to be a highly dramatic location. "She brought him into her father's house", assumingly meeting him on the threshold, between the outside space of the road and the cosy inside space, where he is received with kind hospitality.

Allusions in this text draw intertextual attention to Dinah who was raped (*Genesis* 34) through the words "to talk to her heart"; as well as to the story of the binding of Isaac (*Genesis* 22) by mentioning the boy servant and the two asses. Interestingly however, in *Genesis* 22:3 there are two boys and one ass. The careful reader may now anticipate a 'binding'-scene, and will indeed receive one; but here no ram will be offered in place of this Isaac-like female figure. The allusion to *Genesis* 22 – which is reinforced by terms such as "and he lifted up his eyes" or "and he arose early in the morning" – is of particular dramatic effectiveness, mainly because of the totally *un*balanced equation between the two stories, intended by the author as an ironic device. The mythical story of the Binding serves as a correlative to the possible historicity of this one, as we see later in the implied comparison with the story of Lot and his guests (*Genesis* 19).

Act 1, Scene iii (19:3–9) Hospitality

"and when the father of the damsel saw him, he rejoiced to meet him. And his father-in-law, the damsel's father, retained him, and he abode with him three days; so they did eat and drink, and lodged there." The girl's father plays a perfect, somewhat tedious, almost ridiculous host. The following verses portray an overwhelming hospitality which can be explained in various, partly overlapping ways. Does the girl's father want to keep his son-in-law in his home until complete peace and reconciliation are achieved between his daughter and her husband? Does this scene function as a deliberately exaggerated 'homey' atmosphere so as to enhance, as a pseudo-sweet premonition, the horror to come? Does it insinuate that at least this particular father takes better care of his daughter than the Levite treats his concubine? Or that fathers always treat their daughters better than husbands treat their wives? Within these and many other interpretative possibilities, the 'father of the damsel' is soon to be thwarted, as another old man, the one in Gibeah, will offer his daughter to the rapists.

Throughout the scene it is made clear that the Levite is not a strong-willed person, since he had wanted to leave on the third day and on the fourth he even got up to do so – but assented to stay two more days. On the fifth day, however, he refused to stay despite the implied threat that "the day draweth toward evening", another hint that nights on the road are dangerous.

The one-sided dialogue in this five-day long scene, in which only the father speaks and the Levite's reaction is given indirectly, is dedicated exclusively to the concubine's father's attempts to keep his daughter's husband with him in his own home, tempting him with comfort and food while warning about the dangers of approaching night:

1　"Stay thy heart with a morsel of bread and afterward ye shall go your way" (19:6);
2　"Be content, I pray thee, and tarry all night and let thy heart be merry" (19:6);
3　"Stay thy heart I pray thee, and tarry ye until the day declineth";
4　"Behold, the day draweth toward evening, tarry, I pray you, all night; behold, the day groweth to an end; lodge here that thy heart may be merry and tomorrow get early on your way that thou mayest go home" (19:9).

In using gradually longer speeches, the father is shown as becoming more and more insistent. Retrospectively he can be regarded as expressing a premonition regarding the departure of his daughter. Textually, he addresses his daughter's husband; subtextually he may have his daughter's safety in mind. The dialogical text reveals an adherence to male-oriented customs, according to which the men rather than the women carry the conversation and make the decisions as to whether to leave or stay longer. At the same time, the stage instructions of the indirect text reveal the Levite's wish to leave as soon as possible; but he is either not strong enough or too polite to do so. His weakness or politeness will soon be shown in a different light.

Between the four 'speeches' of the father and the implicitly almost comic descriptions of the Levite rising to go and then 'sitting down' again, the concubine is not described except indirectly. Her semi-offstage presence is nevertheless quite strong, especially in retrospect: obviously the playwright did not ignore her presence, but chose to portray her through her silence in a non-verbal way. The scene emphasizes the passive and silent role of the woman through 'drawing at' her future fate. Though at this point we may wonder whether her silence as an obedient woman is a deliberate technique, we later learn that her portrait as an explicitly silent character enhances the horror of the entire story. Like Cassandra in *Agamemnon*, Katrin in Brecht's *Mother Courage* and many other silent female figures in world drama, the highly dramatic effect of the un-speaking character is very powerful. It is indeed her very speechlessness that encourages the biblical authors to write about her.

Act 1, Scene iv (19:10–14)   Wrong Lodging
"But the man would not tarry that night, but he rose up and departed, and came over against Jebus – the name is Jerusalem; and there were with him a couple of asses saddled; his concubine also was with him. When they were by Jebus – The day was far spent – the servant said unto his master: 'come, I pray thee, and let us turn aside into this city of the Jebusite and lodge in it.' And his master said unto him: 'We will not turn aside into the city of a foreigner, that is not of the children of Israel, but we will pass over to Gibeah'."

Here again one could expect a minimal dialogue between husband and his newly re-wed wife, but it is the boy servant who speaks. This scene re-emphasizes the concubine's silence and the gradually growing motif of trouble in the air, perhaps trouble that comes from within: what would have happened had the Levite spent the night in Jebus (Jerusalem)? It is noticeable that the future calamity will not come from non-Hebrew strangers, but from the Israeli tribe of Benjamin, the Levite's own people *en large*. The gradual dying of the day, of which we are constantly reminded, as a lighting direction implying danger, serves as an active stage direction. The little phrases about the dying of daylight amplify the tension and the drawing nearer and nearer of the horror. Both the dialogue text and the authorial text underline the tension between 'outdoors' and indoor spaces as well as the theatrically oriented differences between light and darkness.

Act 1, Scene v (19:14–22)   Invitation to Lodge
After the hospitality in the father's house, the Levite, his servant, the concubine and the two asses find themselves in the street of the town Gibeah, for there is no one to offer them lodging. An old man comes by from his 'work out in the field'. As in a Hitchcock film, the momentary tension is partly relieved only in order to be increased further, because the old man too is not of the Benjaminites but of Ephraim. Is the man a poten-tial threat as we have often been warned? He 'raises his eyes' (compare *Genesis* 22:4, in which this phrase anticipates the place of binding which Abraham saw from afar!) and "saw the wayfaring man in the broad place of the city". To the polite question ensuing from the old man's recogni-tion that the strangers have nowhere to lodge, the Levite answers: "We

are passing from Bethlehem in Judah . . . and I am now going to the house of the Lord, and there is no man that taketh me into his house. Yet there is straw and provender for our asses and there is bread and wine also for me and for my hand-maid . . ." (19:19).

Since the reader has not been informed of the Levite's intention to visit the house of the Lord, we may wonder whether the very mentioning of the holy place was not intended as a subtle religious qua emotional black-mail, through which (as a pious, harmless man . . .) to achieve an invitation to lodge at the old man's home. And indeed the old man fulfills the Levite's expectations and calms his fears by answering: "howsoever let all thy want lie upon me; only lodge not in the [street] broad place" (19:21), again stressing the danger of remaining outside. In this scene the tensions of familiarity versus estrangement, warm hospitality versus danger and loneliness and tribal differences versus family ties are played against each other and used in order to give the text an extra twist. In slowly developing male–female affairs, then father–daughter relation-ships, then adding guest–host issues against the background (soon to become foreground) of tribal tensions and on the way to national matters – women are constantly ignored and left aside in deliberate narrative silence, reflecting and simultaneously criticizing their socially silenced status.

Act 1, Scene vi (19:22–26)   Evil Doers

The implied, hair-raising comparison in this scene between homosexual and heterosexual preferences was perhaps a shock to people of the period, especially since biblical law promises death to men who perform the 'wanton deed' of male intercourse. Imagined as theatre, the implied spec-tators are invited to 'direct' the scene with their mind's eyes. A male pact in the name of hospitality and local morale is juxtaposed with the women's bodies, which will be so 'generously' offered. How would the Levite have felt if he, and not his concubine, had been attacked by the molesting 'evil-doers'? As part of the plot, yet also functioning as sub-plot, the old man offers his own virgin daughter to the people who knock at the door of his house. Following Bachelard, a typical biblical similarity can easily be seen between the house and a woman's body. The daughter, somehow, escapes the brutal night-long rape whereas the Levite "laid hold on his concubine, and brought her forth . . ." (19:25). An additional indi-rect lesson to be learned is that in dire straights it is still a little safer to be a daughter than a concubine. However, both father–daughter and husband–wife relationships are now seen from an entirely different perspective.

Leaving aside obvious questions pertaining to what these four characters might have felt, a few factual details can still be raised, such as why did the Levite not go out to reason with the 'base fellows' in order to spare the woman he had just brought back from her father's house? How and why did the virgin daughter of the old man escape? Did the concubine go out willingly or was she, as the text suggests with subtle cruelty, dragged 'softly' out by the force of her husband's fear for his own body? Did the Levite not want to overstretch the hospitality of his kind host and therefore 'took out' his concubine? Did he really have a choice? The indeterminacies in the text indicate that the biblical playwright of this drama was well aware of the emotional and moral implications of the occurrences, that he enlisted a number of typically theatrical means to convey his opinion, and that he was also interested in letting the readers complement the details according to their own sensitivities.

Act I, Scene vii   Outside
The biblical text spares the reader all the gory details but makes the essence clear enough: "and they knew her and abused her all night until the morning; and when the day began to spring, they let her go" or, in the original: "they sent her away" (19:25). She was still alive when she arrived on the doorstep.

Act I, Scene viii (19:26)   Threshold
This short scene: "then came the woman in the dawning of the day and fell down at the door of the man's house where her lord was till it was light" is as short as it is intense. Instead of indulging in emotionally charged physical details, the intensity of which is evoked often enough by police officers making precise inquiries after women complain of rape, the biblical playwright concentrates on key words like Man (lord . . .), Woman, House and two extremely powerful descriptive images of the light of day. This deliberate and tactful silence serves to demonstrate the sympathy felt for the victim.

Act I, Scene ix (19:27–28)   None answered
"And her lord rose up (it does not say 'early' in the morning as the formulaic phrase usually tends to continue in biblical Hebrew) in the morning, and opened the doors of the house, and went out to go his way; and behold, the woman his concubine was fallen down at the door of the house with her hands upon the threshold. And he said unto her: '[Get] Up, and let us be going'; but none answered . . . then he took her up upon the ass and the man rose up and got him unto his place . . ."

The movement, the light and the body postures of the characters in this scene deliver dramatic information that is even more revealing than the dialogical text. Furthermore, the two kinds of texts, the dialogical and the authorial, are juxtaposed as complementary conflicts. While the direct speech portrays a uniquely gross and insensitive man, the stage directions show a woman with a stunning, indeed expressionistic gesture of 'her hands upon the threshold'. Indeed the real dialogue is not (and cannot be, because she does not answer), between a totally silenced woman and her speaking, now (all of a sudden!) quite energetic lord and husband, but between speech and silence; between he who escaped brutal rape and she who did not; between the now sun-lit exterior and the (probably) dark interior of the house. It is clearly the body language of the woman that 'speaks'.[5] Not long ago the outside was dark and the inside was lit. And safe. For the woman and the house, the threshold is the meeting point.

Opening the house doors is a highly charged theatrical gesture, shifting the focus to the husband, getting up in the morning. We don't know whether and how he had slept. How did *he* spend the night? What did he think or feel right before opening the house doors? Did he expect the sight the spectators had already seen? Was he surprised? Amazed? Overwhelmed with shame? Glad to see his concubine still alive? Was she?

Act I, Scene x (19:28–29)   Body on the Ass

"Then he took her up upon the ass and the man rose up and got him unto his place . . . " This scene is verbally short but in real time may take at least a few hours. A creative dramaturge or director is invited to fill in all the emotional gaps concerning everything from the woman's physical and mental state, to the potential reaction of the accompanying servant or the Levite's thoughts. Dramatically, sensitive observers may conclude that the journey to the concubine's father – without her – was quite different from the journey back, with her (already dead?) body on the ass's back.

Act I, Scene ix (19:29)   Limbs

"And when he was come into his house, he took a knife, and laid hold on his concubine, and divided her, limb by limb, into twelve pieces, and sent her throughout all the borders of Israel."

The important question here is whether she was already dead when he approached her with the knife (the Hebrew uses *ma'achelet* – the kind of knife Abraham used for slaughtering Isaac), since the biblical narrator does not specify the precise moment of death. Did she die on the threshold? While on the ass? Or actually under her master's knife.[6] Strangely, the text uses the same word 'held' – when the man sent the woman out to the rapists and when he cut her body. While this scene emphasizes action, the following demands speech.

The epilogue of this act ends with the public reaction of whoever "saw it [and] said: 'such a thing hath not happened nor been seen from the day that the children of Israel came up out of the land of Egypt unto this day; consider it, take counsel, and speak'. "

Israel	Benjamin
Forces: 400,000	26,000 + 700
Casualties: 22,000 (of Judah) – 1st day	
18,000 – 2nd day	
30 – 3rd day	
then – 18,000	
5000	
2000	
25,000 + 100	

The Levite succeeds in turning – perhaps justifiably – his personal affair into a national matter. Furthermore, concerning his own (moral? emotional?) responsibility for the previous events, he probably did the only thing that would indeed have let him off the hook.

Act 2 presents the development and events of the war between the Israelites and the tribe of Benjamin, who would not hand over the culprits. The beginning (20:1) is a description of a national assembly, in which 400,000 armed men on foot, representing all the tribes of Israel, come to Mitzpah. Upon being asked how this abomination happened, the bereaved husband answers: "I came into Gibeah that belongeth to Benjamin, I and my concubine, to lodge. And the men of Gibeah rose against me, and beset the house round about me by night, me they thought to have slain and my concubine they forced ('tortured') and she is dead. And I took my concubine, and cut her in pieces, and sent her throughout all the country of the inheritance of Israel; for they have committed lewdness and wantonness in Israel. Behold, ye are all here, children of Israel, give here your advice and council."

Obviously, he hides the fact that rather than 'kill him', the evil-doers had actually wanted from him what they in fact took from his woman and, wanting to save his manly image, he understandably also fails to mention his own behavior under the circumstances. Before letting the Levite speak, the biblical dramatist introduces him as 'the husband of the woman that was murdered', thus shifting at least a touch of responsibility to him. However, in his very eloquent speech, the man himself uses the first-person singular as though the major evil had been done to him.

The decision arrived at is that 10 percent of all the men of the entire people of Israel will be enlisted "knit together as one man" to demand justice. Unity is emphasized here as well as in the term "their brethren"

(20:13), creating a certain air of male bonding, caused by the dismembering of a woman's body. The text is meticulous in describing preparations for a great war (the forces and casualties are detailed overleaf): Six hundred men of Benjamin fled to the rock of Rimmon and remained there for the same length of time that the concubine had stayed at her father's house – four months. After the victory over the tribe of Benjamin, the Israelites took an oath that "not any of us give his daughter unto Benjamin to wife . . ." (21:2) and immediately after we find they "lift up their voices, and wept sore" for losing an entire tribe. Cynics note a parallel between behavioral patterns of the individual Levite and the collective of the entire people: first the killing, then the crying. If this assumption may seem far-fetched, one should take a closer look at the almost explicit parallel between the taking of Bath-Sheba by King David and the ironic parallel of conquering Rabat, at the same time (II *Sam.* 11). Further reinforcement for this claim can be found in the phrase mentioned later: "when their fathers of their brethren come to strive with us, that we will say unto them: 'Grant them graciously unto us, because we took not for each man of them his wife in battle; neither did ye give them unto them, that ye should be guilty'" (21:22). This pseudo-diplomatic excuse reflects retroactively and on a national level, the Levite's previous glib speech in which he explained what had happened in Gibeah.

Act 3 reintroduces back the leitmotif of the drama, namely the silent heroines and victims, the motivating forces of the initial crime and its totally disproportionate punishment, the women, conceived of as birth-machines. While nothing is mentioned explicitly, it is more than clear that throughout the war a very great number of women were slain, for otherwise the entire ordeal of trying to find wives for the surviving men of Benjamin does not make sense: "And the children of Israel turned back upon the children of Benjamin, and smote them with the edge of the sword, both the entire city, and the cattle, and all they found; moreover all the cities which they found they set on fire" (20:48). Had not all the women been murdered too, it would be impossible to make sense of the rest of the story. Nevertheless, here again the playwright does not mention one single word in regard to females. I assume that this deliberate omission draws more attention to itself than would any detailed description of additional rapes and killings.

Treating women as objects is well portrayed in the third act. The solution found for the discrepancy between killing all of the tribe of Benjamin, except for the 600 men hiding at the rock of Rimmon, and the tragedy of losing an entire tribe, is found in the need to supply the 600 with women, however difficult this may be because of the oath they all took "not any of us give his daughter unto Benjamin to wife . . .". After further offerings and prayer (in which women neither participate nor are mentioned), the men of Israel now ask: "How [what] shall we do for wives for them that remain . . ." and they decide to take these missing partners from the Jabesh-gilead, a town that had not participated in the mass murder for unknown, because unspecified, reasons. Whoever had wondered about the previous lack of mention of women is now abundantly compensated: "And the congregation sent thither twelve thousand men of the valiantest, and commanded them, saying: 'Go and smite the inhabitants of Jabesh-gilead with the edge of the sword, with the women and the little ones. And this is the thing that ye shall do: ye shall utterly destroy every male, and every woman that hath lain by man" (21:10–11).

In Jabesh-gilead 400 virgins are found. The 600 men still at the rock of Rimmon are addressed and offered the women, although 200 of them receive none. At this point, it seems that the playwright makes his pro-feminist textual strategies almost explicit, probably in order – yet again – to balance the extreme harshness of the facts with his (?) own much more sympathetic undertone, subtext and insinuations. " . . . and they gave them the women whom they had saved [literally – let live] live of the women of Jabesh-gilead; and yet so they sufficed them not" (21:14–15). The previously only hinted at fact is now made explicit: "how shall we do for wives for them that remain, seeing the women are destroyed out of Benjamin . . . " (21:16).

Another motif is now brought to the foreground, linking between the 'feast of the Lord' that was mentioned previously in a different context, and another violent act, the abduction of the dancers of Shiloh, during a religious folk festivity. Perhaps it is not too far-fetched to assume that the playwright, through the already well-known technique of subtle insertions of certain words, utterly disapproves of the events. It is as though attention is being drawn to the Levite's sanctimonious attitude on a national level, precisely because of the omission of the real cause of these events: the inhuman cruelty toward women.

"And the children of Benjamin did so, and took them wives, according to their number, of them that danced, whom they *carried off* [the Hebrew uses a verb similar to 'robbed']" (21:23). The very end of the drama is another such hint to sanctimony: "And the children of Israel departed ('walked away' is the Hebrew strongly understated term) thence at that time, every man to his tribe and to his family . . ."

The sweet, almost idyllic ending to the rape and murder of the concubine in Gibeah receives a sharply critical, pseudo-formulaic ending, now heavily charged with moral and emotional indignation.

We recall the hands of one woman on the threshold, the unheard cries of the Jabesh-Gilead virgins, the happy then desolate cries of the 'Dancers' in Shiloh, and the silenced cries of the tens of thousands of Benjamite women in this drama. And we recall the final words in the book of Judges, "In those days there was no king in Israel, every man did which was right in his own eyes": no mere formulaic ending, but a masterful condemnation of the status of women.

The full dramatic text reveals an 'objective' description on the one hand and an attitude that is highly sympathetic, embarrassed and charged with indignation on the other. The two mutually complementing attitudes are also mutually corrective, juxtaposing historical facts about the ways in which women were treated with abomination concerning those very same facts.

The plot carries the implied spectator from a private husband–wife affair to a family matter, on to the larger circle of a host–guest situation taken further to inter-tribal complications, and finally to a civil war. In this war, in order to correct an injustice done to one female individual, far greater cruelty takes place against many, many other women. War as well as peace with the tribe of Benjamin is achieved through women's bodies. Of course many men die too; but it is the women whose (theatrical . . . !) silence is outstanding; and whose silence must speak for them. The overtly theatrical means used by the playwright must be internally (at least) activated by the implied spectator in order to fully perceive the drama of the concubine in Gibeah.

Deborah: Anti-Feminism in Text and Stage Directions

Among about 150 women mentioned by name in the Old Testament, the prophetess Deborah stands out as one of the most dominant. Under her leadership, the war between the Israelites and the Canaanite king Jabin and Sisera, commander of his army, is described in the prose of Chapter 4 of *Judges*. The chapter portrays Deborah as a decisive, strong-willed and God-fearing woman. In contradistinction to the relatively objective but nevertheless complimentary depiction of the prophetess in the prose part, Chapter 5 is a vindictive song, a dramatic-poetic presentation of the 'facts', which Deborah herself performs to the victorious Israelites. In contradistinction to the deeply emphatic stage directions in the Concubine in Gibeah story, I read Chapter 5 as reflecting Deborah as a conceited, self-glorifying woman who is, perhaps, ironically criticized by the author, especially in comparison with the previous chapter, in which the author gives the same woman her full credit.

Whereas the prose of Chapter 4 contains certain dramatic elements, the poetry of Chapter 5 reconstructs the war as a story-poem, a grand public oratory, part of a victory celebration. As such, the poetic victory speech renders itself to explicitly theatrical modes of analysis. The speech is rich with direct appeals to the 'dramatic personae' as well as to the audience. No Old Testament judge or king is reported to have feasted on a military victory as blatantly aggressive as Deborah. The following dramatic and theatrical reading of both chapters reveals Deborah's complete 'drama' as tensely stretched between the two versions, seemingly conflicting but in fact mutually complementary. The prose version on the one hand and the poetic on the other can be described as engaged in a dialogue with one another, together constituting a third, 'dramatic' whole.[1] The discrepancy between them invites the readers/spectators to decide for themselves whether Deborah was indeed a fiery super-woman, and/or a petty, cruel, envious and bragging female leader. It may also be suggested that the male author would not allow the woman Deborah to enjoy her victory without his own implied envy.

Deborah's song, as will be shown, is particularly theatrical. However, a high degree of drama and theatre can also be found in the Yael–Sisera encounter, as a play-within-a-play in both versions. Indeed, the actual killing of the enemy general Sisera seems to be a sophisticated attempt to steal the Deborah (and Barak) show. Moreover, the full text of Chapters 4–5 contains not only excellent dialogues, but numerous stage instructions that complement the purely 'verbal' picture. Observed from yet another angle, the Deborah play is a fascinating study of women's roles.[2]

The entire story is replete with conflicts. The principal, typically biblical conflict exists between the Lord God of the Israelites and all the other gods. Then, there is the long and bloody conflict between the Israelites and their enemies, in this case the Canaananites, which marks the entire book of *Judges*. Next, there is a particular personal conflict between the heads of the two camps: Deborah and Barak (son of Abinoam) on the side of the Israelites; King Jabin and his chief commander Sisera on the enemy side. Furthermore, a unique conflict underlies male–female relationships in these two chapters: Barak against Deborah, Jael against Sisera. Last but not least is a finely depicted conflict between the two 'winning' women in the plot, Jael and Deborah.

Dramatically (ideologically and otherwise), God is always presented as the main protagonist throughout the entire Bible, and particularly so in this drama.[3] He is not only the main figure in the national-religious drama of the Hebrews, but also the overall universal director, designer and special-effects engineer of the entire play. His roles, as such, vary throughout the Bible. In the Deborah play, however, He is given full credit, though the other actors-participants, and Deborah in particular, try to appropriate some of the applause.

A brief introduction to the preceding events of this Canaanite-Israeli war may be useful. In the pioneering period covered in *Judges*, the Israelites fought against "the Canaanites, the Hittites, the Amorites, the Perizzites, the Hivites and the Jebusites;" but they also "took their daughters as wives for themselves, and their own daughters they gave to their sons; and they worshipped their gods" (3:5–6). A sensitive reader soon observes that in this pioneering period (as in other periods of hardship), women play specially active and important roles. Following the historical survey presented in Chapter 1 of *Judges*, which reports how the Israelites fought their enemies and partly conquered them, an angel appears in Chapter 2 to warn them: "do not make a covenant with the inhabitants of this land; tear down their altars . . ." God demands an exclusive fidelity, and the Israelites, collectively, react like a woman being admonished for her infidelity: "When the angel of the Lord spoke these words to all the Israelites, the people lifted up their voices and wept. So they named that place Bochim . . ." (2:5).

National and political independence is perceived in the Bible as a divine reward for religious faithfulness. This faithfulness is often portrayed in images directly related to sexual and family relationships. In *Judges*, the typical model of God and his people's behavior is:

Betrayal → Retribution → Outcry → Redemption and Forgiveness

The people of Israel betray their exclusive relationship with God, they marry with other peoples and worship their gods (indicating a direct physical link between faith in God and marital relationships). God punishes his unfaithful people qua wife 'homoeopathically', by having them oppressed by those same 'other' peoples whose sole purpose of existence is to test the Israelites' fidelity. The Israelites then cry out for help to their intimately known God, who in turn sends a judge to rescue them. Then 'the land rests' for forty or eighty years, until the whole dramatic process beings again.

The authors of *Judges* were well aware of the secular nature of the inter-tribal tensions among the Israelites, but the entire book is nevertheless imbued with personal, family-and-tribe erotic imagery of the intimate relationships of God the husband with the Israelite community as wife; and also of a father–sons relationship. The judges are called to perform various national-religious missions, usually of military character. The subtext indicates that they behave like sons defending their (god-) father's reputation against their (people-) mother's prostitution. Some of them, alas, though successful in their military tasks, still fail the religious challenge and later commit adultery with other gods. According to this repeated model, Deborah, the only woman judge (and a prophetess prior to the rebellion against Canaanite oppression), in Chapters 4–5 fulfills the much less common role of mother. She encourages her people and calls Barak to lead the rebellion. Barak's role in the story, as part of the dramatic process of settling in the promised land, in a generally male-oriented society of fighters, is clearly secondary.

Prior to Deborah, three judges had rescued Israel: Othniel son of Kenaz vanquished Cushan-Rishataim of Aram; Ehud son of Gera, a skilful commando-fighter, managed to kill the obese Moabite king Eglon; and Shamgar son of Anath (called after his mother!) succeeded in killing 'six hundred of the Philistines with an oxgoad', a sign that God was on his side. Here and in many other instances, military success is always attributed to God, rather than to the ingenuity of the performing judge.

Securing His absolute sovereignty, God says to Judge Gideon, for example: "Israel would only take the credit away from me, saying, 'my own hand has delivered me' . . . " (7:2). God, or His biblical authors, editors and representatives, use this as an anti-hubris device. Deborah, too, warns Barak: "the road on which you are going will not lead to your glory, for the Lord will sell Sisera into the hand of a woman"(4:9). Power, skill, ingenuity and success are permanently ascribed to God alone. He lends some of His qualities to the judges, but only temporarily, on an ad-hoc 'per mission' basis. Samson, for example, must return the special combat equipment he was given, until allowed, at the very end, to use it just once more, and die.

Deborah indeed gives God full credit, but in between the lines in her song she does not forget to crown her own head with a few laurels. In pioneering times, women carry their own and the community's weight more than in periods of relative affluence. These are also the times when male chauvinism develops. From Deborah's story, one learns about the chauvinistic as well as the egalitarian aspects. Nonetheless, it becomes clear that the Old Testament is at times less of a totally male-oriented text than some of its later Jewish and Christian interpreters may have wished the coming generations to believe.

As further background to Deborah's drama, we should recall certain other women's deeds in *Judges*. It was a woman who killed Abimelech in Thebetz, by dropping a millstone on his head. Dying, he still managed to utter to his armour bearer: "Draw your sword and kill me, so people will not say about me, 'a woman killed him'" (9:54). Even in a relatively egalitarian society it was considered a humiliation to be killed by a woman. Joab reminds David of that same historical incident many years later, through the messenger he sends to the king during the Bath-Sheba affair. Jephtah, the son of a whore, suffered humiliation due to his low social status in the eyes of his brothers. From a psychoanalytic aspect, he went out to defend his family-people, perhaps as a mode of protecting his mother's honor, but then sacrificed his daughter (11). Micah's mother is another interesting woman, who saved money for religious purposes (17:1–6). Samson pursued women and was pursued by them. His mother, as described, proved to be an intelligent, cool-minded woman who calmed her awe-stricken husband after the angel of God had ascended to heaven: "If the Lord had meant to kill us, he would not have accepted a burnt offering and a grained offering at our hands, or shown us all these things or now announced to us such things as these" (13:23). Samson himself followed the woman from Timna and then fall victim to Delilah's emotional blackmail (16:4–22). There were three thousand 'men and women' on the roof of Dagon's temple, shortly before Samson brought it down, a rare example of mentioning women as part of an audience at any biblical public event. One may therefore see this note as ironic: women caused Samson's eventual fall as well as his loss of sight.

Chapter 4 opens with "The Israelites again did what was evil in the sight of the Lord, and (or 'but') Ehud died." The last two words can be understood as a tribute to the dead hero, who had brought eighty years of rest to the country and was rich in deeds though sparing in his use of words. The only direct quotations from him are "I have a secret message for you" and "I have a message from God for you" (3:19; 20) when entering Eglon's quarters, and "Follow after me, for the Lord has given your enemies the Moabites into your hands" (3:28). Compared with Deborah's dialogues with Barak and her long song later, one may assume that the repeated mention of Ehud's death at the beginning of Deborah's story is not accidental. The author may have juxtaposed Ehud's heroic deeds with hers as a slightly ironic reminder, especially in the light of her self-glorifying speech.

"Then the Israelites cried out to the Lord for help" (4:3). The direct cause for the Israelites crying out for God's help is mentioned at the beginning. The Canaanites had 900 'chariots of iron' (tanks or armoured vehicles in today's military terms), which the oppressed Israelites did not have. The more advanced technology enabled the northern king to levy high taxes from his poorer southern neighbours, take their sons for slaves and their daughters for pleasure.

In the next scene, following the exposition, Deborah is drawn in grand terms. The text presents her as 'A woman Prophetess', a grammatical redundancy, since the Hebrew 'nevi'ah' is the feminine form for a woman-prophet. She is also 'eshet Lapidoth', which may mean a fiery, torch-like woman, or simply the wife of a man called Lapidoth. Though vicariously present through their names, neither Deborah's husband, nor the husband of Jael, the other important female character in the drama, will ever appear. Both women think and act independently from men in general and from their husbands in particular. But the husbands' names must nevertheless be mentioned, at least as an identity-card showing their existence.

Deborah was judging Israel at the time, while sitting 'under the palm of Deborah'. Either she was named after the palm, or the palm was called after her. The metaphoric value of Deborah = palm is significant. Trees in many different cultures have a ritual, sometimes mystical significance. A tree signifies, among many other qualities, rootedness, growth, fruitfulness. Similarly, a subtextual meaning may be ascribed to the difference between the (so far 'offstage') 'iron' technology of the Canaanites and, in this scene, the onstage 'tree' culture of the Israelites, which is more agricultural and idyllic. The wood will subdue the iron. As stage-props, Jael's tent-peg and hammer (or mallet) were probably also made of wood. Theatrically, the biblical playwright prepares the space in which the action is about to take place, as well as some of the materials for the props to be used.

Deborah's position is rapidly built-up by a series of stage instructions. The instructions not only provide the necessary information as to where things happened, but also function as anticipating Deborah's verbal entrance. "The Israelites came up to her for judgement", indicates that she is 'on top', geographically and sociologically. The phrase "she sent and summoned Barak son of Abinoam from Kedesh in Naphtali", fully establishes her authority as leader, prophetess and judge.[4]

Barak has arrived from the far north and after having climbed Deborah's hill he is now ready to listen to orders under Deborah's palm! A masterfully theatrical dialogue develops between the powerful woman and the army general. It must have taken place in the presence of the large and curious crowd standing around, or else Deborah would have chosen a private, rather than a public place for the meeting. She may also have made deliberate use of her authority-radiating 'space' as an added device to pressure Barak into action. Skipping formalities and small-talk, Deborah gets straight to the point. She is nevertheless tactful enough to give her orders in God's name, not hers.

She chooses a military commander from the north, because the northern Israeli tribes, especially Naphtali and Zebulun, had suffered most from Jabin's oppressive means: "Does not ['halo'] the Lord, the God of Israel, commands you: Go take position at Mount Tabor, bringing ten thousand from the tribe of Naphtali and the tribe of Zebulun." Her orders are specific and strategic. She mentions numbers, tactical moves and the exact arena for the battle: "I will draw out Sisera, the general of Jabin's army, to meet you by the Wadi Kishon with his chariots and his troops; and I will give him into your hand." The shrewd rhetoric of the text suggests a parallel between King Jabin and General Sisera on the Canaanite side, and the Prophetess, Judge (and almost Queen?) Deborah and General Barak on the Israeli side. The military order is followed by the absolute assurance: "I will give him into your hand." Another rhetorical device is the two different modes of the verb 'to draw': once in the second person singular (you will draw); and the other in the first person singular (I will draw), which maintain a deliberate (?) blurring of the possible speaking voices. Is Deborah speaking for God or for Deborah herself?

Barak's answer must be comprehended within the right theatrical context of space, of other silent participants in the scene, etc. He says: "If you will go with me, I will go; but if you will not go with me, I will not go." Deborah started her address to Barak with 'halo', equivalent to 'is it not that? . . .', but Barak ignores the divine source, and does not react to Deborah's implicit demand that he should have known in advance what he is hearing now, namely, that this is the right time for an uprising against the oppressor. His answer is an immediate response to Deborah's authority. It is important to note that already at this stage of planning, Sisera himself is not promised to Barak, only his chariots and troops. We may regard this as dramatic irony, or at least anticipation.

Barak is revealed as a hesitant commander, willing to 'go' only if she comes with him. Whereas Deborah's style is laconic and manly, Barak's response, according to stereotypes, is weak, childish, womanish. The Bible, however, does not seem to have a problem in presenting strong women and weak men. Deborah reacts: "I will surely go with you, nevertheless, the road on which you are going will not lead to your glory, for the Lord will sell Sisera into the hand of a woman." Her answer is rhetorically complex. She implies that since he was not satisfied with her command but wanted her actual presence, he will not enjoy a glory that could have been his. She may also have been hinting that God would give Sisera into her hands; or did she really prophesy that Jael would kill Sisera?

In the next scene Deborah 'got up', again signifying, in the non-verbal theatrical language of movement, that she is the active partner. The verb 'to get up' will soon be used more frequently, connoting that Barak was indeed a relatively passive, mentally slouching partner, in dire need of constant prodding. He will summon the troops, but not without Deborah who 'came up with him', and 'went with him'. The by now almost comic repetition suggests that General Barak needs a prophetic baby-sitter.

Already in *Judges* 1:16 the Kenites, descendants of Moses's father-in-law, are mentioned, and at this point in the drama they reappear, dramatically foreshadowing Jael's act. The Kenites have "encamped as far away as Elon-bezaananim, which is near Kedesh". The importance of this clan and their geographical and political mid-way location between the Israelites and the Canaanites will soon be evident, but the very fact of mentioning them indicates the centrality the author ascribes them in the seemingly exclusively Deborah focused story. This subplot receives minute attention.

The rhythm and intensity of the scene shifts is heightened, and the main plot returns to Sisera who learns that the Israelite troops have gone up to Mount Tabor. There on the slopes, Sisera has no tactical advantage with his chariots, and Barak plans an infantry ambush against a much stronger military force, near wadi Kishon. Sisera calls up all his immensely powerful, portrayed as anonymous mass of troops, at which point in the rising tension the playwright wisely chooses to focus on Deborah, prodding Barak into action: "[Get] Up, for this is the day on which the Lord has given Sisera into your hand. ['halo', namely again 'is it not that?. . .', connoting that Barak should have shown more initiative, perhaps] the Lord is indeed going out before you." The appeal 'Get Up' (*Kum*) has developed to be Deborah's habitual way of addressing Barak, as will become even clearer in "Get up, Barak" in Chapter 5. The repetition of 'get up!' can be seen as accumulating scorn toward Barak, as Deborah tells him that "the Lord is indeed going out before you".

A short scene is dedicated to the descent of the troops from Mount Tabor, and soon after the entire battle is fully appropriated and directed by the Lord, who "threw Sisera and all his chariots and all his army before Barak . . . " (4:15). The text makes it evident that Barak is not much more than a tool in God's (and Deborah's) hand to perform His will. Moreover, the entire military action is depicted as fulfilling Deborah's prophesy. In this Deborah oriented text, Barak appears to function not only against his own hesitant will, but almost by pure chance.

Having lost his whole army, "no one was left", the beaten Sisera "got down from his chariot and fled away on foot". Whereas the prose text pokes slight ironic darts at Sisera for having lost the chariots that had constituted the main source of his military advantage, in "fled away on foot", Deborah will really feast on the same in her song: "Then loud beat the horses' hoofs with the galloping, galloping of his steeds" (5:22). This little poisonous poetic peg is driven not only into the injured pride of the enemy, who now must flee on foot; it serves also as an aside directed toward, and meant to be overhead by, Barak. In the prose text of Chapter 4, the author is ironical toward both male generals, overcome by women. In the military pursuit that follows, Barak destroys Sisera's chariots only after God has executed the militarily more difficult mission. From a tactical point of view, Barak's task is presented as a secondary, mere 'cleaning-up' project.

The dramatic mode implied in the dialogues of the previous sections turns in the following scene into an overtly theatrical presentation, in fact, the most theatrical part in the prose section of the entire story. Sisera runs for his life to Jael's tent, "for there was peace between King Jabin of Hatzor and the clan of Heber the Kenite" (4:17). The author now engages the dramatic mode, becomes a playwright and concentrates not on epic, showy 'long-shot' war-tableaux; rather, he focuses on the human aspects of the battle. Instead of a big open field, the following scene takes place first outside, then inside a tent. The dramatic time of presentation corresponds, roughly, to the duration of the events presented. Instead of whole armies clashing, drowning, killing and wounding, etc., only two people are now intensely involved in a thoroughly theatrical situation.

Reflecting the Deborah-Barak tensions, the two participating characters 'happen' to be, again, an army general and a woman. As a subplot or indeed a play-within-a-play, the theatrical mode delivers the emotional and moral ramifications of the war, undealt with in of the previous scenes. The playwright designs a multi-leveled dialogue of action and speech between Sisera, the fleeing general, and a so far unknown woman, Jael. Her sudden appearance, however, is not entirely unprepared, and the reader or spectator is now able to identify the previous anticipation and connect Jael with the earlier hints about the Kenites. Sisera, the only survivor of a vanquished army, exhausted and frightened, is about to fall victim to the heroic act of a weak woman; or, alternately, to one of the most atrocious acts of betrayal and cold-blooded murder. For the time being, Barak and Deborah disappear from the stage. The dramatic mode overshadows the epic.

"Jael came out to meet Sisera, and said to him" – She must have heard him approach, perhaps when occupied with some work inside her tent. She may have recognized the man "for there was peace between . . .". As we soon learn, Jael is alone by the tent, and must therefore decide immediately what to do. The biblical playwright lets the potential spectator wonder about the precise distance between the standing Jael and the running, approaching Sisera, when she addresses him: "Turn aside, my lord" [or "come in"]. The repeated appeal indicates that Sisera hesitated; again she repeats "turn aside to me, have no fear". The implied spectator's imagination will supply the exact tone of voice that Jael used, and perhaps also answers to some of the additional gaps of information: Was she afraid too? Did she use an erotic undertone? Was she young and ugly? Old and very beautiful? Was it still raining? Were there any children around? Did Sisera breathe heavily? What exactly did he think of Jael? What did she think he though? Was she big and strong? Was he small and slight?

From our greater perspective of the entire scene, we must remember that Barak too was hesitant in accepting Deborah's call. However, the indication that there was peace between the Kenites and the King of Hatzor enhances the (emotional) option of understanding the first encounter between them, as Jael's attempt to turn the national tension of the situation into a pretended man–woman encounter. She does not ask about the reasons for Sisera's unexpected appearance, alone and on foot, but reacts to the apparent self-evidence of the situation at hand. Her words 'have no fear' obviously mean that he was indeed afraid. Jael, equally obviously, was reacting verbally to Sisera's non-verbal body language. Through her text, we learn about his behavior: insecure, exhausted, afraid.

"So he turned inside to her into the tent, and she covered him with a blanket." Whoever wants to imagine directing this scene will recognize that under the circumstances, Sisera had little choice. Whether real or pretended, the hospitality extended to him was irresistible. He may have believed that he had arrived at least at neutral if not friendly grounds. He may also have relied on the sacred tradition of hospitality which protected guests in those days and places. Sisera performs a double entrance: the first, from the cold and apparently rainy weather outside, where Barak is still pursuing him, into the warmth of a woman's home. His second 'entrance' is his hiding under Jael's blanket. The non-verbal gesture of covering Sisera with a blanket is a true mark of theatrical ingenuity. The blanket, first-aid for exhaustion, provides physical warmth and emotional safety. It offers, moreover, a visual cover against whoever may be pursuing Sisera, as the text itself will presently make evident. Furthermore, the blanket serves as a visual cover for Jael too, for she, by covering him, can hide her own intentions and deeds and gain time either to decide what she really wants to do, or to set in motion her plan to kill him. The blanket is the theatre curtain of this play-within-a-play.

From under the blanket, in his sheltered, weak position, Sisera "said to her: 'please give me a little water to drink; for I am thirsty'." The first words uttered by the general in this scene are courteous, almost meek. Indeed, like Barak's plea to have Deborah go with him, or "give me a hand", Sisera is begging for water. She, in turn "opened a skin of milk and gave him a drink and covered him". The giving of the milk intensifies the dramatic action from a number of theatrical aspects. This activity, which necessitates a moment of preparation, intensifies the dramatic tension with a moment of tense silence. From Sisera's point of view, the act can be perceived as extra tender loving care, while Jael might have decided to give him milk as a light sedative to both body and soul. On yet another level, the giving of milk rather than water can be performed as follows: She props the lying man up, and lets him drink as she holds him in her arms, leaning him against her breasts. The pair may now look like a mother nursing a child; a mock-pieta. After the nursing, she covers him again. At a first reading, the scene builds up toward Sisera's long-sought sweet and peaceful rest. A second reading retrospectively decodes the structure of Jael's activity as a devious means to mollify Sisera and prepare for his murder.[5]

A particularly ironic 'dialogue' develops between the spoken text and the stage instructions. Sisera, appeased with milk, is still not totally at ease: "Stand at the entrance of the tent, and if anybody comes and asks you, 'is anyone here?' say, 'no'." Was his head under the blanket when saying this, or did he half raise himself? Interestingly, the blanket, a central prop in the scene, separates Sisera and Jael, and similarly separates deeds from intentions, the text from the subtext in the spoken repartees, and the dialogical text from the stage instructions. The blanket enables Jael to fetch the peg and the hammer while Sisera is actually hiding under the blanket, as clarified by the previous speech. The blanket, the skin of milk, the peg and hammer – all serve as stage props, masterfully creating a theatrical language of their own, a richly connotative language communicating with the sparse verbal exchange between the two characters.

The biblical text, sophisticatedly, enables yet another interpretative possibility. After giving Sisera the milk, Jael lay under the blanket with him. Therefore he, perhaps suddenly anxious again, asks her to 'stand at the entrance' rather than lie there with him. This interpretation, subtly suggested in the prose text, namely that Jael used her erotic charms to seduce Sisera in order to weaken him yet more and then kill him, is almost explicit in Deborah's song, later on.

"Jael, wife of Heber the Kenite, took a tent peg, and took a hammer in her hand, and went softly to him and drove the peg into his temple, until it went down into the ground – he was lying fast asleep from weariness – and he died." If Jael stayed with Sisera under the blanket, following his request, she must have then got up, searched for the tools, waited till he fell 'fast asleep', approached him again, checked that he was asleep, looked for the best angle to hammer in the peg, and found the best spot in his temple, because he was lying on his side with his right or left temple exposed. The killing itself is performed in a typically energetic biblical series of verbs: She took (the peg), she put (the hammer), she came (to him), she drove (the peg with the hammer) – then 'she dropped' (*vatitznax*). Her activity, decisive and almost surgically precise, is theatrically enhanced by Sisera's passive posture. The original Hebrew, however, does not clarify who or what exactly 'dropped', was it Jael or the peg. 'Yathed' (peg) is a feminine noun, and if it was the peg that 'dropped to the ground', Jael, in 'driving it in', must have employed enormous vigour, because she spiked Sisera's head to the ground. If it was Jael who 'dropped to the ground', she was surely tired after the tension, the act itself, not to mention the emotional and moral ramifications of the killing. Sisera's death is described with an amazing, unique mixture of tender cruelty. Literally translated, we read: "and he fell asleep, and he was tired, and he died" – "*ve'hu nirdam, va'yaf, va'yamot.*" The playwright describes Sisera's sleep as merely a prelude to his death. One wonders whether this suggests that he did not suffer.

As noted, the killing began on the threshold between indoors and outdoors, at the entrance to Jael's tent. Whereas Barak's sword received a divine blessing through Deborah, Jael's peg and hammer acquired their own physical and metaphoric function through their exclusively theatrical usage. Deborah indeed prophesied that Sisera would be killed by a 'woman's hand', but did she really believe it would be another woman's hand rather than her own? This scene, analyzed according to stage-movement, begins outside the tent, glides into it (who enters first, Jael or Sisera?), continues with Sisera under the blanket, and Jael serving milk; then, perhaps, both lie together, after which Jael gets up, prepares the killing and performs it. The ironically dangerous space is, no doubt, the opening of the tent, although the true danger for Sisera lies within the tent. On a smaller scale, yet another pattern of movement can be discerned: Sisera may make little moves over and under the blanket, Jael 'moves' between the milk-skin and the hammer-and-peg. Shortly before the killing, attention is drawn once again to the potential danger outside.

In the next segment Barak is heard approaching, pursuing Sisera. "Jael went out to meet him, and said to him: 'Go, and I will show you the man whom you are seeking'." Like Sisera shortly before, Barak arrives, and again Jael goes out to meet the man, another general. She has already done what he had intended to do. Barak is invited to the scene of the killing. Jael, like Deborah, uses the imperative form 'go!' in addressing Barak, and we remember that she used 'come!' toward Sisera. The front theatre curtain is drawn (again) when the tent-cloth is opened for Barak to enter. The inner curtain drawn (again) is the blanket under which Sisera is lying dead. Barak's moment of *anagnorisis* has come. He realizes that not only did the initiative to start the war come from a woman, but the *coup de grâce* to end the war has also been taken away from him, once more by a woman.

Jael might have covered Sisera's body before going out to meet Barak, or she might have left it exposed. In either case, she stole the possibility of performing the 'most unkindest cut of all' from both Barak and Deborah. The biblical text allows any actress playing Jael to express and interpret her feelings in whatever way she may choose: full of remorse for the act; or relief; perhaps happy and gleeful.

The end of the prose chapter is significant: "So on that day, God subdued King Jabin of Canaan before the Israelites. Then the hand of the Israelites bore harder on King Jabin of Canaan, until they destroyed King Jabin of Canaan." This ending restores the real dramatic balance in the eyes of the Bible. It reconfirms Deborah's warning to Barak, that the results of the battle "will not lead to your glory, for the Lord will sell Sisera into the hand of a woman". The finale provides a cold shower for any potential human hubris the protagonists may have been likely to develop.

For the Bible surely endows God with all the credit. Deborah, Barak and Jael do not appear in this final curtain at all. The collective 'chorus' of Israelites, however, are brought back once more, as those who had completed the job, after God.

These lines, moreover, serve not only as an antidote to the hubris of the previous section, but also as an excellent preparation for Deborah's highly hubristic song that follows. She will open her song with praises to God the Saviour, but we are given a clear glimpse of her own ego too from time to time.

The second, poetic, explicitly-theatrical part of Deborah is as important as the first prosaic one, in that it provides a second view-point that acts as a corrective to the first one. From our specific angle, this performed story poem also enables us to closely observe how biblical fact becomes biblical theatre. It is difficult to know precisely how, when and where the verbal re-enactment of the battle and its particular circumstances took place. We may assume, though, that the event happened a few days after the war, under Deborah's palm, at a huge feast for the populace, a victory celebration. We should also remember that events of this political calibre remain in people's private as well as collective memories only if they are made into a text, aural–oral as well as written. In order to eternalize the victory and imprint its particular socio-religious and ideological significance upon people's minds, the event must be told, interpreted, fictionalized. To be effective, this retelling is turned into a public oratory, a theatre show. Deborah's song is her story, on its way to history.

It is possible that Deborah and Barak stood there on top of the hill, perhaps lit by the rays of the afternoon sun, and spoke their lines as a rhythmic, musical declamation: "Then Deborah and Barak son of Abinoam sang on that day . . ." From the situation and from the opening lines it follows that Deborah chanted the first 'voice' and Barak, if at all – the second. It may also be that the two singing leaders alternated roles and parts, as in a duet. Their mutual poetic–rhetoric interventions might have added an extra theatrical flair to the show, especially in the alternate 'prodding on' lines. Such lines reflect the relationships described in the prose part, where a hesitant Barak is instigated to go to battle, and now, perhaps, he pays Deborah back. For example, Deborah sings "I will sing to the Lord", and Barak answers "I will make melody to the Lord, the God of Israel" (5:3). Perhaps it was Barak who realized that Deborah had stopped for a moment, in itself a wonderfully effective public–rhetorical device, and 'woke her up' with "awake, awake, Deborah! Awake, awake, utter a song!", to which (once awake) she answered: "Arise (in fact a repetition of her previously mentioned 'kum', i.e. 'get up' appeal in the prose

part), Barak, lead away your captives, O son of Abinoam . . ."
Noteworthy in this case is the fact provided by the more objective prose
part, that the only captive Barak could have possibly brought in, had
already been killed by Jael. All the other Canaanites had been killed, as
the reader and audience remembers, and "no one was left" (4:16). Is
Deborah paying Barak an ironical tribute? It can only be surmised that
while standing there chanting, there was a lot of subtextual tension
between the two leaders.

Judging by the repeated lines "until I arose, Deborah, I arose as a
mother in Israel", the prophetess did not suffer from an excess of humility,
unless one prefers to think that the line, as some English translations
would have it, is spoken in the second rather than the first-person singular.
The cry "until I arose, Deborah, I arose as a mother in Israel . . ." suggests
that the prophetess wished to be likened to the founding mothers of the
Hebrew nation – Sarah, Rebecca, Leah and Rachel. She wished to become
a founding mother endowed with spiritual leadership, of an entire nation,
rather than a mere tribe. If God is the Father, she will be the Mother.[6]

The verse following the presentation of the speakers already conflicts
with the report delivered in Chapter 4. It says: "*bifro'a pera'ot be'Israel,
behitnadev am, barchu adonai* . . . " ["Praise ye the Lord for the avenging
of Israel, when the people willingly offered themselves"]. Following the
earlier text itself, no one had really volunteered, but it was Deborah who
had sent for Barak. In order to find grace in the eyes (and ears) of the audience, it is rhetorically wise to flatter them. Once victorious, people tend
to forget that they had not been at all keen on risking their lives, miserable as they were. Embellishing the pre-war facts has been known to
happen, both before and after Deborah. "Hear O Kings, Listen, O
Princes" may constitute an address to the Israelites, or else to the kings
and noblemen around them. The possible subtextual implication is that
'we are not as weak as we may seem, watch out!'

Only then does Deborah appeal to the Lord with "I sing to the Lord,"
etc. The similarity between Deborah's song and Moses's song (*Exod.* 14)
is neither accidental nor a plagiarism. As a mytho-historical event,
Deborah alludes to her audience's collective memory of the nationally
unforgettable dry crossing of the Red Sea. Whereas the prose text only
says "and the Lord threw Sisera's chariots and all his army into a panic"
("*va'yehom*"), the poetic play-text is more explicit: "the torrent Kishon
swept them away", which most probably means that on that day their
was a flood in the wadi, and all the iron chariots were either carried away
with the waters or stuck in the mud.

Allusions link the source text with the target text, and create a tension
between the two. This particular allusion to Moses's song, in relying on

the miraculous element in both, and God's manipulation of water, implic-itly suggests that the present miracle be seen as historically significant as the one in Egypt, long ago. Certainly, the allusion comes to prove God's continued providence for his people. The resemblance between the orig-inal *Exodus* poetry (equally theatrical!) and Deborah's presentation is based on the common denominator of water. But Moses was not only more humble, he was a better poet as well.

Whereas the Exodus is strongly emphasized because it happened long ago, it is interesting to note that Deborah also mentions Shamgar son of Anath, the judge who preceded her. Shamgar managed to kill 600 Philistines with his oxgoad, but is otherwise considered a minor figure, for lack of any further biblical information about him. Deborah recalls that "he too delivered Israel" (3:31). While (deliberately?) ignoring the courageous deeds and feats of Ehud son of Gera and those of Othniel son of Kenaz, Deborah might have found it efficacious to mention only a minor judge whose reputation would not overshadow hers, and who would steal her show, especially on this particular day. Deborah, either because of her personality (which I believe to be the case), or because she was a woman (who must work harder to assert herself in a patriarchal society), or because of contemporary rhetorical conventions (hardly ever found elsewhere in the Bible) or else because she was carried away in her own sweeping speech – invented the "Until I arose" (*Ad shakamti*) syndrome. This syndrome has been ever since typical to many leaders and other heads of institutions: 'whatever happened before I arrived, is less important.' Jael is given some credit, later to be developed in Deborah's unique way.

Deborah describes the hard situation in the country, when people were forbidden by the Canaanite oppressors to carry weapons. She also sati-rizes the local leadership who "ride on white donkeys, who sit on rich carpets", because they, probably, had not called upon the people to rebel, preferring instead to continue enjoying the privileges given to them by the Canaanites. She was probably right in her accusations. However, in the present context of her grand public appearance, one may suspect a touch of populism here too. She praises the shepherds and the simple folk: "there they sing the triumphs of the Lord, the triumphs of his peasantry in Israel." Handing out praises and reprimands, Deborah clearly sees God as the main protagonist, and next to Him – the people.

After repeating her praise to the volunteers among the people in general (5:9) she turns to a minute political, often satirical book-keeping with the various tribes and their relative contribution to the battle. The audience of the time was presumably more receptive to her hints, which we today are unable to fully decipher. The tribes of Ephraim, Menashe (Machir) and Benjamin, in the central part of the country, are praised for joining the battle in the north. The northern tribes of Zebulun, Issachar and Naphtali were necessarily directly involved in the war because of their geographic proximity, but they are praised nevertheless. Dan and Asher, as sea-faring tribes remained in their ships, and Gilead (namely the tribes of Gad and half of Menashe), on the eastern side of the Jordan, were also not involved. Reuven, especially, is ridiculed for not participating: "Why do you tarry among the sheepfolds, to hear the piping for the flocks? Among the clans of Reuben there were great searchings of heart" (5:16). The town of Meroz receives a real curse "because they did not come to the help of the Lord" (5:23).

Having settled her accounts with most of the tribes, Deborah does not mention Judah and Simeon at all – perhaps because they were not expected to take part, due to their southern location. As a national judge and prophetess, Deborah's song is highly political and as such, quite informative in regard to intertribal relationships among the Israelites. The political aspect of her speech is, nevertheless, subservient to the divine force. "The stars fought from heaven . . ." even "the torrent Kishon swept them away." The forces of nature are enlisted to God's army.

The last part of Deborah's powerful verbal performance is dedicated to one highly tendentious scene, reconstructing the killing of Sisera by Jael, and one quite imaginary scene, ridiculing another woman, Sisera's mother.

About the same amount of space is given to the Jael–Sisera play-within-a-play in both the prose and the poetry sections. Deborah begins with an overall "most blessed of women be Jael", emphasizing Jael's marital status as "the wife of Heber the Kenite"; perhaps, in Deborah's subtext, Jael could not have done what she did without this family affiliation, and adds: "of tent-dwelling women most blessed". The tent-dwelling remark may be the result of sheer poetic licence, or a slight put-down of Jael, not quite a complete Israelite but still socially acceptable. Deborah focuses on Jael's milk-instead-of-water gesture, strangely allowing herself another poetic liberty with "in a lordly bowl she brought him curds". Her inclination towards bizarre if not tactless metaphors is noteworthy in "and [raised] her right hand to the workman's mallet" (5:26), which again draws attention, if this was her intention, to Jael's 'working-class' status. This, however is not the end of this series of poetic–dramatic insinuations, which includes several back-handed compliments.

Whereas the prose part uses three different factual verbs to portray Sisera's death, Deborah's song wallows in the synonyms "she struck a blow, she crushed his head, she shattered and pierced his temple". To her (poetic) defence it may be said that she was performing to a victorious crowd, who must have lapped up such a vivid depiction of the death of their mortal enemy. Deborah's next poetic evaluation of Jael may have been true to fact or not, but here she really went far overboard the somewhat monotonous "between her legs (or feet) he kneeled, he fell, wherever he kneeled, there he fell, lay between her legs (or feet), he kneeled, he fell, wherever he kneeled there he fell dead" (5:27). (Prim English versions opt for the much softer, but misleading "at her feet" instead of the precise Hebrew "between her legs.") The repetition is nevertheless rhetorically effective, ridiculing the enemy, while being not altogether complimentary to Jael. The repeated "between her legs" is not a perfect model for female solidarity. The audience was probably happily ready to fall for Deborah's insinuation that Jael's main mode of killing Sisera was through an overdose of sex. While poking some gross fun at men at large, this line also offers an extra subtextual dart shot in Barak's direction.

Deborah achieves her highest degree of vulgar and sarcastic vindictiveness in constructing an imaginary scene, featuring Sisera's mother as the mock-star. The arch-enemy's mother is described sitting by the window, waiting for her son. All of 'us', Israelite victors, audience and (future) readers, know that he is already dead, killed by a woman. The following scene of offstage theatre is particularly cruel, as well as pseudo-feminist. It begins with the worried mother of Sisera: "Out of the window she peered, the mother of Sisera gazed through the lattice: 'Why is his chariot so long in coming? Why tarry the hoofbeats of his chariots?'" Shrewdly, Deborah uses the image of the chariots, Sisera's main source of power, in her speech to the (probably laughing) audience. She continues with a womanly, equally fictitious conversation, in which the ladies attending Sisera's mother try to calm her: "Her wisest ladies make answer", – but she, worried and impatient, answers before they do: "indeed, she answers the question herself (or: she answers them): Are they not finding and dividing the spoil?" Surely, the audience knows, no spoil was divided. And Deborah goes on with her now explicit sexual insinuations: "A girl or two for every man" – using the Hebrew term 'rehem', namely womb, or more precisely in this context, a relatively clean word for 'cunt'. Interestingly, the Hebrew 'rehem' is also associated with 'mercy', which is certainly not found here. Deborah goes on: "spoil of died stuffs for Sisera, spoil of colorful (died) stuffs embroidered, two pieces of colorful (dyed) work embroidered for (my) necks as spoil?" A woman or two are hence equalled to one or two pieces of embroidered stuff. Deborah reveals herself as an excellent public speaker, a talented cheap actress who knows exactly how to win her audience. A little comic relief at the end is always a sure thing.

Deborah may appear less vulgar and vindictive, however, if we consider that the Israelites had suffered from the Canaanite oppression for many years.

The show ends with "So perish all your enemies. O Lord! But may your friends (Heb. 'lovers') be like the sun as rises in its might" – a return to decorum, though after the last two scenes so well performed by Deborah, the religious impact of the last lines may well have been lost on the happily feasting crowd.

In a 'Rashomon'-like technique of receiving the same basic information twice, once as an objective historical drama of a successful rebellion and once as a text delivered to a live audience, readers of the Deborah–Barak, Sisera–Jael story are extended the invitation to make up their own minds regarding the 'truth' or the poetic-rhetorical exaggerations in connection with a post-war euphoria. God, in both genres, receives the lion's share of the glory. Notwithstanding, the purely military encounter was accordingly unbalanced, because of God's ascribed active intervention. The text of Chapter 4 is a careful, subtle and sometimes ironic prose. The theatrical text of Chapter 5 is poetic (rhythmical, alliterative, loaded with imagery, etc.), rhetorically fast and sociologically most interesting; but it is not great poetry by any biblical standards. One may wonder whether the text of Chapter 4 was written by a man, whereas the poetic Chapter 5 text was indeed first spoken and performed by a woman, and then written down. Is it too far-fetched to assume that in a male-oriented society, the primarily or exclusively male editors of the Bible gave Deborah a rope and let her present herself as she wished? Was this the devious way by which they subtly criticised Deborah? Or did the writers/editors indeed identify with the cruel tactlessness displayed in some sections of Deborah's performance, regarding it as a perfectly justifiable release of emotions after long years of Canaanite persecution? Moses' victory song was not as blatantly vindictive, but now the Israelites have reached the promised land, and things have changed. Clearly, the heroes of the entire story are the two women. One was a prophetess, a judge and a national leader. The other one performed a horrid deed, but since she may have had no other option, and especially since in doing so she made herself 'ours', the murder is not only pardoned but profoundly praised. Only the prose writer of Chapter 4 shows signs of moral ambivalence. The third woman, the offstage Sisera's mother, is mocked in her absence. The men throughout this entire drama are depicted as weak. Barak was prodded by a woman, Sisera was killed by one.

Did Deborah in her speech internalize the male discourse in order to be accepted nationally? As long as she is in the hands of the prose writer, her portrait is that of a strong personality, reserved and intriguing. As soon as she opens her own mouth (if she did), and despite the understandable unique conditions of the public occasion, she loses stature and becomes petty, sanctimonious and vicious. At the peak of her glory she reveals a vindictiveness and a hatred of women which only woman haters would dare call feminine.

The women's roles offer interesting food for thought. Deborah did not allow Jael to steal the show from her completely, whereas the (probably male) writer of Chapter 4 uses the stage instructions to depict Jael with all the moral and emotional complexities of her deed. The editor (I assume) of Deborah's song, also seems to allow Deborah's harsh words against Sisera's mother, hoping, perhaps, that sensitive readers will arrive at their own conclusions regarding the pronounced speaker. Is it that in war times 'even' women become heartless and ferocious, even toward other women? Is this the morale of the story as well as the play? Jael, as one example, may have had no choice but to do a dreadful deed well. Deborah lived in a man's world, and behaved accordingly.

Chapters 4 and 5 must be regarded as one dramatic whole, with two mutually complementary parts. Without the drama of the first party mainly implied (though explicit in the scene of killing Sisera), the second part cannot be properly understood either, and vice versa. The dramatic tension as well as the theatrical potential are revealed in juxtaposing both parts. Without the second theatrical part, the first would be mytho-history. The dramatic tension is revealed not only in regard to the events themselves, but also in relation to the protagonists.

3

Tamar: Acting-out a Role Imposed

———

Chapter 38 in *Genesis* is a dramatic accolade to Tamar,[1] the self-liberated biblical woman. Tamar, the daring, wise and elegant protagonist, takes her destiny into her own hands, and ventures not only to challenge the patriarchal system, but indeed to use its oppressive force against itself. This unique woman receives the approval of the (male?) author,[2] and is later mentioned in *Ruth* as a positive, highly acclaimed national model.

The thirty verses of Chapter 38 are dramatic and theatrical in more than one sense. The plot develops from a reported exposition into a fully dialogical central scene, after which the live, direct theatricality is maintained to the end. The main motivating force of the plot is Tamar's disguise as a whore, in which role she chooses another 'persona' in order to redress the injustice afflicted upon her (and, vicariously, upon many other women too). She plays the role of a whore, falsely ascribed to her, in order to redeem her true personal and social position. Tamar consciously, bravely and wisely, uses theatricality. Equally theatrical is the author's treatment of the entire story, in which Tamar is shown as unable to change the system, but quite capable of challenging it.

The family has always been a favorite issue in drama. Whether linked by blood or marriage, members of any family are inescapably bound to each other by love, desire, death, envy, and various social and economic commitments. They must solve their relationships, one way or another. Even without the classical dramatic constrictions of time and space, family ties alone often suffice to produce highly tense and 'dramatic' situations. The Tamar play, like many other biblical stories, also deals with family problems, but mainly from Tamar's point of view.

The characters in the play, in order of appearance, are: Judah, Hirah his Adullamite friend, the daughter of Shuah (Judah's wife), Judah's sons (Er, Onan and Shelah), Tamar, unspecified people of Enaim, unspecified informers who deliver gossip about Judah and Tamar, a Midwife and, finally, the new born babies of Judah and Tamar: Peretz and Zerah.

Structurally, the story lends itself to a surprisingly precise dramatic division of scenes:

- **Exposition** (38:1–2): Judah sets up his tent, sees a woman, takes her and "comes to her". Immediately thereafter –
- Act 1, scene i (38:3): Shuah's daughter conceives, gives birth and Judah names their son Er.
- Act 1, scene ii (38:4): Shuah's daughter conceives again, gives birth and she names their son Onan.
- Act 1, scene iii (38:5): Shuah's daughter conceives again, gives birth and she names their son Shelah.

This reported sequence must last at least three years, and takes away from Judah's other brothers. Shelah, as indicated, is born in Chezib (38:5). *A few years pass until:*

- Act 2, scene i (38:6–7): Judah takes Tamar as wife for Er his firstborn, Er dies. (Length of time is not specified.)
- Act 2, scene ii (38:8–10): Judah tells Onan, the second son to "perform the brother-in-law's duty". Onan spills his semen. God kills Onan. (Length of time is not specified.)
- Act 2, scene iii (38:11): Judah sends Tamar to her father's house for fear that his third son Shelah might also die, if given to Tamar. She goes. (Length of time is not specified.)

Interlude (38:12–13): Judah's wife dies. Judah goes to his sheep-shearers in Timnah. Tamar finds out where he is. From this time on, the action becomes directly dramatic and fully dialogical.

- Act 3, scene i (38:14): Tamar takes off her widow's garments, dresses like a prostitute with a veil, and waits for Judah.
- Act 3, scene ii (38:15–18): Judah and Tamar discuss the price and the pledge and have sex.
- Act 3, scene ii (38:19): Tamar conceives, takes off her prostitute's clothing, dresses once more in widow's weeds. *A day or two later –*
- Act 4, scene i (38:20): Judah sends Hirah to find Tamar and get his pledge back.
- Act 4, scene ii (38:21–22): Hirah cannot find Tamar.

- Act 4, scene iii (38:23): Judah and Hirah talk.
  Three months later –
- Act 5, scene i (38:24) Judah hears that Tamar has whored and is pregnant, and decrees that she be burnt to death.
- Act 5, scene ii (38:25) Tamar reveals Judah's pledge (signet, cord and staff).
- Act 5, scene iii (38:26) Judah 'recognizes'.
  Six months later –
- **Epilogue** (38:27–30): Tamar gives (a particularly complicated) birth to twins.

One of the subversive messages implied in the text is that men kill and die, whereas women live and give life (except for Judah's wife who must die in order to make place for Tamar).[3] Three woman participate in the play. One is Shuah's daughter whom Judah took for his wife. She has no first name and is known only by her father's name. As an intensely silent character, she is mentioned again as Judah's wife when she dies. Shuah's daughter is not given one single line in the play. Her mute voice is nevertheless particularly noticeable when two of her sons die. In comparison with Judah's impulsive vigour ('saw her', 'took her', 'came into her') Shuah's daughter's silence is even more emphasized. Her deliberately passive role in the story is to give birth and see her sons die. But the text does not neglect to mention that it was she who gave the names to Onan and to Shelah, whereas Judah named his firstborn Er.

The Tamar story deals with women's rights, drawing our attention to other subtly subversive stage instructions in biblical texts concerning the status of oppressed women. Dinah (Shimon and Levi's sister and thus Tamar's relative), for example, does not utter a single word throughout the entire stormy Chapter 34 in *Genesis*. The shocking events of the concubine in the Gibeah drama too, focus on the main victim through one, virtually expressionistic stage instruction, "with her hands on the threshold" (*Judges* 19:27). Muted characters can radiate an enormous power on stage precisely because they do not (or are not allowed to) talk. Sophocles's Cassandra and Brecht's Katrin are but two of many such examples from the world drama. The sexually aggressive Potiphar's wife appears right after the Tamar story (*Genesis* 39), indirectly suggesting that the use of trickery to get with child is acceptable, but cheating on one's husband and enjoying sex is not.

Another nameless woman in the Tamar play is the midwife who performs her professional function when Tamar gives birth to the twins. But, perhaps because Tamar's actions have given her courage, she is not mute, being allowed first to speak about the newborn babies and then to them: "This one came out first," she says about Zerah who reached out his hand, and "What a breach you have made for yourself!" she says to Peretz, who pushed his way out into the world. Retrospectively, these remarks can be understood as a refined, understated criticism on the way men behave right from the moment of birth. Otherwise, why should the playwright have 'quoted' an insignificant midwife's words?

Both the daughter of Shuah and the midwife enhance, in their nameless (or purely functional) identities, the character of Tamar. Tamar, in turning from a passive to an active character, employs a classic theatrical trick, and becomes a voice for other muted women who are invited to create their social (at least) identity through the device of masking and demasking themselves and the male-oriented society around them. Ruth, for one, indeed follows Tamar's model. Tamar, significantly, begins as a voiceless passive character, whose unjust social and personal oppression gradually pushes her into action, once she decides to change her situation. In the beginning she is sent to be Er's wife, then pushed on to Onan, and then sent home to her father. Her passiveness is further stressed in the unspoken but clearly felt morbid competition between her grief as widow over the death of two husbands, tacitly juxtaposed with Judah's agony as a bereaved father.

"It happened at that time that Judah went down from his brothers and settled near an Adullamite whose name was Hirah. There Judah saw the daughter of a Canaanite whose name was Shuah; he took her, and went into her."

The Tamar story is inserted in *Genesis* after the opening chapter of the Joseph stories, and its location suggests that Judah chose to be away from his brothers, the considered result of selling Joseph to Egypt. While influencing his brothers not to kill Joseph, Judah nevertheless collaborated with them by not telling Jacob the truth about his beloved son. An important *anagnorisis* thematically links *Genesis* 37 and the Tamar story in Chapter 38. When the brothers bring Jacob the robe of Joseph soaked with goat's blood they say: "This we have found, recognize whether this is your son's robe or not" (37:32). The text uses the term '*hakker-na*' – won't you recognize.[4] The same motif of recognition appears in Judah's recognition of his own signet, cord and staff, and indeed in his realization that "Tamar is more in the right than I . . ." (38:26). Judah is presented as a doer, not a thinker, and certainly not a feeler. In a series of verbs he 'sees', 'takes' and 'goes into' his new wife.

In the next act, three sons are born. Judah names his firstborn and his wife names the next two. A number of years pass, and Judah is still described as the decisive man who "took a wife for Er his firstborn; her name was Tamar". The reader is invited to again examine Judah's actions, as perhaps ensuing from the emotional aftermath of the recent Joseph affair. Trying to establish his own family, the shadows of the past are hovering and haunting. The next verse reveals an immediate problem: "But Er, Judah's firstborn, was wicked in the sight of the Lord, and the Lord put him to death." Er, when written from left to write means 'wicked' (ra) in Hebrew, as noticed by ancient Jewish bible scholars. At this point, for some unexplained mysterious or arbitrary reason, Judah loses a son and Tamar loses her husband, whether she wanted him, grew to love him, cared for him – or not. Er's mother, as noticed, is not mentioned at all. The text does not waste a word about mourning, which may have been taken for granted. But action is soon to follow:

"Then Judah said to Onan: 'Go in to your brother's wife and perform the duty of brother-in-law to her; raise up offspring for your brother'." But since Onan knew that the offspring will not be considered his, he spilled his semen on the ground whenever he went in to his brother's wife, so that he would not provide offspring for his dead brother: "What he did was displeasing (the Hebrew uses the same grammatical root 'ra' here too) in the sight of the Lord, and he put him to death also."

Whereas Judah's order to his second son Onan is quite clear, the emotional ramifications are extremely complex, for all parties involved. To begin with, Judah's command, following Tora laws, treats Tamar as a piece of family property. But under the contemporary circumstances it also shows consideration for Tamar, that she may not remain husband and childless. One may assume that Judah did not ask either Tamar or Onan whether they consented. Did Onan love his sister-in-law? Was she at all interested in him? Could it be that Judah was (already then) secretly in love with Tamar? What was Shuah's daughter's opinion? Feelings? Each of these possibilities could be further developed within the intricate network of family relationships, especially under the intensifying influence of a son's death.

Once in bed with Tamar, Onan may have sexually performed to the full satisfaction of both – except for impregnating his partner. God, however, was less interested in their orgasms, and much more in fertility. Moreover, Onan is probably not rightfully responsible for the noun derived from his name – 'Onanism', namely masturbation, since his sexual behavior was simply a well-known contraceptive technique. Love, again, is not mentioned, since in this context the 'seed' (a frequent term in the text) and the prospects of inheriting the land count for much more. Tamar, furthermore, in the typically biblical anticipatory-retrospective world-view, will become one of king David's ancestors, like Ruth, generations later.

The second son's death is directly associated by the biblical author with Tamar, but ascribed to Onan's sin in not properly performing his duty, irrespective of his love (or lack of such) for Tamar. Tamar herself is not to blame, but did Judah know this? According to the Hebrew law, it is now Shelah, the third son's turn to perform the duty of brother-in-law and impregnate Tamar. Surely all the emotional complications regarding Er's death must have become by now far more intense? What did Shelah think? Feel? Was he afraid of Tamar? Did she like him as the little brother of Er and Onan? Had they ever played together?

"Then Judah said to his daughter-in-law Tamar, 'Remain a widow in your father's house until my son Shelah grows up' – for he feared that he too would die, like his brothers. So Tamar went to live in her father's house."

Aware of the legal obligation, Judah the twice bereaved father, sends the twice widowed Tamar away. Although personal grief is difficult to compare, it is evident that Judah's legal position as a man is by far more comfortable than Tamar's. She is doomed to 'remain a widow', which, in this social context, means that she is not free to marry anyone but Shelah. In modern terms, she is put into deep freeze and deprived of any real marital status, including children and economic security. The scene in which Judah tells her to go is absolutely matter-of-fact, devoid of any emotion. Consequently, one can only imagine the period during which Tamar stayed at her father's house, and what she thought, felt, wanted and finally decided to do, in that course of time.

"In the course of time the wife of Judah, Shuah's daughter, died; when Judah's time of mourning (in Hebrew *va'yinahem*, one word only, meaning 'and he was comforted') was over, he went up to Timnah to his sheepshearers, he and his friend Hirah the Adullamite. Tamar was told, 'Your father-in-law is going up to Timnah to shear his sheep'."

Judah's habitually abrupt actions are described with the particularly short "when the mourning was over" (or "and he was comforted"), thus raising a question about his real grief over the death of his wife (who had herself perhaps died of heartbreak?). Instead of indulging in feelings, the text characterizes Judah with yet another action. Judah goes with his friend, perhaps a comforter too, to shear his sheep, both because it is time, and as a means to distract his mind from yet another death in the family. Some good though unnamed souls bother to inform Tamar about Judah's trip, proving, as later reconfirmed, that there was indirect communication between Tamar and Judah.

The text, however, does not mention explicitly whether Tamar was informed of Judah's wife's death. This omission, if deliberate, sheds a certain light on Tamar's action. If she did know of Shuah's daughter's

death (the more likely opion), she may have assumed that Judah had not
had sex lately.[5] If she did not know of his wife's death, she would still try
to seduce him.

One of the most dramatic scenes in the Old Testament follows,
performed in theatrical deeds, not feelings.

"She put off her widow's garments, put on a veil, wrapped herself up,
and set down at the entrance to Enaim, which is on the road to Timnah.
She saw that Shelah was grown up, yet she had not been given to him in
marriage."

The scene opens with Tamar's exquisite change of costume, a change
of personality. She plans a sexual ambush, in which the sex-act is not
planned for pleasure or for money, but in order to get pregnant. Tamar
chooses the obvious location: town outskirts have long been favourite
locations for prostitutes to solicit lustful businessmen who, in turn, prefer
to enjoy quick anonymous sex away from the center where they might be
recognized. Tamar, moreover, must have planned (or enjoyed the coincidence?) of her ovulation day as well. Delicately balancing Judah's
previous "for fear he [Shelah] too would die . . .", as Judah's reason for
denying Tamar his third son, the text introduces Tamar's very similar
motivation as well: "she had not been given to him . . .".

"When Judah saw her, he thought her to be a prostitute, for she had
covered her face."

From the surface of the text we learn that prostitutes in those days,
whether they exposed their bodies or not, usually covered their faces. But
in this highly individualized context (and subtext) Tamar had, naturally,
yet another reason to hide her face from her father-in-law.

"He went over to her at the road side" (the verb 'yet' is the same as
that used for Judah's 'went down from his brothers' in the beginning of
the chapter). The irony of the situation in which Judah 'just' 'went over
to her', lies in the fact that this will turn out to be no mere 'side issue'. It
may also suggest the difference between the masculine attitude to the
possible consequence of sexual intercourse, which the feminine partner
will bear for nine months. It is precisely this difference that the text underlines in Tamar's plan.

> And (JUDAH) said: "Let me come in to you" [for he did not know that
> she was his daughter-in-law].
> SHE said: "What will you give me, that you may come in to me?"
> HE answered: "I will send you a kid from the flock."
> And SHE said: "Only if you give me a pledge, until you send it."
> HE said: "What pledge shall I give you?"
> And SHE said: "Your signet and your cord, and the staff that is in your
> hand."

The reader (and definitely the implied spectator) can enjoy this classic case of dramatic irony, for the stage instruction minutely specifies: "he did not know she was his daughter-in-law." Tamar's answer can be enjoyed even more, because what she really wants from him will be contained in the act itself, for it is not money that she needs. One wonders that Judah does not recognize Tamar's voice. Or perhaps he suppresses his own recognition? His answer (especially, though inadvertently ambiguous in English), is that he will send her a 'kid' from his flock. Since Judah had already once promised Tamar a human child, this promise will not be taken seriously. Tamar needs a pledge to ensure, on the superficial level, that Judah will indeed 'pay'; but what she is really after are Judah's undeniable signs of identity. His "What pledge shall I give you?" sounds disarmingly naïve. Her final response in this repartee works on two levels. She does not want just one, or even two – but three indisputably highly personalized props, in order to prove later on that he is the only possible father. The signet, the cord and the staff can, in today's terms, be compared with a passport, a driver's license and a credit-card. Alluding to the 'staff' in his hand, a Freudian could well suggest that Tamar was refering to Judah's obvious sign of his desire, not just his personally carved walking cane or symbol of dominance. Indeed, he gives all these signs of his (blind?) eagerness to Tamar, who has not only succeeded in tempting him but, as will become clear three months later, has also 'got him' where he was weakest.

"So he gave them to her, and went in to her, and she conceived by him." Interestingly, the text hurries to declare that Tamar has 'conceived', even before she stands up. The scene ends, beautifully, in a reversed dressing ritual. Having conceived, Tamar returns to her widow's weeds in an entirely different mood.

"Then she got up and went away, and put off her veil and wore the garments of her widowhood."

Within a few moments Tamar has turned from widow to whore, then to mother and then again to widow. Her veiling and unveiling functions theatrically on the realistic as well as metaphoric level.

Horny but honest, as well as eager to receive his status symbols back, "Judah sent the kid by his friend the Adulamite, to recover the pledge from the woman. He could not find her." Hirah deserves the 'best supporting actor' award. Judah, possibly too proud to return to the scene with a little kid in his arms (or dragged reluctantly behind him) sends his friend Hirah, who cannot find Tamar. The scene emphasizes Judah's position throughout the entire story. He does not want to give Tamar his son Shelah (strangely, the name 'Shelah' in Hebrew also sounds like 'hers!'), and by sending Hirah he again avoids having to do something himself.

Tamar wants Judah's children, and since she will not be given Shelah, she takes the children directly from the source.

"He (Hirah) asked the townspeople, 'Where is the temple prostitute who was at Enaim by the wayside?'

But they said, 'No temple prostitute has been here'."

Hirah, embarrassed to inquire about a common whore, raises the woman's social status to that of a temple prostitute. Ironically, again, Tamar was indeed no prostitute, but Hirah does not know this.

"So he returned to Judah, and said, 'I have not found her'; moreover the townspeople said, 'No temple prostitute has been here.' Judah said, 'Let her keep them, otherwise we will be mocked; you see, I sent this kid, and you could not find her'."

The text repeats the term 'temple prostitute' three times, and thus draws attention to Tamar's mysterious identity. Judah gives up the attempt to recover his belongings, for fear that further publicity might ruin his reputation. His remark suggests that he is rather particular about his social status. Moreover, his fear of being a laughing-stock will soon be all too disastrously born out.

"About three months later Judah was told, 'Your daughter-in-law Tamar has whored; moreover she is pregnant as a result of whoredom." Parallel to Tamar being told of Judah's going to shear his sheep, gossip now tell Judah of her situation.

"And Judah said, 'Bring her out and have her burnt'." In his usual abrupt, impulsive way, Judah uses only two Hebrew words to have Tamar killed for doing the same thing he had done three months ago; whether with her or any other woman. Tamar's trick relies on the sexist ramifications of economic and social inequality between men and women. The oppressive, indeed deadly meaning of the law can be fought against by using its own power – male sexuality.

"As she was being brought out, she sent word to her father-in-law, 'It was the owner of these who made me pregnant.' And she said, '(Do, or 'please') Recognize, whose these are, the signet and the cord and the staff.' Then Judah recognized and said, 'She is more right than I, since I did not give her to my son Shelah.' And he did not lie with her again."

This scene is the climax of the drama. Tamar must have been aware that she was risking her life, but at the proper moment, after waiting years for Shelah and another three months for her pregnancy to be observed and reported to Judah, she finally unmasked herself – and him. On her humiliating way to be burnt, Tamar is very favorably described in using courteous, ironic and fine words, juxtaposed with Judah's previous "get her out and burn her". Here the text also juxtaposes their mutual family ties: 'His daughter-in-law' versus 'Her father-in-law'.

One may fill in the theatricality of the scene with a prepared stake waiting for Tamar. The text, however, does not make it explicit whether Tamar reveals Judah's signet, cord and staff in public, or whether she tries to save his face and show him his things in private. I suggest that her act of exposing the truth was two-fold. She probably indeed 'sent' a general statement in the vein of "It was the owner of these who made me pregnant", but having been brought to him, she told him straight out, in the necessary presence of other people: "Recognize, whose these are, the signet and the cord and the staff." As a classic act of recognition, this one too comes as both an inevitable dramatic result of the previous events, and as a complete surprise to Judah and the rest of the community. One may assume that the other women present did not bother to hide their smiles. Wisely, Tamar does not say 'these objects are yours, Judah', but invites him to come up with the confession. The text skips Judah's direct admission of 'These are mine'. As a sign of tact, and, more importantly, because all involved knew it anyway.

Judah, thus exposed and probably shamed in public, is honest enough to admit, "She is more right than I, since I did not give her to my son Shelah." From that day on he did not (know) lie with her – either because the Tora law forbids a woman to sleep with both a father and the sons, or because Judah was so angry with Tamar that he punished her by avoiding any physical contact with her – or both.

The Epilogue is dedicated to the birth of Tamar and Judah's children. There is a unique poetic justice in the birth of their two sons, replacing Judah's sons who had died. However, Tamar did not substitute for Judah's dead wife.

"When the time of delivery came, there were twins in her womb. While she was in labor, one put out a hand; and the midwife took and bound on his hand a crimson thread, saying, 'This one came out first.' But just then he drew back his hand, and out came his brother; and she said, 'What a breach you have made for yourself!' Therefore he named him Peretz. Afterward his brother came out with the crimson thread on his hand; and he named him Zerah."

This birth is not a regular happy end to the story. In fact, it re-emphasizes two main motifs around which the entire story revolves: the firstborn's right, and the women's reaction to the male-oriented laws.

One of the most striking qualities of this drama is the discrepancy between the characters' respective active or passive behavior and their distinct actions (or biography) on the one hand, and the lack of expressed feelings on the other. The plot deals with a highly intense family situation, in which the death of two sons and later their mother, is merely stated in passing. Love does not seem to play an active role at all, at least not on the overt level, although one must assume that this basic emotion – or the lack of it – must have motivated at least some of the action. Even mourning, at the other extreme, is mentioned cursorily with one single word. Whereas the plots of many plays are tightly stretched between Eros and Thanatos, love and death – the Tamar play compensates the loss of some lives with other lives, and leaves love for the reader or the spectator to fill in. The unique theatricality of Tamar's drama lies precisely in this gap. In fact, if treated on-stage from the approach of having each of the family members tell the story from their angle, we would probably end up with totally different emotional versions of the very same facts. Hirah's version too, as Judah's friend, might be yet another story.

4

Ruth: the Shrew-ing of the Tame

Ruth and *Esther* are the only books in the Old Testament called after women. Like *Esther*, the *Book of Ruth* has often been dramatized in the Hebrew theatre. Both texts are inherently dramatic due to the plot, the many dialogue-scenes and the wealth of stage instructions. In fact, *Ruth* is one of the most 'dialogical' biblical texts. Of a total of 85 verses, 54 are exclusively or predominantly a directly delivered dialogue. When read aloud in synagogues on the Jewish holidays of Purim (*Esther*) and Shavu'ot (*Ruth*), the performative elements in the text come alive even more intensively, since the reading is indeed a ritualistic-theatrical performance (though in a strictly religious context).

But whereas *Esther* can be considered a 'Jewish'-dramatic text, from its reception-oriented perspective, *Ruth* is more typically 'Israeli'. *Esther* was particularly suitable in the historical context of the desire to educate through the Old Testament that crystallized during the Enlightenment period. The text describes how the exiled Jewish community in Susa was saved by Mordechai's advice and Esther's intelligence, charm, courage, and resolution. The story offers a vicarious means of interpreting, as wishful thinking, the fate and fortune of the Jewish interpreters themselves, *vis-à-vis* their own lives in many exiles throughout history, personally and collectively. *Ruth*, on the other hand, has been well received and re-interpreted, dramatically too, ever since the Jewish people began returning to the Promised Land in the 1870s.[1] Because the biblical text describes a foreign, non-Hebrew character's decision to integrate into the Hebrew society of Bethlehem, into the agricultural ambience as well as the dramatic space of the country itself, it readily invited identification by its readers and spectators.

Ruth and *Esther*, as the only Old Testament books called after their female protagonists, prove these women's importance in the eyes of a dominant male establishment. The texts maneuver Ruth the Moabite girl into her key position in Hebrew history as the great-grandmother of none other than King David; and ascribe Queen Esther an intensive involvement in the politics of the Median–Persia empire. The main similarity between the individuals Ruth and Esther, however, lies in the roles these two women played for the benefit of the entire nation: Esther in King Ahasuerus's court, and Ruth on Boaz's threshing floor. Both women made active, intelligent and virtuous use of their bodies as well as their feminine charms, in order to gain a position for themselves and for their people. Esther, the almost completely assimilated Jewish girl, planned in advance her intention of saving her people upon attaining her high position in court; while Ruth, the Moabite, insinuated herself into Hebrew society and the dynasty of kings.

Both start their careers as the good souls of Moab and Susa. The major change (*peripeteia*) in the plot occurs, in both cases, in Esther's and Ruth's contact with a male symbol, physically and metaphorically. Esther touches the king's golden sceptre, and Ruth touches Boaz's euphemistic 'feet'. This chapter deals with Ruth's integration into the Bethlehem clan. It is devoted, primarily, to the theatrical elements in the already dramatic book of *Ruth*, in which the beautiful young Moabite woman undergoes a gradual, therefore perhaps more realistic, but also idyllic integration process into the Hebrew community.

Esther seems to undergo a relatively sudden identity crisis, and the entire story reads much more like a fantasy, later developed into a black comedy indeed. The sheer threat of killing all the Jews is answered by the actual or legendary murder of some 75,000 (mostly innocent) people. However, even the schematic structure of Esther testifies, theatrically at least, that the text contains more than just a gruesome story of sex and devious courtly machinations of power.

In the Jewish exegetical tradition, *Ruth* is considered a particularly 'pleasant' book, a model, indeed, for personal dedication and self-sacrifice, as well as retrospective testimony to ancient Hebrew liberalism toward strangers. It is also regarded as a mildly proselytizing text, which praises mainly Ruth herself as the archetype-mother of all – especially female – converts to Judaism. The Israeli, more secular reading of *Ruth* emphasizes the positive influence of the cycle of nature and agricultural work in enhancing healthy social behavior. Ruth has therefore often been staged in kibbutzim and socialist youth movements in Israel, in the pre- and early state years. In such nature-culture oriented readings, emphasizing the return to the land, the reinterpreted plot served as an antidote to the Jewish 'unnatural' and non-agricultural life in the Diaspora. However, a closer observation of the text, paying special attention to the stage instructions, reveals an intricate and not quite so pleasant message.

The ingenious biblical playwright balances Ruth's individual character against the reserved, even slightly hostile, family, society and religion that she chose as her new home. As a Moabite, she came from a people who were enemies of the Israelites. As a stranger in any case, she is initially deprived of any social rights. The playwright portrays her as a decisive young woman who seems resolved to follow her destiny in joining her mother-in-law and a foreign culture. She is also depicted as an intelligent, fully aware person who does not hesitate to use a number of womanly tricks to achieve her goal. Ruth turns her alienated 'otherness', her social and personal frailty, into a source of strength. Is Ruth a victim of Naomi's subtle but efficient emotional blackmail, or is she capable of thinking ahead of her own interests? As a theatrical text, *Ruth* presents these and more possibilities, which can be observed in the discrepancies between the authorial and the dialogical texts.

Ruth is associated with Tamar within the text itself. Tamar too performed a sophisticated biblical reverse tactics (*Genesis* 38) in employing the oppressive impact of the patriarchal system against itself. Like Ruth, she too used her erotic appeal as a lever to extricate herself from an inferior position, and gain minimal social and personal rights. Both women suffered a gender-oriented discrimination, and used their womanhood as a tool to assert themselves. *Ruth*, like the Tamar story, is a drama of personal choice and social integration, in which, nevertheless, being used and using others are neither mutually exclusive nor frowned upon by the author(s).

The story renders itself divisible into a typically dramatic structure of twelve distinct scenes, marked by entrances and exits and major shifts in time and space. The following outline presents only the non-verbal elements, which will later be integrated in discussing the interrelations between the dialogical text and the stage instructions. The Hebrew verb always carries the action of the biblical text, and can therefore indicate the dramatic movement of any particular section. The following structural outline of the play, covering the complete text of *Ruth*, reveals some of its main theatrical elements.[2]

- **i** (1:1–6) *Exposition* The prologue describes a family's move to Moab, over more than ten years, and features six characters: Elimelech, his wife Naomi, Mahlon and Chilion their sons, Orpah and Ruth, their wives. The three men die, the three women survive. Hunger drives the family to a foreign country across the border, and the prospect of bread drives Naomi back home to Bethlehem (Heb. 'House of Bread'). Verbs used (from here on, literally translated): go, dwell (or 'live'), come, be, die, remain, marry, stay, die, remain, rise (to go), hear, consider, give. The verbs, even without their proper conjugation of tense and person, clearly create an outline of an existential situation, indeed a whole life: living, marrying, dying, moving.

When the dialogues are added to the theatrical structure, the complete play can be presented. The prologue, as often in biblical narrative (and 'drama') reveals the time, space, and characters. It also indicates the main motivation: hunger – together with two other crucial notions, death and exile. "In the days when the judges ruled, there was famine in the land." An Ephratite family of husband, wife and two sons goes to live in Moab. Ephratite may mean 'from Ephrat in Judea', well-off people or indeed from the tribe of Ephraim. The man Elimelech dies, his sons marry Moabite girls, and ten years later both of them die too.

The answer to the question 'What's in a name', is often very clear in the Bible, and the characters' names in *Ruth* draw immediate attention. Elimelech means 'God is my king'. 'Naomi' stems from the Hebrew 'Naim', pleasant; Mahlon is derived from sickness, while Chilion is directly associated with 'perish', or 'expire'. Orpah is 'she who turns her back' (or 'neck'); and Ruth is connected with drinking to satiety, 'Revaya'. Five of the characters indeed die or live up to their names: Mahlon and Chilion are disposed of; Orpah turns her back on Naomi; Naomi later on even plays consciously with the meaning of her own name, and temporarily calls herself Mara, the bitter one, but is redeemed by Ruth, whose thirst for life is quenched to the full. Elimelech's name too will finally be eternalized.

The text, as noted, kills all three men and concentrates on the three, then two surviving women all the way to its happy end. Moreover, the deep structure of the drama is cyclical, in regard to time, space, and plot. The characters' personal time turns, retrospectively, into a historical time-perspective.[3] In this sense, the text focuses on the life-giving force of women. The move from Bethlehem to Moab is corrected at the outset with the motif of the return, typical to classical (biblical included) folktales and sagas. The dead characters of Elimelech and his sons will not return to life, but their memory, hovering over the plot and mentioned in the dialogues, will continue to follow the living, and be 'redeemed' both legally and emotionally through the new-born child. The embittered Naomi will be compensated with the new life of her grandson and be given a home she thought to have lost. Ruth, the protagonist, will also be richly rewarded for her decision to follow her mother-in-law.

- ii (1:7–18) After the general exposition, covering ten generally depicted hard years, the second scene begins with the bereaved Naomi about to leave Moab and go westward to a 'house' in which there is bread, Bethlehem. Under the title *"Where you go, I will go . . ."*; the second scene is a concentrated, emotional farewell encounter with Naomi, Orpah and Ruth, at the beginning of the road to Bethlehem. The time is not indicated. The typical verbs are: go (out), go, kiss (2), (re-)turn (6), weep (2), cling, determine(d). The stage instructions establish the predominant emotion of 'weeping'.

> NAOMI (to her two daughters-in-law): "Go back each of you to your mother's house. May the Lord deal kindly with you, as you have dealt kindly with the dead and with me. The Lord grant you may find security, each of you in the house of your husband."

Naomi's speech is a masterfully executed piece of bitter compassion for the young women, as well as a shrewd emotional blackmail. In starting her address by telling Ruth and Orpah to go to their mothers' house, Naomi implies that she herself cannot be their mother anymore. Perhaps she paused for a moment, as befits such an emotional scene, and they may not have answered. Adding that "you have dealt kindly with the dead and with me", Naomi gives them credit as good and faithful daughters-in-law. Implied, again, is also "now they are dead, it's all over". Wishing Ruth and Orpah God's security in their now empty houses of their dead husbands, in the third dramatic segment, however, verges on the sarcastic, because the husbands are dead, and neither rest nor security can be found in the empty houses. Naomi kisses them, and they all weep. The scene is replete with crying and physical contact between the women. Naomi's farewell words enhance, contradict, and finally complement the intimate and sad body language of all three women.

> RUTH AND ORPAH: "No, we will return with you to your people."
> NAOMI: "Turn back, my daughters, why will you go back with me? Do I still have sons in my womb that they may become your husbands? Turn back, my daughters, go your way, for I am too old to have a husband. Even if I should have a husband tonight and bear sons, would you then wait until they are grown? Would you then refrain from marrying? No, my daughters, it has been far more bitter for me than for you, because the hand of the Lord has turned against me." ["Then they wept aloud again."]

At this point "Orpah kissed her mother-in-law but Ruth clung to her." The authorial text tactfully refrains from mentioning Orpah's actually turning her back and departing, and puts this recognition in Naomi's mouth. Orpah, apparently convinced by Naomi's words as well as her own considerations, departs. Noticeably, other than letting Orpah act out her name, the text does not blame her for her decision. Nevertheless, the text does contrast her behavior to Ruth's. Naomi's understandable but blatant sarcasm may be more than Orpah is willing to swallow, at the present moment or in the future. The playwright, moreover, contrasts Naomi's tactlessness in appropriating the greater share of suffering with Orpah's tactful silence, kiss and departure. On stage, actions count at least as much as words.

Ruth's clinging (the same verb 'davok' appears later to retrospectively illuminate Ruth's demeanour) to Naomi emphasizes Orpah's leaving. The deep structure of the scene is based on a model of the conflicting emotions of all three women involved. Naomi is torn between her honest care for the younger women's destiny, and her own fears of remaining poor and totally alone. Orpah and Ruth are equally torn between their wish (or duty?) to stay with Naomi, and their natural inclination to return to their Moabite homes.

> NAOMI: (to Ruth) "See, your sister-in-law has gone back to her people and to her gods; return after your sister-in-law."
> RUTH: "Do not press me to leave you or turn back from following you. Where you go, I will go; Where you lodge, I will lodge; your people shall be my people, and your God my God. Where you die – there will I be buried. May the Lord do thus and so to me, and more as well, if even death parts me from you."

This beautiful, often quoted performative speech-act does not describe a situation. Rather, the speech is a promise, fulfilled as soon as it is uttered.[4] When closely observed, nevertheless, the speech is a partial repetition of Naomi's text. Naomi says to Ruth "See, your sister-in-law has gone back to her people and to her gods . . . ", Ruth picks up these key words and uses them in her independent response. She is a fast learner, who will continue to follow texts and instructions and develop them into an authentic personal expression; she is definitely not portrayed as naïve.

"When Naomi saw that she was determined to go with her, she stopped talking to her." Though we may assume that the meaning is 'she did not try to convince Ruth to stay in Moab', one still wonders whether Naomi indulged in an aggrieved silence all the way to Bethlehem. In this context, Fewell and Gunn note on 'five notable silences in the book of Ruth, having an important bearing on the reader's understanding of Naomi',[5] which are indeed highly theatrical silences.

- iii (1:19–22) *Is this Naomi?*" The difficult road leading through at least forty kilometers of a steep desert climb up to Bethlehem (from about 350 meters below to 800 meters above sea level) is only mentioned in passing in "So the two of them went on." This scene takes the two women to Bethlehem and only then into the town.

Naomi and Ruth meet the people of the town, especially the women. The verbs: go, stir, go–return, call, do evil. The text specifies Ruth's silent presence.

The women's entrance is divided into "until they came to Bethlehem", and "As they came to Bethlehem", thus distinguishing between their lonely march and the tumultuous reception. Upon meeting them, the women, rather than the people, say "Is this Naomi?" Ruth, obviously present, is not mentioned by the women of the town. Naomi, recognised despite her long absence, has aged and suffered lot. She says to them:

> "Call me no longer Naomi (the pleasant one), call me Mara (the bitter one), for the Almighty has dealt bitterly with me. I went full away, but the Lord has brought me back empty; why call me Naomi when the Lord has dealt harshly with me, and the Almighty has brought calamity upon me?"

The spectator or reader, still impressed with Ruth's resolution, dedication and love, may be rightly taken aback by Naomi's complaint of being brought back 'empty'. The tactful playwright corrects Naomi's inadvertant insult in the next verse: "So Naomi returned together with Ruth the Moabite, her daughter-in-law", as though making a specially detailed effort to fully recognize Ruth's presence, and indirectly credit her for it. From a different point of view, nevertheless, Naomi may have been correct in not presenting a Moabite, a stranger, immediately upon their arrival, thus enabling Ruth to prove herself independently as a positive character. The indication of the time of the year "at the beginning of the barley harvest", suggests a bright light, joy and affluence, in the authorial text. This is contrasted with Naomi's indirect suggestion of begging. Harvest, at the same time, also promises at least a minimal livelihood for the two widowed women.

- iv (2:1–2) *"Let me go and glean . . ."*, Naomi and Ruth alone inside an unspecified location, probably a small shack, a temporary shelter they have found in Bethlehem. Morning. The verbs, in future tense, indicate Ruth's active intention, as the motto for the scene suggests. The stage instruction, in present tense, creates a hovering offstage anticipation: "Naomi had a kinsman . . . "

  RUTH: "Let me go to the field and glean among the ears of grain, behind someone in whose eyes I may find favour." She does not yet know of Naomi's prominent kinsman, Boaz. The dramatic function of the scene is to endow Ruth with the initiative. Chance, or is it God, plays an active role too, collaborating with Ruth's activity. "As it happened, she came to the part of the field belonging to Boaz."

Ruth's personal efforts and qualities are first contrasted with the social ambience around her, and then conciliated through God's help.

- **v** (2:3–17) *"Do not go to glean in another field."* Out in the wheat-field, shortly before lunch-time, bright sunlight. Ruth, reapers (men and 'girls'), Boaz, Servant (foreman?). Possible 'props': Sheaves, various tools, bread (or toast), vinegar etc. The key verbs are: glean (7), go (4), com e (3), find grace (2), leave (2), eat, drink. Characteristic to the scene is the instruction: "and he heaped up for her some parched grain."

This mass-scene focuses on Ruth as a gleaning beggar at the fringe of the field, 'behind the reapers'. The dramatic structure shifts from the previous dark, secluded indoor scene, to a bright, densely populated outdoor picture, and from women to men. Boaz's entrance into the scene is masterly: "The Lord be with you!" he greets his workers, and they answer: "The Lord bless you!" The first encounter between Ruth and Boaz takes place in the presence of many people. Having noticed Ruth, because she is a stranger, or beautiful, or both, Boaz's first natural action is to inquire about her: "To whom does this young woman belong?" (Or "whose is this girl?") The first (perhaps reciprocal) eye contact has been established from afar. A gradual approaching follows, as the foreman of the reapers explains to Boaz who she is, presenting her as "She is a Moabite who came back with Naomi from the country of Moab." This is in fact the first time Ruth is openly talked about in Bethlehem. Then the foreman quotes Ruth's words: "She said: 'Please let me glean and gather among the sheaves behind the reapers'." This man, judging by the three distinct parts of his answer to Boaz, was certainly impressed by the young woman. He does not neglect to mention that "she has been on her feet from early this morning until now, without resting for a moment" (or "bringing home only little", or "she was not much at home but worked here"). He probably pities her.

The dialogue between Boaz and the foreman takes place in front of the other reapers, while in the meantime Ruth is approaching the two men. Perhaps she has already reached them by the time the foreman finishes his favorable report. A dialogue is about to begin between Boaz and Ruth, creating a delicate balance between text, possible subtext, and the social context. The actual lines are duly courteous, although the subtext connotes an implied intimacy that the public circumstances of this talk do not allow feelings to be revealed openly. Boaz's attention to Ruth, seen retrospectively, can be interpreted as love (or any other 'interest'?) at first sight. The social and emotional realms are exquisitely measured. Boaz's first words to Ruth are particularly warm, very personal and considerate.

> Boaz: "Have you not heard, my daughter, do not go to glean in another
> field or leave this one, but cling to my young women. Keep your eyes on the
> field that is being reaped, and follow behind them. I have ordered the young
> men not to bother you. If you get thirsty, go to the vessels and drink from
> what the young men have drawn."

Boaz addresses her as 'daughter', an endearing appeal to a stranger,
which also asserts the age difference. His first words (like her first words
in her answer), suggest that he has already fallen in love with her.
Metaphorically, the 'field' he refers to can hence be interpreted also as his
soul. Boaz tells her to cling to the girls, i.e. not to mix with the young men.
As a foreign and poor young female, she could fall easy prey to sexual
insinuations or actual molestation. Boaz is certainly aware of his young
reapers' behavior, and may want to protect Ruth as well as to keep her
for himself. At the same time, he behaves generously and in accordance
with Hebrew laws regarding the poor. The many Hebrew laws and Torah
commandments prescribe allotting 10 percent of the harvest to widows
and orphans (See *Exod.* 22:21; *Deut.* 10:18–19; 14:28; 15:7; 24:19, etc.).
Boaz is portrayed as just, correct, caring and in love. In *Ruth*, this scene
shows how personal interests, social codes and religious laws are used
(rather than ab- or mis-used) by the protagonists and harnessed to one
another in a mutually complementing fashion.

Ruth "fell prostrate, with her face to the ground, and said to him: 'Why
have I found favour in your sight, that you should take notice of me, when
I am a foreigner?'" Like him, she begins with a (implied, rhetorical) question, as though inviting further talk. Whereas her falling prostrate signifies
acceptance of his graceful superiority, her spoken words are more
complex. Already at this stage she explicates his words to her benefit, by
saying "I found favour in your sight."

> BOAZ: "All that you have done for your mother-in-law since the death
> of your husband has been fully told me, and how you left your father and
> mother and your native land and came to a people that you did not know
> before. May the Lord reward you for your deeds, and may you have a full
> reward from the Lord, the Lord of Israel, under whose wings you have come
> for refuge."

Who told Boaz about Ruth and her wonderful deeds? Was it the result
of Naomi's public relations passed on through the women of Bethlehem?
In a small village rumors about foreigners, and especially those who return
to the clan, certainly spread quickly from one to the next. Boaz makes
Ruth's story public, thus affording her extra protection. His main motif

concerns the reward that God will give her. Mentioning God is probably both a rhetorical device and a recognition of divine power. This sophisticated anticipation of "God's wings" protecting Ruth will soon be cleverly used by Ruth herself. In her response, now noticeably more daring, she says:

"May I continue to find favour in your sight, my lord, for you have comforted me and spoken kindly to your servant, even though I am not one of your servants." In already behaving and presenting herself as a servant at the beginning of the encounter, Ruth rapidly understands Boaz's special favors, and ends her speech suggesting she "will not be one of your servants". Her message to Boaz can be seen as deliberately ambiguous.

The first encounter between Ruth and Boaz could have happened with the two of them at a distance from one another, after which they got closer and talked, with Ruth finally at Boaz's feet. On the third encounter, at lunch time, she is invited to eat with him: "Come here, and eat some of this bread, and dip your morsel in the vinegar." Now both are sitting. This pretended gesture of simple hospitality is beautifully underlined with the stage instruction: "So she sat beside the reapers and he heaped up for her some parched grain." His tender attention to her gradually reveals his enamoured state of mind, which he must nevertheless conceal from the group of reapers. Did he really reach out the parched grain straight to her mouth, or just offer it to her outstretched hand? Whereas Ruth was 'behind the reapers' while gleaning in the field, now she is 'beside' them, slowly but surely gliding into the center of the action. Ruth's proxemic (space and movement) pattern changes from distant to close, and from a low body posture to an erect one.

In the last part of the scene, after the meal, Boaz instructs his workers: "Let her glean even among the standing sheaves, and do not reproach her. You must also pull out some handfuls for her from the bundles, and leave them for her to glean, and do not rebuke her." Boaz, very particular in establishing Ruth's position among the reapers, due to her personal qualities on the one hand and his (growing, we assume) love for her on the other, is at the same time functional in integrating her into a new society.

- vi (2:18–23) *"Blessed be the man who took notice of you."* Ruth and Naomi in their place, evening, dark. Verbs: cling, glean. Inserted in this scene is Ruth's daily rhythm of working in the vast, brightly lit field, (in the strong June sun), then returning to her dark and narrow (?) dwelling with Naomi, where she 'sits' with her.

In the dramatically opposed dark again, in an indoor and intimate two-women scene and space, Ruth tells Naomi, albeit selectively, what has happened in the field. Whenever a speech is repeated in a biblical text, the observant reader is invited to examine slight but crucially important differences. It is natural for any hungry person to first eat, then give to others. However, almost imperceptibly, the text raises the possibility that Ruth knows how to take care of herself in this respect and in other areas of life as well.

"Her mother-in-law saw how much she had gleaned. Then she took out and gave her what was left over after she herself had been satisfied."

> NAOMI: "Where did you glean today? And where have you worked? Blessed be the man who took notice of you."
> RUTH: "The name of the man with whom I worked today is Boaz."
> Naomi: "Blessed be he by the Lord, whose kindness has not forsaken the living and the dead."
> RUTH: (Silent. Smiling?)
> NAOMI: "The man is a relative of ours, one of our nearest kin."
> RUTH: "He even said to me, 'Stay close by my boys, until they have finished all my harvest'."
> NAOMI: "It is better, my daughter, that you go out with his young women, otherwise you might be bothered in another field."

"So she stayed close to the young women of Boaz, gleaning until the end of the barley and wheat harvests; and she lived with her mother-in-law."

Shrewd Naomi may already have guessed that Ruth had gleaned in Boaz's field, but she lets Ruth say so for herself. She obviously understands that Ruth could not have brought back that much grain without somebody's help. Naomi brings up the memory of her dead husband and sons, a reminder that even in Ruth's present happiness, the dead must not be forgotten. The text does not indicate 'pause', but does add: "Naomi also said to her", which functions to the same dramatic effect. Ruth, whose Hebrew was perhaps not yet fluent, could nevertheless not have mistaken male for female, boys for girls. In reporting to Naomi that Boaz told her to cling to the boys, she deliberately distorts Boaz's words, and certainly with intention. She may have wanted to test Naomi, or hide her feelings for Boaz, so as to keep the emerging relationship with him to herself. Assuming that older people are better acquainted with the way young foreign girls are treated among a group of reapers, we must still consider the alternative: namely, that Ruth was not that naïve. Naomi indeed plays into Ruth's hands in repeating Boaz's advice to cling to the young women. From her perspective, this is an implicit encouragement for Ruth to pursue the budding relationship with Boaz.

- vii (3:1–5) *"Go down to the threshing floor"*; Naomi and Ruth at their place, evening. Verbs do most of the planned activity for the immediate future, with the possibility that the washing, anointing, and dressing of Ruth may take place in the present, while Naomi is instructing her daughter-in-law what to do: seek (security), winnow, wash, anoint (perfume), put on (best clothes), go down, lie (appears three times!), do not make yourself known, observe, uncover, tell, say.

Sometime after the previous scene, at the end of the harvest, Naomi repeats another key phrase of hers: "My daughter, do I not seek security for you, so that it may be well with you?" Naomi plans the next move in order to find security and rest for herself as well:

> NAOMI: "Now here is our kinship Boaz, with whose young women you have been working. See, he is winnowing barley tonight at his threshing floor. Now wash and anoint yourself, and put on your (best) clothes and go down to the threshing floor; but do not make yourself known to the man until he has finished eating and drinking. When he lies down, observe the place where he lies; then, go and uncover his feet and lie down; and he will tell you what to do."
>
> RUTH: "All that you tell me I will do."

Naomi is the director of the subsequent scene. She designs the space, the action, the costume, and the movements. Ruth is supposed to act in it, and re/present her own and Naomi's desired results. But in following the directions, she will yet surpass even her instructor's advice and add authentic, unrehearsed texts and gestures, because she plays her "self," indeed in a role decisive for her future life.

- viii (3:6–15) *"Spread your wing"* (or cloak); Ruth and Boaz in the threshing floor, night time. Darkness. "Props": Ruth's (special) clothes, Boaz's clothes (cloak?), Ruth's cloak (or shawl), six measures of barley-seeds from the big pile. Verbs: eat, lie (5), come, uncover, startle(d), spread, get up, put on (barley), "redeem" (in the legal sense of 'act as next of kin'). Among the important indirect instructions in this (primarily dialogical) text we find: "So she lay at his feet until morning, but got up before one person could recognize another."

The beautiful, slightly and deliberately misleading authorial text of the scene opens with: "So she went down to the threshing floor and did just as her mother-in-law had instructed her . . . At midnight the man was startled, and turned over, and there, lying at his feet, was a woman."

BOAZ: "Who are you?"

RUTH: "It is I, Ruth, your servant; spread your wing (or cloak) over your servant, for you are the redeemer (next-of-kin)."

BOAZ: "May you be blessed by the Lord, my daughter; this last grace [*hesed*] of yours is better than the first; you have not gone after young men (boys) whether poor or rich. And now, my daughter, do not be afraid, I will do for you all that you ask, for all the assembly of my people know that you are a worthy woman. But now, though it is true that I am near kinsman, there is another kinsmen more closely related than I. Remain this night, and in the morning, if he will act (the verb 'gaol', to 'redeem') as next-of-kin for you, good; let him do it. If he is not willing to act as next-of-kin, then, as the Lord lives, I will act as next-of-for you. Lie down until the morning."

Startled as he is, Boaz is still able to tell that the person at his feet (or 'legs') is a woman, because he speaks to Ruth in the feminine second person singular. She, in return, uses '*Anochi*', a self-assertive form for 'I', then states her name, and only then adds 'your servant.' She then catches him by his own words, and continues with the wing image Boaz himself has generously offered her. However, rather than asking for God to spread his wing over her, as he had suggested, she requests Boaz himself to do so.

Theatrically, Ruth is at center-stage, and Boaz 'at the edge of a grain-heap'. The startled Boaz indulges in an excitedly grateful monologue. He realizes that she has not only refrained from following a younger man, her first 'grace' – but that she has chosen him, her latest 'grace'. The endearing twice repeated 'my daughter' suggests, in this particular situation, appreciative love rather than age difference. Rapidly gaining his presence of mind, having been awoken in the middle of the night, he does not fail to notice that Ruth has not followed any young men, rich or poor. Hopefully he implies that she may be interested in him as a person, not only because of his social and financial status. He also realizes that Ruth has come to collect her 'reward' from him, not from 'under God's wing', as he had suggested.

Boaz pays tribute to Ruth's good reputation in town, thus complimenting her, but at the same time he may be assuring himself that she is not simply a whore. Truly appreciating her initiative, he plans the next step. Realizing there is another, closer next-of-kin, he subtly insinuates that he must get rid of him, but without disclosing to Ruth precisely how this will be done. He may consider her mind to be not quite geared to the legalistic procedures of the Hebrew law, or else fear she might be bored. In any case, from a dramatic point of view, the tension of the untold details must be kept for the coming scene. At present, Boaz is too excited anyway. He begs Ruth twice to stay the night: "remain this night" and "Lie down until morning". Emotional outbursts are interspersed with his necessarily cooler plans for later in the morning. Ruth stays on the threshing floor, but gets up "before one person could recognize another" (or "his friend", in the original), because Boaz has wisely suggested that it would be better if no one finds out there was a woman on the threshing floor. This advice may ensue from the need to keep the relationship secret prior to the upcoming public hearing; and also in order to protect the reputations of both parties. But in the meantime they have indeed 'recognized' each other, and established an exclusive intimacy.

The scene ends with what I consider to be one of the most touching actions in the Bible, when Boaz says: "'Bring the cloak you are wearing and hold it out.' So she held it, and he measured out six measures of barley, and put it on her; then he went into the city." Pouring out six measures of barley into her lap is, primarily, a gift. It is also an advance payment to make sure she will not gossip. Furthermore, it is a poetically (and theatrically highly charged) refined way to suggest that Boaz and Ruth had experienced a most enjoyable night, and that Ruth was perhaps already impregnated by Boaz. Six measures of barley seed poured into a woman's opened 'cloak' is a clear enough metaphor.[6] Bearing the barley to the place she shares with Naomi, Ruth must even look like a pregnant woman. The barley image is a metaphor and not a metaphor at one and the same time.

- **ix** (3:16–18) *"How the matter turns out"*; Ruth and Naomi, very early in the morning, in their location. A cloak with six measures of barley. "Then she told her all . . ." – or, perhaps, only carefully chosen parts of what had happened on the threshing floor.

It is still early in the morning when Ruth returns from the threshing floor. Whereas Boaz was unable to recognize Ruth, it is definitely with a touch of humor that now even Naomi only half-recognizes her. Is it the darkness, or has Ruth changed?

NAOMI: "Who are you, my daughter?"
RUTH: "He gave me these six measures of barley, for he said: 'Do not go back to your mother-in-law empty-handed'."
NAOMI: "Wait, my daughter, until you learn how the matter turns out, for the man will not rest, but will settle the matter today."

Following the pattern of indeed telling the truth, but not always only the truth, or nothing but the truth, Ruth shows compassion, tact and consideration for Naomi, who has given up any hope of remarrying. Boaz may perhaps have intended the barley for Naomi, but he had not mentioned anything specific to that effect, and I suggest that Ruth had simply not wanted Naomi to feel left out. This deliberately 'invented' quotation is reminiscent of the 'adjusted' conversation in which Ruth told Naomi about Boaz telling her to cling to the young men. Naomi, scheming, but still careful and not overly optimistic, suggests they should both wait for Boaz's real action. Totally ignoring the barley, her subtext may be: 'the barley is fine, but let's wait for the real thing.'

- x (4:1–12) *"I will redeem it"*; Boaz, The "Next of kin", Ten Elders, "All the people", obviously only men, are gathered by the city gate. Broad daylight. Necessary prop: a shoe. Characteristic verbs: Redeem, acquire, take off (shoe, or sandal). The stage instruction is a summary of the entire previous plot: "So Boaz took Ruth and she became his wife."

The play shifts from the dark, intimate, and personal scene on the threshing floor to another dark indoor scene of Ruth and Naomi's dwelling, and then into the open public town square, where Ruth is mentioned but perhaps not present. She may be hiding in a corner to see how Boaz will carry out his promised plan. Ruth has played out her honest role on the darkness of the threshing floor, and it is now Boaz's turn to act out his role publicly on the social level. Unlike Ruth who was obliged to act discreetly, his is a public appearance, in which he tells the truth, most of the truth and almost nothing but – and yet he conceals his real motive. Boaz encounters – by the same coincidence that had caused Ruth to glean in his fields? – the other next-of-kin, and tells him, in a commanding tone: "sit down here." The man does. Then he assembles ten of the elders, and commands them, similarly: "Sit down here." They do too. Consequently, Boaz dominates a public court-scene, masterfully balancing between the objectively correct and legal state of affairs, and his own, emotionally vested interests.[7] While Boaz, for obvious reasons, does not mention the night on the threshing floor, the trial scene is a lever on the way to securing his love for Ruth. Combining the erotic-personal with the legal-social aspects endows the scene with an extra tension, and an added subtextual flavor.

The other 'redeemer' hears from Boaz that "The day you acquire the field from the hand of Naomi, you are also acquiring Ruth the Moabite, the widow of the dead man, to maintain the dead man's name on his inheritance." Boaz uses the plain truth as a means to scare off the other redeemer, with a stunning talent for public rhetoric (not unlike Mark Anthony's famous speech). Subtly emphasizing that Ruth is included in the deal, in itself a religiously and socially recommendable deed because it is a commemoration of the dead man's name, Boaz cleverly inserts

Ruth's Moabite origin. This, as Boaz planned, is precisely the argument exploited by the other redeemer in order not to perform his legal duty: "I cannot redeem it for myself without damaging my own inheritance. Take my right of redemption yourself", he says to Boaz, "for I cannot redeem it". In saying so, as the text explains, the other redeemer "took off his sandal" (shoe) signifying by this legal deed that he relinquishes Ruth. It is very likely that he threw the shoe into Ruth's hands, as in a traditional Jewish divorce ceremony. But from that moment, Ruth was already under Boaz's 'wing'.

This longest scene in the play is divided into three parts: the preparation, the 'hearing' (in which the text explains the law of 'redeeming'); and the final public approval, which includes a blessing. The text is performative in more than one sense. The taking off of the sandal is a typical ritualistic gesture, connoting 'getting rid' of the duty to redeem. Boaz's finalizes event with a performative speech, the function of which is mainly to establish a new legal, financial, and social situation for himself and for Ruth in front of the entire community. His speech does not describe anything, it creates: "Today you are witnesses that I have acquired from the hand of Naomi all that belonged to Elimelech and all that belonged to Chilion and Mahlon. I have also acquired Ruth the Moabite, the wife of Mahlon, to be my wife, to maintain the dead man's name on his inheritance, in order that the name of the dead may not be cut off from his kindred and from the gate of his native place; today you are witnesses."

"All the people who were at the gate, and the elders, said: 'We are witnesses. May the Lord make the woman who is coming into your house like Rachel and Leah, who together built up the house of Israel. May you produce children in Ephratah and bestow a name in Bethlehem; and, through the children that the Lord will give you by this woman, may your house be like the house of Perez, whom Tamar bore to Judah'."

The public blessing of Boaz's deed connects the individual aspects of the play to the collective historical drama of the Israelites. However, even here the speaker(s) seems more sophisticated than meets the unsuspecting eye. According to the redeeming law, Boaz and Ruth's children will be called after Elimelech, Mahlon, and Chilion. This means that Boaz's interest in Ruth was, most probably, not a financial one. Moreover, he was independently wealthy and in no need of the Elimelech property. Contrasting with the other redeemer, who was willing to take the property but did not want Ruth, Boaz was willing to take the property mostly because of Ruth.

The (indirect) warm public approval gives Boaz credit for his love for Ruth, and praises her for willingly joining the Hebrew clan. The blessing may serve as compensation for Boaz, who will inherit neither the land nor the 'name' of the deceased. The entire town fully accepts his deed as well as Ruth, but not without hinting that they are all well aware of Boaz's scheme. Comparing Ruth with Rachel and Leah is a great compliment; but mentioning Tamar's story may indicate that the elders as well as the people, retrospectively understood very well the rhetorical, emotional, and legal trick that Boaz had performed in the redemption deed. Interestingly, the image of the House links the private, the communal and the overall historical layers of the story.

The field (emotional, legal, and social) is now clear and ready for Boaz's deal, and he marries Ruth. In this scene the double interest of the main characters is strongly stressed. Boaz, Naomi and Ruth have all used each other, but none have been abused or misused. And the elders and the people know this. There seems to be a common unspoken agreement upon the difference between the overt and the underlying motivation. This scene is, predominantly, a typical male business, due to the nature and content of the event.

- **xi** (4:13–17) *"And the women said"*; A group of women, Naomi, Ruth, Baby Obed. Probably Boaz's house. Verbs: love, give birth, lay (child in bosom), name. The instruction "And Naomi took the child and laid him in her bosom, and became his nurse", completes the idyllic happy end.

The playwright dedicates this scene to the women, though not necessarily to Ruth herself. In the previous men's scene Naomi was not even mentioned and the focus was on Ruth. Once married and with a son, she has already achieved the goals planned for her and carried out by her. The women then turn to Naomi and to the new-born child, rather than to Ruth: "Blessed be the Lord, who has not left you this day without next-of-kin; and may his name be renowned in Israel. He shall be to you as a restorer of life and a nourisher of your old age; for your daughter-in-law who loves you, who is more to you than seven sons, has borne him."

The women's blessing appoints Naomi as a surrogate mother, indirectly presenting Ruth as a womb-for-hire, a (praiseworthy) tool through whom Naomi is now comforted in her old-age. Naomi "took the child and laid him in her bosom, and became his nurse. The women-neighbours gave him a name,[8] saying 'A son has been born to Naomi.' They named him Obed . . ." The play is a living commemoration for the dead, and throughout the plot the dead play a vivid role. The organic cohabitation of the living and the dead is part of a huge historical cycle. The bereaved are comforted with a new birth.

- **xii** (4:18–22)   *"Now these are the descendants"*; The last verses are not a scene, but an epilogue, locating the entire play in its proper historical, meta-personal dimension, as a link between the past, through the (dramatic) present into a future, when King David will be born.

The verses provide an extra emphasis on what the men in scene 10 and the women in scene 11 have already alluded to, this time from the meta-temporal superplot's point of view. The previous scene ends with "They named him Obed; he became the father of Jesse, the father of David . . ." and the genealogical (highly poetic!) list completes the drama: "Now these are the descendants of Perez: Perez beget Hezron; Hezron beget Ram and Ram beget Aminadab, Aminadab begat Nahshon, Nahshon begat Salmon. Salmon begat Boaz and Boaz begat Obed. And Obed begat Jesse and Jesse begat David." Though legally called after Elimelech's family, Obed is part of the David dynasty and his birth is linked with his loving natural father, Boaz. Women are, no doubt, indispensable, but biblical history is nevertheless carried by men. Even in this very woman-friendly drama.

Theatrical Elements: an Overview

Space and lighting

The play opens with a description of a broken, destroyed house (or 'home' – the same Hebrew word for both). The house is not only frequently mentioned in the beginning, but because of death, poverty and hunger, is presented as empty. In the middle parts of the play, Naomi and Ruth live in an unspecified, temporary 'house'. Ruth and Boaz's meetings takes place in the open field and on the threshing floor, not in any house. The 'hearing' scene is an outdoor scene. But the play ends with a strong emphasis on a house (and a home) in the personal as well as national and dynastic sense, which is both restored and built anew.

The playwright leads the (implied) spectators through various spaces along the plot, with a well-marked contrast between open public spaces and closed intimate locations. The dramatic space-pattern of the play is dynamic, changing and atmospherically richly suggestive. However, not one scene takes place explicitly inside a house. Even Ruth and Naomi's dwelling is never explicitly mentioned. It is an offstage image, hovering above the plot as shattered in the beginning, temporary in the middle and metaphorically restored at the end. Opening with three 'destroyed' houses, Orpah returns to her Moabite house while homeless Naomi and

Ruth go to 'A house of bread' (Bethlehem), but find shelter in a Bethlehem 'somewhere' – perhaps the playwright deliberately denies them 'a house,' and places them in an unspecified kind of 'nowhere'. The threshing floor is 'a house' for grain, a womb for seeds. The final 'naming' scene may take place inside or right in front of Boaz and Ruth's house – the text does not say. But the House of Perez and of Israel is explicitly compared with Boaz and Ruth's house. Theirs becomes a house both for the old and for the new. Old Naomi represents the past; the baby – the future. The future, in the exquisite final scenes, is cradled, like baby Obed, in the bosom of the past. A house, finally, is the spatial translation-interpretation for a temporal issue, as in 'The House of Israel'.

The dramatic space of *Ruth* gradually develops from an unfriendly location into a cordially inviting personal, social, national and even re/symbolic womb (to women whose wombs will eventually produce King David). Consequently, the potential lighting design of the play follows indications pertaining to the locations and to the hours of the day in which the scenes occur: early morning, morning, noon, evening and night.

Dramatic characterization through naming

Ruth, perhaps more than any other biblical figure, is called different names by the characters who communicate with her. In a biblical story so concerned with eternalizing the names of the dead, Ruth's various name-masks therefore indicate the personal and social attitudes of the author, the other figures and even Ruth herself. The names serve as a splendid dramatic device, and establish a socio-metric chart of the relationships between the characters. Ruth is called, among others, the Moabite, a woman, this girl (or young woman), a daughter-in-law, daughter, Mahlon's wife, a servant, a 'worthy woman', and finally 'better than seven sons'.

In the beginning, Ruth appears as one of a pair of women, together with Orpah. Then her own name is mentioned, but the text at this stage turns to her as daughter-in-law, emphasizing her function in the family relation to Naomi. Naomi addresses both Ruth and Orpah as 'my daughters', but only Ruth will really justify her daughter-hood. The objective narrator in the authorial text refers to her mostly as Ruth, though in the beginning she was, for him too, 'a Moabite'. In fact, as a 'good' Moabite, Ruth ever really gets rid of her origin . . .

Naomi usually addresses Ruth with the endearing 'my daughter.' Boaz's servant in the field characteristically calls her by the depersonalized 'Moabite girl', certainly representing the attitude of the other reapers too. Boaz himself identifies her initially as 'whose is this girl?' namely as 'belonging' to some man; then as 'my daughter', an expression which connotes both differences of age and love; and later as 'worthy woman'. He presents her, diplomatically, as 'the Moabite' and 'the wife of Mahlon' in the city-gate scene. He may be suggesting that the other woman who had married Chilion had not 'joined us' and therefore Chilion had indeed perished. The other redeemer does not call her by any name at all. But the elders, as noted, compare her with the most distinguished women of the nation. The women, on the other hand, perhaps envious, or even jealous of Ruth, avoid her altogether in their final speech, but they do indirectly refer to her as 'better than seven sons'.(!) The naming-pattern corresponds to the space-and-movement pattern of Ruth who begins her integration on the fringes of Bethlehem society and ends in its very center.

Of special interest is how Ruth calls herself. In the field she presents herself as a stranger, a servant. After Boaz's words, she corrects her self-address to "and I will not be as one of your servants." On the threshing floor she moves from the festive 'I' form (anochi) which is the way she may perceive herself, to 'Ruth', which is her known name, and known, positively, to Boaz too. Then she says 'your maid', which is her polite, if inaccurate mode of accepting Boaz's patronage. Having uncovered Boaz's 'feet' she gradually uncovers her own identity. First her 'I' in her own eyes; then her known, 'objective' name Ruth, which Boaz is already acquainted with, then her social mask as a maid, according to the etiquette. It is a truthful, though diplomatically brilliant way of self-re/presentation under the circumstances.

The *Ruth* play presents an organic cohabitation of the living and the dead, past and future, poverty and hunger *vis-à-vis* affluence, barrenness and fertility, youth and old-age. It molds the conflicts between the major components of life in a cyclical optimistic pattern. Accordingly, the characters are arranged in a concentric pattern. Ruth, Boaz and Naomi are in the center. Around them are the living or dead characters of Orpah, Elimelech and his sons, the foreman in the field and the other, nameless redeemer. In a yet wider ring are the reapers, elders, men and women of Bethlehem. Finally the entire community is surrounded by multitudes of the already long dead or still unborn Hebrew generations. Hence a specific plot pertaining to an individual persona is fundamentally just one act in the large historical drama.

Props and Costumes

The stage-instruction text of *Ruth* indicates a number of important costumes and props. Among them we find sheaves, water jugs, vinegar and bread, perfumes and body-oils, one very central shoe; Ruth's dresses and her most significant cloak. Regarded theatrically, these props and costumes share a common denominator: all of them relate to basic human need for food, clothes and sex. As such, they create a basic pattern which motivates the plot but is nevertheless also elevated to a metaphoric-symbolic level. If the props and costumes would be allowed to 'act' on stage in pantomime only, they would still make sense.

In the conflict between Naomi's agony of bereavement and Ruth's viduity, there are, finally, no winners, no losers. Naomi is given the new-born baby as a surrogate mother, Ruth gets a husband–father. A new family has been created, snugly bedded in the entire tribe.

5

Esther and the
Head of the Sceptre

The *Book of Esther*, one of the most dramatic, thrilling and comic scriptures in the Old Testament, has served as a basis for many Jewish and Christian plays in the last centuries, most of them adaptations. The story of *Esther* is a dramatic plot, replete with theatrical effects from the very beginning. As drama, it is charged with conflict between (and finally reversal of) the private–personal realm and the ethnic–political one; between men and women; and between the strong and the weak. The story has also a moral sub-plot, not necessarily in favor of saved Jews. *Esther* contains similar materials and motifs to those found in some of the best-known plays in world drama: political scheming, ambition, honor, sex and power; and existential questions of life and death, not only for the individual, but for a whole nation.

The very structure of *Megilat Esther* (The Scroll of Esther) is easily recognizable as dramatic. The story is constructed in clearly discernible scenes, in which the intricacies of the plot are presented according to basic dramatic components, such as characters, different spaces, rapid or gradual shifts of scene, etc. There are (relative to most biblical texts) many dialogues, which enhance the dramatic value as well as theatrical potential. Even a basic reading of *Esther* reveals it to be a complex and sophisticated text that, especially as a play, opens up not only artistic, but also numerous aesthetic and ethical interpretative possibilities. Traditionally each Jewish generation is re-extended an invitation to interpret itself through *Esther* and vice versa, in the light of its own particular cultural and historical circumstances. The *Megila* continues to present relevant contemporary issues such as the forceful Jewish reaction to the threat of genocide, which nowadays has a special meaning unknown in Ancient times; or the equally relevant attitude toward women. Examining the theatrical potential of *Esther*, in this chapter I deal with the 'feminist' issue, concentrating on the 'double talk' on women, as reflected on the one hand by the dialogical text which the characters exchange among themselves, directly and indirectly; and by 'stage instructions' on the other.

The magnificence and pomp, power and affluence of King Ahasuerus are splendidly demonstrated by both the Persian King and the Jewish biblical playwright in the exposition. This grandeur will, however, soon be understood as ironical. Irony has long been proven an efficient weapon in the hands and pens of the (politically) weak, as well as an exquisite dramatic device, able to transmit potent subversive messages over the same 'textual frequency'.

While the immense Persian empire is described by means that can be regarded as epic, they are also typically dramatic: a huge geo-political 'dramatic space', a long period of 180 days of feasting, culminating in a seven-day feast, before peaking in one grand *Finale* on the last day at the beginning of the drama. The opening stage design features an extremely rich decor, expressed through numerous 'props' of expensive materials, precious stones, silver and gold. The minutely described design ends with "drinking . . . by the flagons, without restraint, for the king had given orders to all the officials of his palace to do as each one desired."

The stage is set to receive the *dramatis personae*, waiting in the wings. The anticipated central figure in this big show is undoubtedly the king himself, but the playwright postpones his actual entrance. Between the 127 provinces stretching from India to Ethiopia, gradually narrowed down to the main celebration hall (but still hovering somewhere in an offstage space), and the "as each one desired" – the fascinating plot will take place. It will be played out by the main characters, a particularly interesting series of secondary figures, and the unique person of Esther, the protagonist. In addition to being a key narrative of 'relief and deliverance' in the Jewish exile history, *Esther* is also a biographical quest-play of an individual transformed from a manipulated, passive and erotic doll into a brave, intelligent and independent woman. Toward the end she is willing to risk her own life in order to save her people, and accepts full responsibility for her own actions.

Once the main stage has been set, the playwright turns to the sub-plot, and tells of Queen Vashti's special "banquet for the women in the palace of King Ahasuerus". Obviously, the main party was meant for the men alone. The king sends seven eunuchs to bring the queen, in order to display his wife's beauty to the "peoples and officials". These erotically harmless men are given the task of exposing her to less harmless men, who, in turn, may also only look at her, and envy the king. However, the biblical playwright ironically shows that what has been planned, or perhaps merely arose as an amusing idea "when the king was merry with wine", as a cherry to top the icing on the cake, turns out to be a complete fiasco.

Vashti refuses the summons. The proud King Ahasuerus must consequently suffer not only personal humiliation, as a result of his evident
inability to master his own wife, but also a total diplomatic and political
disaster, the public shaming of the strongest male in the ancient world of
the period. Vashti deflates the king's hubris, together with the
surrounding pomp, with her laconic, unexplained yet clearly understandable refusal. The tightly constructed dramatic text uses Vashti's behavior
to anticipate the behavioral patterns of the two other women, Esther
herself and Zeresh, Haman's wife. The sub-plot never really disappears –
it just moves to 'offstage' where, hovering there almost to the end, it serves
to influence and activate the main plot of *Esther*.

Vashti's highly theatrical refusal to display herself as an erotic-diplo-
matic sex-object is masterfully depicted. For example, the verse 'to do as
each one desired' can now be interpreted in an ironic light, rather than
how the writer may have led the reader/spectator to believe only four
verses back. Throughout the entire empire, and particularly in the celebration of the king's third year on the throne, certain people are indeed
trying to do 'as each one desired'; but the king himself, already at the
outset, has proven to be bereft of true will-power, although he does act
according to whim. Character-wise, the king's impotence is revealed in
choleric outbursts. It is also shown that the first person to act according
to 'desire' in its more serious sense is not 'a man' but Vashti; and her
replacement, Esther, will go even further in this direction.

The major dramatic shift from displaying "the great wealth of his kingdom and the splendor and pomp of his majesty", to "at this the king was
enraged and his anger burned in him", indicates in the opening how the
plot will develop. Unlike the free, resolute and daring Queen Vashti, King
Ahasuerus needs advice from his ministers and councilors, and is rapidly
revealed as dependent, emotionally excitable, and therefore arbitrary and
rash in both thought and action. Many other characters in *Esther* are
equally clearly depicted. Haman, Zeresh and Mordechai, for example,
sometimes move between extremes of situations and moods. The spectator, consequently, may empathize with their social and personal
upheavals, and experience with them their fluctuations between the personal–emotional and the public–political realm, so typical of the *Esther*
drama. Nevertheless, most characters in *Esther* are highly theatrical.

Following Memucan's advice, Ahasuerus dethrones Vashti (the
medieval Jewish scholar Rabbi Shelomo Itzchaki [Rashi] suggested that
he had her killed because of the Hebrew term '*gazar*' that appears in the
text), because "she has not performed the commandment of King
Ahasuerus conveyed by the eunuchs". It is always rewarding to examine
some of the uses biblical narrative makes of messengers. In *Esther* there

are many such instances, mostly due to the hierarchical structure of the court. Eunuchs rush back and forth, delivering messages and bringing people in and out. In a theatrical-oriented reading, except the obvious potential for on-stage commotion, the messenger's role gains a unique status. The 'messenger' device, which may appear anti-dramatic because it indirectly 'tells' rather than directly 'shows', can nevertheless prove theatrically potent. For instance, when the king conveys his orders, the messenger/actor may choose a particular intonation. The discrepancy between the content of the message and the tone in which it can be delivered is indeed the essence of theater. Of particularly dramatic potential is the role of Hathach, who acts as a go-between for Esther in the palace and Mordechai who remains by the king's gate.

The following analysis focuses on three scenes: Esther's invitation to the king and Haman for a private get-together; the first banquet; and then the second one. These scenes highlight the theatricality of the entire book. They cause the *peripeteia*, and bring about a major change as well an *anagnorisis* of sorts.

Prior to the banquet, however, Vashti is disposed of, and Esther is introduced first into the story, then into the king's harem. There she is duly treated with cosmetics, oils, perfumes and myrrh. Even Hegai, the women's keeper, likes her because of her proper behavior. During this one year of preparation, not only is her body massaged, but her soul too is trimmed and modeled to become an obedient erotic slave who will follow the court etiquette with grateful subservience. Throughout this period, Esther not only conceals her origins, as Mordechai has commanded her, but she does not speak much at all. As already noted, the silence of biblical women is frequently quite eloquent. Esther is virtually molded into a soft and silent pleasure-giving body. Well trained and properly oiled, a year later she is chosen as the next queen, to replace her rebellious predecessor. Through Esther's later reaction we learn that even as the first lady and queen, she may not approach the king freely, but must wait for the summons of the golden scepter. When staged, this part must surely concentrate on touch, gesture and movement.

In the meantime Mordechai has managed to prevent the assassination of King Ahasuerus. Chapter 3 of the book describes Haman's promotion and ascent to power, but while all the king's servants bowed to him and "did obeisance to Haman . . . Mordechai did not bow down or do obeisance". His deliberate disobedience, though stemming from different motivation, is clearly reminiscent of Vashti's refusal to show respect, as a reappearing motif of rebellion against the regime, dramatically enhancing the tension. The infuriated Haman plans to destroy not only the rebel. Understanding the national-religious motivation behind Mordechai's disrespect, Haman proposes to annihilate all the Jews, Mordechai included. "When Mordechai learned all that had been done", he tore his clothes and put on sackcloth and ashes.[1]

In this latter scene, which brings us closer to Esther's banquets, and in the one to follow, a great deal of the action is delivered through a refined, certainly ritualistic, and thus also highly theatrical usage of costume. In ritual and theater clothes always signify a consciously externalized inner attitude, easily deciphered by members of the same culture group. Rather than indulging in psychological, perhaps sentimental, verbal descriptions, the biblical playwright prefers to let the (potential) audience draw their own emotional, sympathetic conclusions. Esther sends her uncle 'proper clothes'; he refuses. But after the three days of his fasting, Esther puts on her own royal clothes, from which we learn that she too wore sack-cloth. The phrase "and Esther wore royalty", may better reflect the metaphoric meaning of clothing: Esther 'wore royalty' would be the literal English translation, as though for the first time she has become really resolved to behave like a queen. The costume is hence an external, theatrical sign of Esther's inner conversion.

In this particular context, the 'props' of food and drink can be explained in a similar way. Not only is fasting believed to cleanse both body and soul, but in refraining from eating Esther is simultaneously rejecting the bountiful food of the king's court, together with everything cruel and arbitrary that this food symbolizes, and identifying with her own people.

The playwright, having supplied the external conditions and the inner resolution for the protagonist to act, describes Esther as ready to stand now "in the inner court of the king's palace, opposite the king's hall". The dramatic as well as designed stage-space itself, no less than the costumes and the props, is metaphoric of any scene's message. While Esther is standing outside, probably in a lit area, at one end of the courtyard, the king is sitting "on his royal throne inside the palace opposite the entrance to the palace", in a shadowed area. (Or else, she is in the shade in a corner, whereas he is in the lit area!) Again, rather than indulging in emotional details pertaining to the characters' feelings, fears, expectations etc., the playwright makes the non-verbal elements speak a clear body-language. Ahasuerus and Esther's body postures, the two different spaces they occupy and the space-gap of the courtyard between them, the lighting and the imminent movement are eloquent signifiers of the dramatic tension.

"As soon as the king saw Queen Esther standing in the court, she won his favor" – which again draws attention to her way of standing, whether mysterious, obedient or erotic, but certainly expectant. The term 'won favor in his eyes' implies that he may not have recognized her from far off, but that even from a distance she was impressive. "And he held out to her the golden scepter that was in his hand." The regal act expresses power disguised as grace. On stage, the scepter acquires extra strength as a heavily charged prop, which in this scene serves as the acute meeting point for the two characters. In the particular context of this scene within Esther's function in the royal court, the phallic symbolism of this royal prop is almost melodramatic, as an object with which the king chooses his ladies.

Esther approaches the scepter, silently crossing the physical distance of the courtyard, and the perhaps greater distance from her resolution to the beginning of carrying it out – a magic theatrical moment. Now she touches the top of the scepter, and an indirect, subtle and humiliating contact has been achieved between the two. Despite her royal status, Esther cannot penetrate the palace, as the king's space, without expecting to be symbolically (and physically) penetrated by him.[2] Knowing this all too well, she will turn the dominant male (as husband/owner – '*baal*', in Hebrew) power against itself, for her own purposes. This wonderfully effective stage prop is both the king's key to Esther, and her key to him. Their real intentions, obviously, are diametrically opposed. It is therefore the broader context of the protagonists' motivations that turns the scene from melodrama to high drama.[3]

The first direct dialogue between them is about to begin, some nine years after the expulsion of Vashti, which Esther certainly retains as a lively, potentially threatening memory of what might happen to her. She first touches his symbol of pride, as a sign of submission, and he is the first to talk – a sign of dominance. "What is it, Queen Esther? What is your request? it shall be given you, even to the half of my kingdom." From his words it is clear that her facial expression is not quite cheerful; he also perceives that she wants something. Perhaps her very being there implies her desire for something – unusual for Esther, who has been noted as asking for nothing at all. The king's liking for Esther is expressed with "even to the half of the kingdom" – or perhaps this is merely a typical royal idiom. Her answer is duly polite, almost laconic and likely to arouse curiosity: "If it please the king, let the king and Haman come today to a banquet that I have prepared for him." However, what does the 'I have prepared for him' really mean? Firstly, Esther is in fact presenting the king with a *fait accompli*, thus delicately pressing him to accept the invitation.[4] Secondly, is the 'him' form a courteous third person address to the king, or does it indeed refer to Haman, whom Esther pretends to honor, though in fact she intends to trap? Esther does not reply to the concerned and unsuspecting king's question: "What is it?" – more precisely, 'what is the matter with you?'

He must have noticed that she is troubled (as ironically known, of

course, to the spectator), yet she asks for nothing, but only offers a celebration. Theatrically, a discrepancy is created between her spoken,
dialogical text, and her non-verbal behavior, correctly deciphered by her
partner to the scene. The two languages transmit opposite messages. On
the other hand, Esther never expressly states that she has no request.
Ahasuerus may assume she will tell him her real wish in the intimacy of
the prospective banquet, later that night. From Esther's point of view,
remembering her predecessor's fate, it is surely better to dare her planned
intervention in affairs of state in the privacy and relative security of her
own space, rather than take a chance on (again . . .) embarrassing the
king in public.

Esther's scheme is clarified in retrospect. She designs a three-stage move
to foil Haman's scheme for mass murder. First she invites the king and
through him Haman. Then, on the first evening she does not yet reveal
her cards, keeping them for the second banquet. She must be extremely
careful, since the issue at stake is not only that of her own life. Another
evidence of the playwright's subtle irony is noticeable in Ahasuerus'
response. He seems eager to attend the banquet, as we know from Esther's
words to Mordechai that she had not been called to the king for the last
thirty days. Ahasuerus immediately summons Haman, probably not only
to invite him to this special evening, but also to make the necessary preparations: "Hurry Haman to do what Esther said".

The next verse "So the king and Haman came to the banquet that
Esther had prepared", is a bridge to the following scene.

In the first banquet scene the set changes. No longer the king's official
audience chamber, it becomes the queen's personal chambers, her home
base, a friendly space to her and therefore the best trap for the two most
powerful men in the entire empire, one of them evil (at least from her point
of view), and the other pompous and impressionable. She will use her
reputation, her charms (already proven to have influenced the king), her
excellent sense of timing – and a glass of wine or two, since the king likes
to drink, and alcohol, as we have seen, affects his clarity of judgment.

In this scene Ahasuerus repeats the formula of his previous question,
with one slight but important variation: "What is your petition? It shall
be granted. And what is your request? Even to the half of my kingdom, it
shall be fulfilled." He no longer asks: 'What's wrong with you?', since
Esther must have made a special effort to look her best; neither does he
repeat the formal appeal 'Queen Esther', unnecessary in these less formal
circumstances. Whereas the king's lines are a little shorter now, Esther, no
longer under the scrutiny of the king's courtiers in the hall, allows herself
a longer speech: "This is my petition and request: If I have won the king's
favor, and if it pleases the king to grant my petition and fulfill my request,

let the king and Haman come to the banquet that I will prepare for them, and tomorrow I will do as the king has said." Esther's rhetoric is well thought of, witty and effective. She uses the king's own words (petition and request) twice, manifesting utmost respect for the almost 'holy' words of the monarch, though biblical narrative often uses redundancy and deliberately excessive repetition as an ironic, even sarcastic means. We also learn, retrospectively, that her choice of grammatical tenses is deliberate: 'I have prepared a banquet' is quite different from 'I will prepare . . .'. In her diplomatic maneuver, a brilliant and frequently used dramatic strategy, in which one partner employs texts said by or about another partner, she knows that she has 'found grace in his eyes'. Moreover, he has already promised her 'even the half of the kingdom', and yet another discrepancy is created between what dramatic irony conceals from the king and Haman, but the spectator already knows.

Esther postpones her real request once more, but promises to raise the issue – now clear to all that there is one – on the following day. In the meantime she has succeeded in arousing both Haman's flattered pride at having been invited to this special event, and the king's curiosity.

Only one day goes by between Esther's first banquet and her second, but the plot of *Esther* gains velocity and intensity in a a series of six scenes and a short interlude.

1 On his way out, Haman encounters the rebellious Mordechai yet again.
2 At his home Haman boasts of his successes, especially of the banquet, "yet all this does me no good so long as I see the Jew Mordechai sitting at the king's gate." The idea of the hanging-tree arises at this meeting.
3 Unable to fall asleep, Ahasuerus finds an old report on the foiled assassination attempt, and wishes to reward Mordechai. Haman has just arrived, and is waiting outside in the exterior court to get a permission to hang Mordechai. In this ironic scene of reversal Haman is ordered instead to honor his enemy: "Thus shall it be done for the man whom the king wishes to honor."
4 Following the typical *Megilat Esther* pattern of hubris/humiliation, Haman carries out the king's orders.
5 Mordechai is back at the king's gate, while Haman, "hurried to his house mourning and with his head covered". His wife Zeresh and friends promise Haman a 'complete fall'.
6 In a short but viciously funny interlude, the king's eunuchs arrived and 'hurry' Haman to Esther's banquet.

The main banquet scene opens with a hint to an even less formal evening than the night before. Not "And the king said to Esther at the wine-banquet", but "And the king and Haman came to drink with Esther" or as we might say today, 'to have a drink or two' with her.

The king turns to her, probably very curious by now to find out "what is your petition, Queen Esther, and it shall be granted; and what is your request? Even to the half of my kingdom, it shall be fulfilled." This third version contains elements of both the previous ones. This time Ahasuerus uses a slightly more formal approach, perhaps to back up his former promise with a little more royal authority. Esther's answer is also based on her previous, almost excessively polite but intentionally vague message, which she now constructs differently. She turns to the king using the second-person singular – "If I have found grace in your eyes, oh king, etc." and if it pleases the king – shifting back to the third person. It is a smart, manipulated rhetorical tactic to stimulate the king's sensitivities through alternately approaching and alienating him – verbally, at least. Instead of only 'my petition and request' as she had said the previous night, she fills the hollow, etiquette-ridden verbal formula (possibly in a deliberately ridiculing way) with a most unexpected and very concrete plea. As far as the stage characters are concerned, these last words constitute a double shock. We know little about the king's mood, except that his curiosity regarding Esther's twice postponed desire has not yet been satisfied. Haman, in contradistinction, has had a ghastly day and is in a miserable state. We can only guess whether he has any notion at all of what to expect tonight. Before going on, the actress playing Esther may take a little pause to increase tension: "let my life be given me – that is my petition – and the lives of my people – that is my request."

The banquet for three has turned into a theatrical pearl. It is thick with dramatic irony, extreme gaps between text, context and personal as well as political subtext. Esther goes on: "For we have been sold, I and my people, to be destroyed, to be killed, and to be annihilated" (Possible long pause!). "If we had been sold merely as slaves, men and women, I would have held my peace; but no enemy can compensate for this damage to the king." The immense tension between Esther's two listeners arises from Haman's devious plans being brought out into the open in a most precise way, and from the king's amazing moral indifference; when we remember what he had said to Haman – "The money is given to you, and the people as well, to do to them as it seems good to you" (3:11). Furthermore, the seemingly innocent word 'good' now acquires horrid meanings, when employed so sarcastically under the circumstances.

Esther dilutes her crude and certainly un-diplomatic words 'kill, destroy, annihilate' with the bitter but pseudo-polite "if we have been sold merely as slaves . . ." – a now established rhetoric typical of her character. Stunned Ahasuerus seems to stutter: "And king Ahasuerus said, and he said to Esther: who is he and where is he, who has presumed to do this?" Esther: "A foe and enemy, this wicked Haman."

Haman has been a silent, though definitely very attentive partner in the scene. In two ingenuous stage instructions, the playwright describes the two men's non-verbal reactions, implicitly maintaining that they were indeed practically speechless, though for different reasons: "And Haman was terrified before the king and queen, the king rose from the feast in wrath and went into the palace garden." Haman's reaction is understandable, the king's – less so. But Ahasuerus's confusion and miserably poor reaction is nevertheless an exquisite peace of stage-craft, utterly commensurate with the king's normally irregular behavior.

Dramatically it is important to get the king out. Firstly, to give him and the spectators an opportunity to digest the news. He himself has unwittingly collaborated with Haman and now discovers that not only is Mordechai his savior Jewish (which he knew), but so too is his wife. He exits to enjoy his *anagnorisis* alone. Secondly, the playwright might have wanted to mock Ahasuerus's continued indecision, and so left the exact motivation for this wonderful 'exit' somewhat unexplained. Thirdly, this royal exit is absolutely necessary to prepare the *coup de grâce* for Haman as well as expose the king as a person whose final motive for independent action will be seen to be sexual jealousy.

Haman, alone with Esther, wants to plead for his life, but we can only guess at what she feels or desires. There is no mention of direct dialogue between the two, in this scene within a scene. It may be a silent one. Returning from his few moments alone in the garden, the king sees Haman falling on the queen's bed. Did she really trap him with erotic insinuations? Did she simply make him trip over the bed? Did the king misinterpret Haman's posture as an attempted rape? Did Esther 'direct' such an ambiguous posture and plan it in advance? These and many other questions are not answered in the biblical text, and are open to a director's own intentions. However, Ahasuerus, perceived as stupid in Jewish exegetical traditions, must indeed have been either quite drunk or overwhelmed by a combination of unpleasant feelings, to believe that Haman could possibly have dreamed of making a pass toward the queen at this particular moment.

This magnificent scene ends with "And Haman's face 'dropped' or 'was covered'" to show that sometimes one well-aimed spotlight can do the job of many words.

Esther is the only character in the *Megila* who undergoes real change. She

is transformed first from an orphaned refugee child to an object of pleasure, then to the frightened wife of a monarch; and finally she becomes a
courageous, self-willed intelligent independent woman. While she was
indeed subjected to the influence and pressure of Mordechai, her acts
could nevertheless not have been performed without her own great resolution. The many highly theatrical events, as well as specific promises and
decrees in the *Megilah* that function as virtual speech acts, are commensurate with the protagonist's own performance, theatrically and
personally.

Part III

———

WOMEN AND MEN,
PHYSICS AND METAPHYSICS

6

"The Voice of my Beloved Knocketh"

The assumption in the following discussion is that Chapters 4 and 5 in *The Song of Songs* form a dramatic and poetic unit, harmonious and complete in itself, located at the center and pinnacle of the eight chapters that comprise the book. Like the other chapters, this section too is erotic, daring and breathtaking in its beauty. An examination of several of the literary and dramatic devices of these two chapters will reveal not only the beauty within the poetry, which is well evident even from the first reading, but also its complexity and sophistication. From a wide choice of possible criteria for analysis, I have chosen the following: poetic structure, images, and specific use of verbs and sound patterns. In particular, I wish to draw attention to the dramatic/theatrical approach both within and beyond the literary basis. A dialogical relationship exists between these fundamental components, corresponding to the relationship between the individuals described – the lover and his beloved. The poetic elements reinforce one another and, finally, merge in the description as well, as expressions of the garden of love. Each individual component of the poem is a metaphor for the meaning of the poem in its entirety. The harmonious compatibility between structure, images, verbs and sound patterns indicates that Chapters 4 and 5 not only constitute a superb work of art, but one that also reveals a clear-cut dramatic quality, presenting characters, situations, plot and suspense, as well as suggestions for costume, scenery, lighting and movement – all as befits a text meant for performance and not merely for a silent reading. The following treatment of the text is intended as dramaturgical preparation toward a possible staging of the two chapters.

Structure

Each of the two chapters, 4 and 5, comprise a total of 16 verses, according to the traditional biblical phrasing. In Chapter 4 the lover describes his beloved and in Chapter 5 she describes him.

The following subdivision accentuates the quality of the relationship between the two lovers:

Part 1: (a) Appeal to the beloved; visual description.
           (v. 6 implies a self-addressed appeal of the lover)   4:1–7
           (b) Attraction and responsiveness.   4:8–9
           (c) Appeal to the beloved; intimate sensual description; further closeness.   4:10–11
           (d) The poetic penetration into the garden.   4:12–15

Part 2: Mutual internalization of points of view
    (a)   The lover speaks in his beloved's name.   4:16
    (b)   The beloved speaks in her lover's name   5:1

Part 3: Point of view of the beloved.
    (a)   A missed nocturnal meeting.
           (v. 2: quotation from the lover)   5:2–6
    (b)   Encounter with the "Guardians of the walls".   5:7
    (c)   Dialogue with the Daughters of Jerusalem   5:8–10
    (d)   Description of the lover by the beloved to the Daughters of Jerusalem   5:11–16

Verbs

If the structure is the skeleton of the poem, then the incorporated verbs are its muscles. A sensitive reading aloud of the verbs alone indicates that they 'make sense' in their own right, as already observed for other biblical sections. Even when taken randomly out of context, they still convey a great deal of the emotional impact that is found in the entire *Song of Songs*. If the verbs are applied to the parts of the poem according to the suggested structural divisions, by grouping them according to different criteria it is possible to draw several enlightening conclusions. It is important to remember that the Hebrew verb form indicates, in one word, gender, tense, person and function and is, therefore, sometimes untranslatable into *one* English word.

I   (a) glided, rose fitting, built, hung, grazing, will blow, will flee, I will go.
    (b) thou hath ravished my heart (2), (to be fair, to be better [verbs in Hebrew], come, sing).
    (c) dropping.
    (d) locked (2), living, flowing.
II (a) awake, come, blow, flow out, let him come, let him eat.
    (b) I came, I gathered, I ate, I drank.
    (c) eat! drink! drink to intoxication!
III (a) asleep/awake, knock/open, filled, I have undressed/I shall dress, I washed/I shall defile, sent (his hand)/(my innards) were moved, I rose to open, dropped, opened/withdrew/was gone, (my soul) went out, I sought/I could not find, I called/he did not answer.
    (b) found me, surrounded, smote me, wounded me, took from me.
    (c) I avow, (if) you find him, (that) you tell him, I am sick (from love).
    (d) prominent, washed, sitting, dropping, passing, filled, overlaid, set upon.

I(a) and III(d) are similar from the viewpoint of structural components and grouping of verbs and the use of the present particple as an *adjective*. Likewise, there is a certain semantic similarity between 'fitted', 'built', 'hung' and between 'sat', 'filled', 'veiled', 'set upon', and also between 'glide', 'rise', and between 'dropped', 'washed'.

The beloved is described as the less mobile of the two, but she herself makes use of almost twice as many verbs as does her more freely moving lover. There is a group of contradictory verbs describing situations of conflict; verbs that are casually interwoven; and a small and prominent group of negative or conditional verbs (except in the beloved's section).

Verbs that appear more than once may be considered as key verbs, such as 'come' (four times), 'eat', 'open', 'pass', 'drop', 'find' (three times each), fill, wash, shut, drip, ravish, blow (twice each). Verbs can be grouped according to their semantic similarity, such as verbs of movement, flow and fluidity: 'glide', 'rise', 'pass', etc., that appear mainly in the past and future tenses; or verbs that describe a static situation, such as 'fitted', 'filled', 'sat', that appear mostly as participles. Likewise, there is a group of verbs indicating acts of internalization and consumption such as 'ate', 'drank', 'drank to intoxication', 'gathered'.

From the declension of the verb (tense, choice of pronoun and participle), it is obvious that the beloved appeals to her lover in the third person, while he is hidden but addresses her in the first person. He, for the most part, relates to the future, while she mainly relates to the past.

The most dynamic section of the entire poem is the second part. (In *Part 1* there are seven verbs in the 15 verses; in *Part 2* there are 13 verbs in two verses; in *Part 3*, 39 verbs in the 15 verses!) Hence, the verbs in I(b) and III(b), for example, bridge the gap between anticipation and fulfillment.

Images

There are at least three different types of images in the poem, classified both according to semantic criteria and to the criterion of 'concealment'. A difference exists between "thy hair is as a flock of goats" on the one hand, and between and "mountain of myrrh" on the other. Whereas the first contains both the X and the Y factors of the metaphor (alternately 'tenor' and 'vehicle'; 'describer' and 'described' etc.) – the second type includes only the describing element. Moreover, there are several verses in the poem where metaphors and imagery are conspicuous by the *absence* of the particular part of the body described. The images in the poem can be divided according to their structural grouping.[1] In addition to the above, one may draw conclusions from the different ways in which the images are developed by both lovers.

Part 4: Phonetic patterns
I shall not attempt to clarify all the sounds and rhymes (including internal rhyming patterns) of the poem, but discuss only the some of the many and rich most predominant sound patterns in the poem, in connection with their suitability to the poem's structure and images under discussion.[2]

Turning now to the text itself, we shall incorporate the aforementioned principles into the discussion in the attempt to present the text as an organic whole. In *Part 1* the lover appeals directly to his beloved and describes her in the second person. He opens with "Behold thou art fair my love, behold thou art fair." The repetition[3] emphasizes the beauty of the beloved and the attitude of the lover towards her; a relationship expressed by 'my love' and by the special use of 'thou' (*hinekh*) in place of 'you' (*at*). It is a sensitive and emotional appeal. The use of "Behold thou art beautiful" is, as will immediately become clear, a general impression, which the lover will then methodically and precisely elaborate. From a general view of the maiden he proceeds to a description of the most prominent features of her face, distinguished by their shining and mobile qualities and by their responsiveness to the onlooker – her eyes. The eye is the organ designed to sense the furthest distance of all the senses, while at the same time also reflecting in itself all that it sees, physiologically and metaphorically. When the subject is love, eyes are the most suitable object for the opening lines of a poem dealing with a love affair, where the intensity increases in direct ratio to the reduction in physical distance. The eyes of the beloved are compared to doves, but they are seen through her tresses (hair, veil, shawl?). Had the lover's description been entirely schematic, from top to bottom, he would have begun with her hair and not her eyes. He describes the eyes first and foremost because the effect caused by their veiling adds an aura of mystery and enhances the image of doves copped up, as it were, in their dovecote. From her eyes he moves on to her hair, that can be seen both above and below the eyes; flowing "like a flock of goats". The movement itself, and not merely the order of description, is once again from top to bottom. The direction of movement is reversed in the image of a flock of "newly shorn" ewe that *come up* from the washing rather than glide down, continuing with the description of her white teeth "whereof all are paired, and none is bereaved among them". The alliteration of the letters 'sh', 'k', 'l', that will continue mainly with 'l' and 'sh', emphasizes the flawlessness of her teeth and their perfect match, in the same way as the contrast between 'all are paired' and 'bereaved' (and later "that I am sick of love" which sound like 'shekhola' rather than 'shakula'). In the same way that the lover gives the description of his beloved's eyes precedence over her hair, he also describes her teeth before her lips. Usually lips are visible before teeth, but here too there is a purpose behind the deviation from regular description. The lover suggests in this way that his beloved is smiling, for thin lips were not considered particularly sensual and thus also the image "thy lips are like a thread of scarlet", strengthens the impression that she is smiling. Otherwise, why describe lips as *a thread of scarlet* instead of (as she describes his lips) as lilies. The mysterious and remote effect of the eyes, which enhances their erotic attraction, is balanced by their unveiled pleasantness and the invitation to approach what is hinted at in her smile.

Three animal images – doves, goats, sheep – demonstrate the compatibility and harmony of a group of objects that go as well together as do the parts of the body of the beloved; and even more so when the lover describes the *pair* of lips as a *single* thread of scarlet. A colorful impression is also achieved from the description of the grey doves, black goats, white sheep and scarlet thread. The lover continues his study from top to bottom and examines her mouth ('your mouth' [*midbarekh*] may also be interpreted as 'your words', but it would appear more reasonable for the lover to continue with his physical description, rather than to deviate to a vocal impression is called to mind by 'your words'). He completes his description of her lips and moves to her temples "like a soft pomegranate". Here the color remains, the shape changes; and it is possible that it is the pomegranate seeds that are suggested here. If this is indeed the correct interpretation, then here too a single part of the body (temple) is described in plural terms (seeds). The image of the temple is linked through the rhyme of the previous image: your mouth/ your temple/ your tresses (*midbarekh, rakatekh, tsamatekh*).

The position of the beloved's head is clearly picturesque. She is half turned toward him (he seems to be seeing one of her temples) and smiling; the image of her neck as David's tower differs from the other images from the realms of nature and agriculture, in that the neck is not only beautiful, proud, etc., like David's tower, but also has jewels hanging from it, i.e., non-organic objects, like heroes' shields. The significance of the sound image is enhanced through the alliteration of 'l': tower (*migdal*), a thousand bucklers (*talpiot elef*), hung like the shields (*talui kol shiltei*). This too is an 'urban' description – 'majestic' being more suitable for the describer than the described. This indicates an element of him that is to be found in her; a sort of literary fable on the deliberate subjectivity to be found in the words and actions of love.

From the neck the lover passes on to a description of his beloved's breasts as two fawns, and apart from the graceful sensuousness that is suggested here, there is also an intimation of the red color that is becoming increasingly apparent, as well as the scent of the pastoral lilies (nipples). The 'sh' sound that dominates in the image of the breasts leads the lover, in v. 6, to inhale deeply and try to reach some sort of conclusion stemming from the passion that his own descriptions might have caused him. At night ("until the day be cool, and the shadows flee away") he tells *himself*, he will go to "the mountain of myrrh and the hill of frankincense".

In contrast to the previous images, the lover uses a restrained image of nocturnal shadow (exchanging the 'h' sound of "two, breasts, lilies" [*shnei, shedei, shoshanim*] for the soft and misty 'l' of "shadows, I will get me" [*tslalim, elekh li*]), in that he does not say *what* are the mountain of myrrh and hill of frankincense. The word 'myrrh' is mentioned six times and always in connection with a physical act of love, with sexual organs, or with his or her love juices. In v. 7, the lover sums up his description that began with the head and ended with the sexual organs, and claims that it would appear that he has proved what he had supposed from the start: "you are *all* fair my love, and there is no spot in thee." Her legs are not mentioned; she may be lying down with her legs covered. Perhaps the quality of sprightliness and strength of leg are his qualities and not hers, as can be seen from other indications ("jumping over the mountains, skipping over the hills", etc).

The verbs used in this part of the poem are mainly in their participle form, that in Hebrew also indicates an adjective: 'fitting', 'built', 'hung', 'shepherding'; only 'glided' and 'come up' are verbs describing the activity of dynamic parts of the body. All seven of the verbs used by the beloved to describe her lover (5:11–16) are also in the participle form and create an impression that what is said about the two lovers is constant and not dependent on any past or present tense. Only in his appeal to himself does the lover use the dynamic form of the verb 'blow', 'flee away' (and the opposite) 'I will go' – verbs that are aimed at the future and form a declaration of intent.

There is a small gap between *Parts 1 and 2*, as if the lover is asking himself "It's all well and good, but what shall I do with all this beauty of yours?"; and, pursuing a line of thought that has already been suggested in the movement toward the mountain of myrrh, he invites his beloved to accompany him: "Come with me from Lebanon . . . with me from Lebanon", to the various mountain tops – a restrained metaphor for erotic heights. The more his desire is revealed, the more *restrained* his images become (this is one of the features that distinguishes eroticism from pornography). Mount Gilead has already been mentioned, myrrh and frankincense have been suggested, and now he names Lebanon, Amana, Senir and Hermon – high mountains that may also be considered as phallic symbols.

The beauty of the poem also lies in the multi-purposeness of the metaphoric focus, and thus myrrh, mountain of myrrh, etc., are both masculine and feminine images. In his excitement the lover puts his invitation and the details of the places they will visit before the reason for the invitation. The reason is a passionate and twice repeated "thou hast ravished my heart". Certainly, "thou art fair", but in fact, he is saying, I am calling you to come with me because it is enough for even "one of thine eyes", and "one chain of they neck" (rhyme: einay'ikh, tsavaronay'ikh) to justify my invitation. He will 'pull' her ("pull me and we shall run") because she 'pulls' (attracts) him. The fiery invitation is also expressed in the transition of sound from the soft 'l' in "from Lebanon my bride, from Lebanon" (*mi'Levanon kala, mi'levanon*) to the 'sh' in "look from the top" (*tashuri mirosh*) that has already previously focused attention on the stimulus and is now transferred to the 'r' in "lion from the mountains of leopards" (*araiyot, meharerei nemerim*). The naïve and harmless animals that previously characterized the beloved (doves, fawns, etc.) have now become creatures of prey – lions, leopards, and from the pastoral serenity of a meadow, somewhat remote due to the visual nature of the images used, we move on to wilder, more savage and predatory geo-erotic scenes. These areas are more untamed due to the height of the mountains; more predatory due to the lions and leopards that prey on goats, fawns and sheep. The 'beasts of prey' then become modified once more into honey, milk, spices and perfumes. The allusion to eating and drinking becomes more explicit and the lover continues to satiate his hunger and his thirst, poetically at least, in the following section.

In *Part 3*, his appeal to his beloved is not in visual terms, owing to the reduced distance between the described and the describer, but, rather, through the senses of taste and smell, which demand a more intimate approach and comprise an important element in the erotic menu. Although at first the lover mentions water, this is the water used for washing both the predator's and her (the prey's) own mouth parts. In the transition from washing water to drinking water (fountain, well, etc.), he mentions various poured or dripping liquids: wine, oil, ointment, honey and milk. These are the dominant images in his description of his sister, his bride. She is flowing, sweet, intoxicating, feminine. We may relate to her 'oil' as if to the natural perfumes of the body, but it is clear that the description will not lose by it if we include the spectrum of taste, as well as the intermingling of flavor and scent, relating to the various perfumes that women are wont to use. The increase in physical closeness of the lover to his beloved is beautifully focused in the musical "Thy lips . . . drop as the honeycombs" (*nofet titofna siftotayich*) that actually perform and not merely simulate the movements of the lips and tongue during a kiss or lick. "Thy lips . . . as honeycomb" may also be interpreted in the same way as 'thy mouth / thy words', and thus also the milk and honey under her tongue. However, it is clear that this interpretation negates the self-evident sensuality that is explicit in a correct reading of the language used.

Although the sense of hearing is somewhat neglected and little referred to in the poem, the very act of speech itself and the pronouncement of words of love are directed towards the ear. Thus, 'your mouth', 'your lips', and 'your tongue' are intended, in this context, for taste and not for speech. Their roles as organs of speech will be fulfilled when the maiden opens mouth. These images deal with real taste and not with 'tasteful' speech. The passion of the lover increases in "how fai . . . how much better . . . ". Her beauty cannot be contained. This stage in the lover's approach to his beloved, and the help he receives from his more intimate senses, is complemented by the tonal quality of 'kh' and 'l', and in the soft consonants of "milk under thy tongue and the smell of thy garments is like the smell of Lebanon" *(khalav takhat leshonekh vereakh simlotayikh kereakh Levanon)*.

In *Part 4*, corresponding to the top-to-bottom description of *Part 1*, the lover passes from the head (lips and tongue) of his beloved through the scent of her garments to the locked garden. The maiden herself is a locked garden, if the expression 'a garden shut up' (and thus also 'a spring shut up', 'a sealed fountain') is also a metonym and she and the "garden" are one. Because the garden is locked (twice) and sealed, the lover bursts into it, poetically, and describes 'thy shoots' in a vast and rich choice of images of taste and aroma. Unlike the other images, described separately, 'thy shoots' alone are described here in a series of comparisons and simulated images in which the comparison itself becomes the focus for image-upon-image. Besides the scent and taste that they evoke, they also represent fertility and plenty, like an orchard replete with pomegranates and bunches of grapes. The exoticism and richness are well expressed not only through the many images evoked for the description of one, central, part of the body, but also through rhyme and alliteration; in the vowel 'ee' and the consonants 'p', 'r' "an orchard of pomegranates with precious fruits; henna with spikenard plants" (*pardes rimonim im pri megadim kefarim im neradim*), the 'r' has been transferred here from the 'prey' of the lions and leopards, but softened in the vowel 'ee' and consonant 'p', as the food here is not a sheep or fawn, but fruit. This tonal quality balances the 'n', 'm', 'l' and the vowel 'oo' in the previous verse, and 'corrects' the locking and the breaking in, even vocally. The young man's description of his beloved ends again with the "flow of clear living waters" and links, like many of the other images, with the previously mentioned image that has become a focal metaphor: the Lebanon. The heavy alliteration of 'n' and 'm' (coming after 'calamus and cinnamon') focuses attention on the onomatopoeia of the sound of sipping and tasting of water. The image becomes the metaphoric summation of all the images of flowing, life, virginity, purity (her characteristics), and also of strength (from the immense potential force contained in 'a wave shut up', evoking a giant tidal wave) and the savageness that is taken from Lebanon and all that has been previously associated with this mountain. This verse summarizes the motif of thirst/ quenching (a variation on hunger/satiation) and the lover's passion.

The second part of the poem is the most interesting, also from the erotic point of view. In 4:16 and 5:1, one can perceive a phenomenon characteristic of couples who are genuinely in love. They each internalize the thoughts or words of the other. In 4:16 the lover speaks in his beloved's name, and she, as if from her own point of view, enheartens herself and invites him to come to her. He uses a packed series of highly dynamic verbs; the first three in the second-person imperative and the last three in the third-person future. The appeal, in the imperative, is to the wind, to himself and to her at one and the same time: the wind is the beloved, the wind is the lover, and the wind is what will come and blow upon the garden. This is the north wind, where the lover imagined making his mountainous journey, and also the south wind (the Yemen), as opposite directions of a man and a woman who will act to attain the same goal. The expression 'to blow' has already been mentioned in 'until the day be cool', and the actual soft blowing of the wind are expressed in the alliteration of 'f' and 'v' "O north wind and come . . . blow upon . . . that the spices may flow out . . . and eat of his precious fruits" (*uri tsafon u'voi'l teman . . . hafikhi gani, izlu vessamav, yavo dodi legano veyokhal pri megadav*).

The garden is a metonym for the lover and the beloved. In 5:1 the point of view changes. The beloved internalizes her lover, and speaks in his name as if he has *already* come and gathered his honey and eaten and drunk. The seven verbs in this verse are divided into a group of four in which repeatedly and dynamically the lover speaks through his beloved's mouth of her heart's desire, in the past tense; these are followed by a group of three verbs in the present imperative. The turning point in the two verses is found in the tonal quality of 5:1, that differs from that of 4:16. The most dominant sound here is the joyous vowel 'ee' (and 'oo' at the end), that can be interpreted as the joyful sounds of the actual act of lovemaking. In this light 'friends' does not mean the friends and acquaintances of the youth, but is an appeal to the couple *themselves*, who are the beloved lovers and those who are also intoxicated by the acts of love. This turning point becomes equally clear from the transition in tenses. What exactly happened between 'come!' and 'I came' is a gap that each reader is invited to bridge according to his own inclinations. The two verses together appear to offer an anticipation whereby each lover expects the reactions of the other, and the precedence of intimacy of the soul over that of physical consummation is expressed; such a strong yearning between them is evoked that for a moment the act of love appears to have already occurred.

At this moment the two parts of this particularly dramatic scene form the crescendo of the entire poem – his from her point of view and hers from his point of view, complement each other in their imagery:

(a) blow upon my garden
spices may flow out
my beloved came into his
garden and eat his
precious fruits.

(b) I came to my garden
I gathered my myrrh with my spice
I ate my honey with my honeycomb
I drank my wine with my milk.

In the act of love (perhaps it is wishful thinking at this stage), tenses, phonetics and images are exchanged, and man–woman each contribute to the poetic development of the other, and to the act itself. The couple are revealed as seen through each other's eyes, in the same act but in two versions: perfumes that from his point of view (as she sees it) are liquid, from her point of view (as he sees it) appear as honey, as is also the case with the images of Lebanon and myrrh.

In the second part of 5:1 we find the essence of the entire poem: unification – through the use of the plural by the two lovers. From the point of view of structure, therefore, 4:16 and 5:1 reflect the complete Chapters 4 and 5, and thus too the actual merging of the couple, which forms the central focus of the book of *Song of Songs* in its entirety. "Eat, O friends, drink, yea drink to intoxication", therefore, relates to the rest of the passage in 4:16 and 5:1 in the same way that these two verses in their turn relate to the two complete chapters, functioning as a play within a play. These two chapters function in the *same* relationship towards all eight chapters of the book.

In the third part and in (a) from 5:2, the speaker is the maiden, who begins her speech in the first person: 'I was asleep', but, as if still under the influence of her lover, immediately reverts and quotes him. In his description the lover waits for night – which has now arrived. This section deals with the development of the meeting previously hinted at in *Part 2*, yet not in the form of a poetic realization of the meetings of two souls and the emotional exchange of a slightly different sort of development of verses and feelings, but in a description of the missed actual physical encounter. This is a dramatic and 'suspenseful' part of the poem, whether we see it as a dream, or as reality with the lover's voice really waking his beloved from her sleep. In any event, she expresses the awakening of her soul even if her body remains dormant.

"The *voice* of my beloved knocketh" relates to the sense of sound, which has been somewhat neglected so far, but now suddenly springs to life, in the deep of the night, when nothing can be *seen* and the path to the closed and locked door cannot be tasted, smelled or touched. The verbs that complement each other in *Part 2* (come, I came; wake, I woke; eat, I ate, I drank, etc.) now become verbs that reflect the contrast between sleep and wakefulness, and therefore also between desired reality and a dismal dream; and thus the enormous tension that has built up: sleep – wake; knock – open; fill (both of them are 'filled'); I put off – shall dress; I washed – I shall defile. The rest of the verbs in the verse do not form contrasts, but it is easy to see among them a link that also expresses, *not just for its own sake*, the relationship between the couple: sent – moved; I rose to open, dropped with liquid myrrh, I opened – withdrawn and gone – (my soul) failed me. This poignant situation ends in an extreme contrast:

"I sought him . . . but I could not find him"; "I called him, but he gave me no answer". The feeling of suspense and loss at the end, along with the dejection, are expressed not only in these verbs, but are equally clearly expressed in the sound pattern. The 'd' that is softened in "my beloved knocketh" (*dodi dofek*) becomes a more and more demanding and attacking 't' in "open, my sister, my bride, my dove, my undefiled" (pitkhi, akhoti, rayati, yonati, tamati), the frequency of the 't' in the sentence increases and becomes more aggressive towards the end and imitates the rhythm of penetration. Echoes of this 't' are found in "I have put off my coat" *(pashateti kutanti)*; the same 't' sound emitted by her and by him.

The word myrrh, as a keyword, like the image 'Lebanon' and the expression 'cousin' *(dod)*, is mentioned here frequently. The images in this section are 'coy' images and their significance is explained in at least two ways. Perhaps the lover is outside, beyond the door of her room (in a reality that may or may not exist in her dream) but preparing for physical entrance. If so, "my head is filled with dew" may or may not be a metaphorical expression. If not, the image is beautifully ambivalent. The beloved, on her side, delays the invasion of her room / garden with a transparently humorous excuse. She appears ingenuous, and not just because she has been suddenly woken in the middle of the night – her heart had been awake throughout! She presents as a reason not to open the door the fact that she has already *undressed*. After all, this is exactly the situation she is ready for. The excuse of dirtying her feet is even more transparent. The repeated 'how shall I'? confirms it. His 'head' filled with dew and the drops of night completely correspond to her fingers dripping with myrrh, and both of them are ready, willing and able. There is no need to elaborate on the keyhole, yet her 'guts' (me'ayim), a less 'romantic' element but more credible from the point of view of feelings, are what respond to her lover's suffering because he is unable to enter. The maiden's *self*-perception and her empathy with her lover are compatible. At this moment the poetic/erotic tension reaches its climax; however, the images, previously mentioned, become restrained whereas the tonal quality becomes bold. When at long last she opens for her lover, he withdraws and is gone, and with him "my soul failed me". The emotional precision is stunning: in a mournful tone "I sought him" (bikashtihoo instead of bikashtiv) and "I could not find him" (in the same tone) the maiden searches for her man, calls him but receives no answer. From a position of near consummation, closeness, and realization of her love and perfect physical and emotional harmony, she is rejected in an instant to a lost and remote place where only a moment before the voice that had spoken to her, the real knocking at her door, now no longer answers. The pattern here responds to the circular patterns in (a) that lead from "thou art fair" to "thou art all fair" and "from washing water" to "drinking water" and from "what is thy lover" to "this is my lover". Perhaps this entire scene of the missed encounter between the lovers is a sort of illustration of "if you waken and if you appeal the love until it is desired" (2:7) – and here love is indeed highly desired. It should be noted that it is unclear whether a 'realistic' meeting actually occurs between the lovers, and if their love, perhaps, remains within the realm of yearning rather than actual consummation. Whether or not this is in fact the general nature of their love – the reader must interpret for herself. In any event the approach here is not that of the romantic style whereby unfulfilled love is presented as a desirable principle.

In *Parts 2 and 3* the beloved speaks of her encounter with the guards on duty at the wall (she herself can be conceived as a 'wall' – VIII:9–10, and they can also be perceived as guardians of virginity). They represent official disapproval and it is clear, of course, that forbidden fruit is sweeter; they punish her for her vagrancy. However, it appears that it is not only the finding, smiting and wounding of her, and the mournful tone in which she recounts the events that form the real punishment, but, rather, the fact of the embarrassing meeting, and the sharp transition from the situation of a wonderful dream-like intimacy to the reality (?) of the rough public encounter.

In *Parts 2 and 3* there are no metaphors, thus possibly indicating that we are dealing here with the ruder reality of the encounter with the guards and less with the meeting with the daughters of Jerusalem. The various meetings of the maiden with different groups – one with members of the opposite sex and one with girls like herself – adds a more social, perhaps interhuman, and more universal touch. A marked difference is shown between the guards and the lover, and the secret nature of the love is emphasized. Her girlfriends, particularly when seen against the background of the meeting with the guards, reveal sympathy and identification, and ask her what makes her lover so special in comparison with others, such as, for example, the guards themselves. It is indeed the particularity of both lovers that makes them 'special' in each other's eyes and in all other organs.

The lover speaks directly to his beloved, but the maiden describes events in the third person when speaking *of* her lover, because he is hidden. The text intensifies the hidden quality of the lover; grammatically and dramatically. She carries on an explicit dialogue with the Daughters of Jerusalem, adjuring them to find him and tell him that she is 'sick from love'. This expression today has somewhat sweet, emotional and more or less positive connotations, but in its original context there is no doubt that it indicated deep suffering, through its very restraint and understated value. In front of her own girlfriends the maiden does not complain of the blows she received or about the cold (they took her mantle from her) and being torn from the warmth and safety of her bed, her dream and her love; her sorrow is for the disappearance of her lover. The Daughters of Jerusalem, for their part, provide her with an opportunity to describe her lover, and to complete the poem that commenced with her lover describing her. This time, in *Part 4*, the images are mostly visual, but are also laden with the additional meanings that have accrued from the other senses during the development of the song in its entirety. The dream itself, and the meeting, provide the direct inter-poetic motive for the description. The maiden's description of the youth completes the symmetric circle of their relationship; but in the same way that it opened, so it now closes: more remote at first, stemming from the use of visual images, to images and situations that flow with the senses of taste and smell; senses that demand physical closeness. The opening question, "What is thy beloved more than another beloved"?, rhetorically emphasized and repeated with slight variations, deliberately ignores the soul searching that accompanied the dream, and allows the beloved to refer to her lover in comparative calm that arises, from her point of view, from the pallid substitution of *about him* for being *with him*. She makes use of certain images that bear some similarity to those used by her lover, but are also different. Her images are slightly bolder because 'like' is omitted (a weaker metaphorical link) and replaced by a direct metaphor: "His head is not 'like' the most fine gold", it *is* the most fine gold – and thus continues the rest of her description of him. Thus too she describes him from head to foot and examines his locks, eyes, cheeks, hands, body; she skips over his loins, but does not forget to praise his legs – for he is agile and light of movement and 'withdrew and was gone'. Her description begins with "is the chiefest among ten thousand" in reply to the first question "what is your beloved?"; a more personal delicate reply is obtained from the words "his mouth is most sweet, yeah he is altogether lovely", and ends in the – according to the times – incontestable evidence: "*This* is my beloved . . . and *this* is my friend."

In the lover's description of his beloved 'soft' images predominate, such as the verbs expressing gliding and gentle dropping and various adjectives that describe flowing. The feeling that is created is one of a richness of movement and harmony, together with a suggestion of physical eroticism. His descriptions also include 'hard' images such as mountains, lions and leopards, and even the neck like David's tower. When the maiden describes the youth there is a blend of 'hard' and 'soft' images: the eyes, cheeks and lips of her lover are likened to 'soft' objects, while his hands, body and legs are 'hard', valuable materials. The hard and soft elements interchange again at the end: "His aspect is like Lebanon, excellent as the cedars" becomes 'most sweet' and 'altogether lovely' that describe the hard and the soft together. The expression "This is my beloved, this is my friend" also encompasses both the 'hard' and the 'soft' aspects. The two together make him the ideal lover; their striking vividness is similar, except for the maiden's words being more explicit: he is white and ruddy; his hair – the most fine gold; his locks – black; his eyes – grey or black (their pupils) 'washed' with milk; his lips – red; his hands – golden, and so too his thighs set on pillars of fine stone. Her description of him is regal, and emphasizes the 'urban' rather than the 'rural' aspect. He calls her by many names: my friend (3), bride (6), sister (5), dove, and undefiled; while she calls him (once) 'my friend' and my beloved (8). The great stability in her relationship toward him ('solid' images . . .) is also reflected here.

Literary criteria, at least insofar as there is no actual vocal performance of the text, bear witness, in spite of their 'literariness', to the considerable dramatic factor. The many verbs, particularly in the sections that are more active and 'suspenseful' from the point of view of the plot, serve, as previously stated, as the muscles of the text, describing the situation while at the same time creating its movements and pauses.

The great musicality of the text cannot of course be fully expressed if it is not brought to fruition and can be compared to a musical score: only a trained musician can hear these notes inside himself. The musical basis points to an almost unavoidable necessity to implement the text through sound and rhythmic movement of one sort or another.

The many images also possess a meaning that is not just dramatic but, rather, theatrical. For, especially in biblical times, the play itself was a metaphor, a physically performed ritual fable of a spiritual moral, presented in an attempt to demonstrate, using space, time and plot, as well as costumes and special accessories, things that belong to the higher spheres of reality and of awareness. The workings of the *imaginatio* – rather than 'fantasy' – as an active and creative force, have, therefore an important place in theatrical usage, in the sometimes even violent joining of elements that at their source belong to totally different realms. The play itself, as an event that 'is and is not' at the same time reality and illusion in one is basically similar to an image. From this issue too stems the validity for imagining a physical act of love as the love of God for his people. An image, whether within the theatre or of the theatre itself, is capable of redefining reality. However, in the *Song of Songs*, and especially in the central chapters dealt with here, there are additional dramatic foundations that are worth our attention.

In the *storyline* of these chapters there are, first of all, many contrasts:

male/female, serenity/violence, village/city, single/plural, imagination and reality, and others. The conflict, as one of the most typical elements of a 'dramatic' situation, although not extreme in this case, cannot be ignored, due to the quality and quantity of its appearance. The contrasts do not exist only on the level of plot, but are also reflected in the musicality, imagery and structure. As it remains unclear to the end whether the lovers 'really' met or not, certainty only exists in the realm of literary-fantasy or theatrical performance, and is expressed, amongst other things, in color, sound and indications of scent, taste and touch, as a complete synaesthetic experience in the way that theatre can and should be.

It is possible to see into the distance and into light years of time. Hearing is generally restricted to a shorter range; the sense of smell necessitates the proximity of the object to be smelled to the nose of the smeller. Touch, of course, requires direct and continuous contact with the object. The sense of taste demands physical *internalization* of the tasted object in order to turn it, physically and metaphorically, into a part of oneself. The effect of gradually bringing closer the different senses, in these two chapters, creates a tremendous dramatic and sensuous suspense. Whether this explodes into climax or whether the climax is never attained remains unclear. Equally unclear is whether the concept is merely at the level of a dream, a sort of play within a play, particularly regarding the height of suspense that is found in the gap between Chapters 4 and 5 – between "Let my beloved come!" and "I came into my garden".

In the text, various accessories are mentioned – jewels and costumes (shields of mighty men, veil, coat, etc.) that can greatly assist anyone wishing to present it on stage, and these objects *are used* in the 'play' and their role is not only descriptive: the maiden removes her coat, the guards carry her veil and mantle. Movement is contrasted with immobility: while in the first part the girl appears to be resting and giving herself entirely to description by the lover, in the third part he is absent and she becomes active in her search. What seems a relatively static description, at first glance, of doves, sheep, goats, fawns, presents images of great harmony, evolving into a more balanced scene from the standpoint of dynamic movement; the lover is compared with valuable but static objects – architectural elements of a palace – pillars, sockets, etc. He, for example, compares her to water 'flowing from Lebanon', and she uses the same metaphor from the point of view of her own love – 'his aspect is like Lebanon'. It is the individual method of comparison that counts. Certainly a more intensive dramatic effect is achieved through contrasting types of movement, in addition to the quality of movement itself as opposed to stasis. The dynamics of approach/retreat increase the suspense.

The location, its landscape and the movement in it that breathes life into the space, is varied. The body is described in scenic terms that metaphorically convert the scenery into a body. Valleys and mountains, gardens and wells, towers and pillars, rooms, cities, flowing fountains, parts of halls and doors and locks – all these are theatrical usages that personify the inanimate object and imbue the human object with beauty. In this way dramatic spaces, open and closed stages and imagination are described and formed as multicolored and glancing impressions of erotic areas. The implied lighting also changes, from daylight, through shadow to night, and adds a highly theatrical quality to the lovers' drama.

The clearly dramatic structure of the 'play' is based on the lovers' monologues and on making the partner in dialogue appear present in his/her absence (or at least distance) as in the verse "with me from Lebanon", which is meant to be considered as the reply to an un-posed question. The 'absent' partners are 'made present' through words. The quest for the absent lover(s) appears and sounds as though the words themselves create the person through their performative function rather than their descriptive one. This effect of the actual presence of the maiden is the flesh and blood of all theatre. Further on we find the mutual internalization of the words of the lovers; the beloved speaks in her lover's name, and 'real' dialogues take place, with more 'realistic' properties, between the maiden and the guards – an indirect and violent dialogue; and between the maiden and the Daughters of Jerusalem – a direct dialogue, pleasant and humorous.

The plural appeal, hinted at throughout the work, whether through use of the plural verb or the plural "Daughters of Jerusalem", indicates the author's consideration of his audience, that large community of lovers who are capable of taking an active role in love.

Throughout the entire poem, through its motifs and keywords, there exists a pattern of motif and variations. Each of the two lovers relates to the act of love and to his/her partner in his/her own masculine/feminine way. They both speak of the other in a way that characterizes the other while at the same time characterizing the speaker him/herself. It must be added, that *Song of Songs* is spoken predominantly from a female point of view (about 60 percent of the verses). Certain passages are regarded as 'so essentially feminine that a male could hardly imitate their tone and texture successfully'.[4]

The traditional Jewish interpretation conceives the lover in the *Song of Songs* as none other than God, and the beloved is the People of Israel. Some of the interpreters, by this allegorical interpretation, wished to justify the inclusion of the book of *Song of Songs* in the Bible, as a book in which not only is the name of God not mentioned, but which also deals with a subject that, despite its potential spirituality, is nonetheless first and foremost extremely physical, mischievous and sexual. Other interpretations recognized the meaningful link between a sexual experience and a religious one, or at any rate the *yearning* for such an orgiastic experience, physical or spiritual. Certainly the interpretative attempts to see the text as reflecting a reality, generally idyllic, that lies beyond itself, are neither new nor original. I have attempted to seriously accept *both* poles of metaphor (in particular) and allegory (in general). In *Song of Songs*, according to metaphoric logic, if the God of Israel is the lover, the lover is described as 'divine'.[5] The theory of speech-acts is concerned with the question, how to do things with words?[6] *Song of Songs* gives a particular answer in a particular field. "But words are also by the mouth of the speaker, a mouth that is itself in the speech *as* speech. The mouths are literally uttering body language."[7] The poem *itself* is an act of love: it is an *expression* of love as well as love itself. It is a hyposthasis of love in the words that express it and through their use. The dramatic elements are only a metaphor for the significance of the poem in its entirety: two lovers describe one another, each hidden in the words of the other, exchanging words of love and their experience of an act of love that is not fully realized (also, and mainly because it is impossible to carry out on paper . . .). "the voice of my beloved knocketh" is, therefore, a phrase that can also be read and understood as such. An ideal performance of the text is an invitation to a theatricality in which body and soul sustain one another.

7

The Educational Theatre
of Proverbs

Large portions of *Proverbs* are devoted to descriptions of voluptuous women who seduce poor innocent men, thus creating a culturally enduring model of "The Bad Woman". *Proverbs* ends, nevertheless, with an accolade to "The Capable Women" (Eshet Chayil) [31:10–31], a positive model for a biblical 'Donna Ideale'. In addition to the many aphorisms and fragments about 'good' and 'bad' women, *Proverbs* also contains a compact, humorous theatrical pearl in Chapter 7. It is a dramatized one-act piece of moral instruction given by a father (or teacher) to his probably adolescent son (or sons), intended to convince him how bad (and easy) it is to be sexually seduced, and how high the moral price will be. This little gem of a piece is divided into five distinctive scenes, and includes the dramatic personae of the foolish seduced young man, the devious whore and the omniscient first-person singular speaker, half-participating, half-reporting.

This one-act picture creates a deliberate conflict between its depiction of sensuality on the one hand, and the inevitable moral peril awaiting the young man, who, if seduced, will be doomed to descend "to the Sheol (hell) . . . [and] to the chambers of death". Although the obvious moral at the end of the act is that one should never, never be tempted, the impression the reader/listener(s) are likely to get – is quite the opposite.

The dramatic space of the presentation is the house of the father and the son, and the time, most suitably, is night. The circumstances of the event, as the text suggests, are a cosy father–son get-together in the peace and quiet of their home, in and from which the father portrays a half-realistic, half-fictitious scene-within-a-scene of seduction, which, in turn, takes place in a nearby street in town. The moral security of the family home is strongly contrasted with the dangers 'outside' and thus echoes to the moralistic ending of *Proverbs*, regarding the importance of the home: "food for her household (Hebrew 'house' or 'home') [. . .] not afraid for her household . . . all her household are clothed, [. . .] she looks well to the ways of her household."

Scene i (7:1–6) Introduction

Following the moralistic style of *Proverbs*, the father opens with an appeal to the son, warning him in advance: "My child (my son), keep my words with you and store up my commandments with you; keep my commandments and live, keep my teachings as the apple of your eye . . ." This individual but stereotype father (figure) not only resorts to the classical biblical rhetorical device of parallelism, but indeed speaks in a God-like style. Keeping the 'commandments' echoes and directly alludes to the "Hear O Israel" (*Shema Israel*) section, which became the most famous Hebrew prayer: "Keep these words that I am commanding you today in your heart. Recite them to your children [this father indeed does . . . .] and talk about them when you are at home and when you are away, when you lie and when you rise. Bind them as a sign on your hand, fix them as an emblem on your forehead, and write them on the posts of your house and on your gates" (*Deut.* 6:4–9). The father reuses the original Pentateuch text in a sophisticated way. Instead of 'tie them on your hands' he recommends that his son: 'bind them on your fingers' but does not neglect the original 'heart' metaphor: "write them on the tablets of your heart", thus enlisting yet another famous religious object, the tablets of the law. Whereas 'apple of your eye' is addressed to the first part of the body that might be seduced from afar, the protection for the fingers is intended against any tactile encounter with a woman, and can then continue, if the heart is not well prepared, shielded with good advice.

Prior to the depiction of the evil woman, the father wisely and in the manner of a liberal, almost open-minded pedagogue, offers an alternative positive model of woman: "Say to Wisdom, 'you are my sister,' and call Insight your intimate friend, that they may keep you from the loose woman, from the adulteress with her smooth words." In other words, 'before I tell you all about bad women, you should know that there are good ones too'. The subtext, however, clearly implied in these lines, expresses a different view altogether: "If you approach women at all, do choose Wisdom and Insight." In Hebrew, both these nouns are conjugated in the feminine form, making them indeed female characters; but being allegorical, an actual sexual relationship with them is not really a very tempting option. Moreover, the father presents these ladies as 'sister' and 'friend', thus suggesting the impossibility of any (incestuous) physical intercourse with them. The son, it is well understood, will not dare make love to his sister. The idyllic, non-physical intimacy with Wisdom and Insight will keep the son away from the 'loose' (stranger, in Hebrew) woman, the adulteress. The text distinguishes between spiritual family intimacy on the one hand, and the alienation and 'strangeness' involved in physical intercourse, on the other. This speech also separates the needs and desires of the body, presented as 'a stranger' (zara), from those of the soul or spirit which are 'intimate'.

Scene ii (7:7–13)

The father–narrator engages in depicting a scene of a gradual, nuptial approximation between a 'wily' (or 'a woman whose heart is besieged or closed') prostitute and the 'heart-less . . . youngster without sense'. The narrator is rapidly revealed as also being the playwright and director, not to mention the skilful designer and an actor in the play. The listener(s) in the scene and the outside spectators/readers alike, learn that the youngster listening to the play and the youngster acting in the scene are identical. The son is the protagonist in this biblical version of the 'Mouse-trap,' a beautifully designed meta-theatrical device of a play-within-a-play, that takes its morally proper place outside this family's window, offstage.

The father is not only the overall theatre-maker, but in his role within the inside play he also assumes the part of a Peeping Tom.

"At the window of my house, I looked out through the lattice, and saw among the simple ones, I observed among the youths, a young man without sense . . ." At the outset of this vivid picture, the father tells how once upon a time, or perhaps right now, he witnessed what was shortly to prove a shocking sight. Surely, the deliberate false naïvity of this 'what a coincidence!' device can only be perceived as truly humorous. A little pun may be suggested in associating the Hebrew 'Pethi' ('silly' or 'without sense'), ascribed to the youngster, and 'Pithui', namely seduction. It is also not too far-fetched to assume that the father has just recently seen his son in pursuit of a woman, and with this cautionary tale he wishes to warn him against any further unruly behavior.

The father's observant eye catches sight of an 'anonymous' young man, and follows him on his pursuit of a whore. Having fixed upon the pseudo-stranger youngster, he continues to follow the lad in an equally mock-naïve "passing in the market by her corner". This time he addresses his educational intentions directly toward his listener, who by sheer coincidence just happens to be there, by the window, peeping through the lattice. However, the omniscient peeper knows very well where his character/listener really wants to go. Indirectly, the father make it clear to his son that there is always someone (he himself!) keeping an eye on his offspring's un-kosher intentions, and he exposes his devious behavior: "taking the road to her house in the dusk, in the eve of day, at the time of night and darkness."

The four synonyms of 'dark' contribute considerably to the theatrical design of the scene. 'Dusk, Evening, Night and Darkness', together and separately, relate to the proper lighting of the prospected event and create the sombre atmosphere fit for the nasty deed. It is somewhat surprising that the father manages to see anything at all in a night as dark as he himself describes. Clearly, therefore, as any theatre critic will claim, under these minutely specified lighting conditions, no one is going to be able to see anything, and if it was really so dark near the whore's house, how could daddy have seen what was going on there? Theatrical realism and truthfulness to facts are hereby sacrificed to a little humorous piece of heavy-handed pedagogy.

Once the truly dark, ominous and frightfully threatening scene has been set, a female figure emerges from the gory shadows of the night: "Then a woman comes toward him." Narrator, listener, the blind implied spectators, and the readers too, get a little closer yet, and behold, the woman is 'a prostitute, wily of heart'. In his gradual close-up technique, the father first designates her as just 'a woman', then exposes her as 'a whore', and in the same breath tells that she is 'with a closed heart', (netzurat-lev). The Hebrew term suggests that she conceals the real intentions in her heart. Only the omniscient narrator, rather than the actively participating 'unsuspecting' son, can know what she is up to. The son, alas, will have to learn the facts of life and sex from his own, probably regrettable experience, just as daddy had done in his own younger years.

The approaching lady is further portrayed as 'she is loud'. The original 'homiya' is traditionally interpreted in this context as 'wild in her sexual desire'. The woman is, furthermore, 'wayward', an expression equally erotic in its Hebrew connotation. This particularly rhetorically ambiguous dramatic section builds up erotic tension while describing it as perilous. The bewildered, or else amused, or perhaps ashamed, sexually aroused, etc. listener may not be sure what to feel, think, want. So far, however, the fine borderline between pure eroticism and eroticism deprecated, has not quite been crossed. The lady's appearance is still more negative than positive. Later on, the father will make the common mistake of depicting Sin too beautifully, in over tempting colors.

One of the ways to achieve the father's desired theatrical effectiveness in the scene is through the contrast between the light and safe indoors, from which the listener in the scene and the readers with him vicariously peep into the dark and dangerous outdoors. This 'out there' darkish urban landscape is, nevertheless, morally (rather than emotionally!) pierced by the narrator's gaze. He tells us that "her [the prostitute's] feet do not stay at home; now in the street, now in the squares, at every corner she lies in wait". The place of a decent woman is, no doubt, at home. It is therefore enough to state that this woman roves the streets to prove her guilty of evil machinations.

As in a good play, here too it is evident that whatever is bound to happen will indeed happen, by force of dramatic inevitability, and the only theatrically-oriented question is how. The whore succeeds in trapping the youngster like a bird, cornering him in the dark alley, recently mentioned and still fresh in the memory. The following juicy scene is meant, of course, to engender in the youngster a profound aversion to such terrible women. Already promised that they are lascivious and lustful, the listening son now hears that 'she seizes him and kisses him'. The objective, sensitive reader will never know whether his counter-part within the text, the listening son, considers such advances to be in fact rather pleasant, or are they indeed appalling as the father describes. In any case, women who take overt sexual initiative are often considered prostitutes by a (gynophobic) male society, and perhaps this is the case here too, as the father warns his son against the whore's erotic aggressiveness. Whereas kissing him is considered in itself too impertinent, the narrator father adds: 'with impudent face she says to him', implying that her verbal appeal to the youngster is even more shameless than the kiss.

Scene iii (7:13–20)

The third scene is the central one, theatrically, structurally and thematically. The father's invading gaze now penetrates the prostitute-as-an-actor, who will play her role and speak her part in his voice. The speech itself is intelligently constructed, tendentiously witty in order to catch attention, and plainly bawdy. Nevertheless, it is delivered by a male figure, invading the portrayed character from the inside and appropriating her 'despicable' womanly qualities from the outside.

"I had to offer sacrifices, and today I have paid my vows; so now I have come out to meet you, to seek you eagerly, and I have found you! I have decked my couch with coverings, colored spreads of Egyptian linen; I have perfumed my bed with myrrh, aloes, and cinnamon."

Erotic discourse is nowhere better to be found in the Old Testament than in *Song of Songs*, in its purest manifestations; or in some of the prophets' metaphors, in its harnessed and enlisted forms. The playwright of this particular one-act *Proverbs* piece chooses a third (and, I believe, humorous) way, in which the obviously sexual images are interspersed with moral condemnations. In order to reconfirm his former declaration that the whore is concealing her true intentions, her speech in his mouth opens with the offerings she had sacrificed and the vows she had paid. This means, in practical terms, that she has a well stocked larder at home, as the Hebrew custom would have it. Part of the offering is given back to the person who offers. In modern terms she could say 'My fridge is full, my bar stocked with drinks, why don't you pop in for a snack?' Presenting herself as a woman who truly pays her vows, namely a chaste, God-fearing lady, 'she' (in fact, the father who speaks through her), actually appeals to the youngster's appetite and taste, in this forked-tongued appeal. 'Therefore', she adds, 'I have come out to meet you', etc. This personal address is of course simply another trick, frequently encountered by many a man on the way to his downfall. In her eyes, so it would seem, he is not just one of a crowd, but has been carefully picked out, because she has made a special effort to find, no other but him

Having titillated the youngster's appetite under the disguise of an 'offering' by the lady, who is in fact offering only herself, the text becomes gradually more explicit, transmitting promises appealing to all the other senses as well, to touch, smell and sight, and to warmth and utter luxury. 'I have perfumed my bed' links touch with smell, preparing the visitor for yet another pleasure, more directly connected with sex. Myrrh, cinnamon and aloes can be understood as such, or else as metaphors, as in *Song of Songs*, to personal body liquids and odours, both masculine and feminine. Perhaps these sensual promises are not sufficiently evident in themselves as an invitation. It is his first time, he is embarrassed, inexperienced or simply foolish, and 'she' therefore says it loud and clear: "Come, let us take our fill with love until morning, let us delight ourselves with love." (In *Song of Songs* the female figure is completely independent, therefore the text can portray 'pure' eroticism!)

Anticipating two still unasked but relevant and hovering questions – Are you married? and Is your husband at home?, the women adds (hastily?): "For my husband is not at home; he has gone on a long journey." In this way the built-in director of the imaginary boy-meets-whore show makes clear that she is married, and therefore not just a lustful woman, but a sinful adulteress to boot. The next verse is of particular interest: "He [the husband] took a bag of money with him; he will not come to his home until full moon." The smart prostitute again delivers an ambiguous message, which comes to reassert her manipulator–impersonator's point, regarding the gap between her words and her intentions. If the husband took his wallet along, so it seems his journey will certainly be a long one. On the other hand, the same words serve as a fat hint that there is no money at home, thus implying a subtext of: 'Don't you forget, young man, the pleasure will not be free of charge.' She also says, perhaps as a little warning, that the husband will return 'for the holidays' to his – neither 'mine' nor 'our' – home.

Scene iv (21–24)

Reflecting genuine erotic propriety, the fourth scene avoids portraying the erotic encounter itself. This prude father will not indulge in the details, which is understandable, regarding his altogether moral approach. Moreover, now even he cannot see anything behind the prostitute's closed door. He can only gaze bluntly and perhaps frustratedly at that imaginary door created by himself, now softly closing behind his son and the woman's backs. So he fades out the scene: "with much seductive speech she persuaded him; with her smooth talk she compels him." Few young men, probably including his son, would want to be 'compelled'. In fact, however, he inadvertently admits that this was from the start an unfair fight between his own real speech and his "words, commandments and teachings", and the woman's slick seductive talk (also his own . . .). As father, teacher and moralist, he has clearly lost the moral battle to his own artistic talents as actor–impersonator of bad women.

He therefore is now left to bemoan: "Right away he follows her, and goes like an ox to the slaughter, or bounds like a stag toward the trap" (or 'like a fool to receive his punishment'). Father, carried away with his own convincing rhetoric, and concerned for his son's morality as well as money (his?), completes this heart-breaking picture of doom with "until an arrow pierces its liver (or 'entrails'). He is like a bird rushing into a snare, not knowing that it will cost him his life." This verse, while still belonging to the scene, functions much like throwing a stone after the danger has long passed. But the one-act play is not over yet.

Scene v (7:24–27)   Epilogue on the moral of the story

The narrator appeals to the listener(s) in his presence, and indeed to all the young and innocent men in the land of Israel and in the big wide world: "And now, children (sons), listen to me, and be attentive to the words of my mouth . . . " By saying 'my mouth' he perhaps wants to remind his sons that the 'show' part is over, and they must not confuse theatre with reality. "Do not let your hearts turn aside to her ways; do not stray in her paths. For many are those she has led low, and numerous are her victims. Her house is the way to Sheol, going down to the chambers of death." Whereas the metaphor for the female sexual organs in *Song of Songs* is a hill of myrrh, here the vagina is described as the gate of Sheol.[1] The bad woman is no less than murderous. As far as the dramatic space is concerned, we have moved from the safety of home to the dangers of the open street, then into her house, a slaughter-house, a trap, sheer hell. The youngster, having listened very carefully to his father's lively enactment, emits a sigh of relief and swears never ever to be tempted by such horrors. If, by any chance, he has already experienced a remotely similar incident, his reaction might well be different; but he most certainly will not utter a single word about it to daddy.

It is difficult to fully assert the exact tone and atmosphere of this one-act play. One tends to believe that in biblical times people behaved, sexually at least, differently. Given the legal and cultural background the Old Testament itself provides, I suggest that the differences, if any, were not so great. This little educational skit must, however, be perceived in the overall context of *Proverbs*, namely as an extension to the commandment "You shall not commit adultery" (*Exod.* 19:14) since the prostitute is presented as a married woman. It is also a semi-enacted piece of moral-sexual instruction to young men. Both aspects are emphasized in the last verses of the previous chapter in *Proverbs*, "but he who commits adultery is heartless, he who does it destroys himself", etc., in which the entire last section in Chapter 6 is dedicated to this topic. Nevertheless, in light of the extreme demonization (*Sheol*, 'chambers of death') of the female figure, the above explanation appears lacking. I suggest, therefore, in accordance with the many witty and sophisticated sections in *Proverbs*, that the author/editor(s) of this book of wisdom, and especially the half-serious playwright of the piece, was well aware of the potential humor in his own educational presentation, and was able to guess that his vivid description may in fact have achieved quite the opposite result from that intended.[2] While aware that must not read contemporary sensitivities and impose them upon ancient text, it still remains true that 'even' the playwright of *Proverbs* might also have been aware of the counter-effectiveness of his drama.

Part IV

PROPHETS AS PERFORMERS

8

Elisha: Religion, Sex and Miracles

The prophet Elisha is first mentioned by his full name as son of Shaphat from Abel-meholah, in God's word to Elijah, in I *Kings* 19:16. Elija must appoint Elisha as his successor, and this successor to Elijah will kill all those who manage to escape the sword of Hazael and the sword of Jehu. The first meeting between Elijah and Elisha is particularly significant, as it explains traits in Elisha's character and serves as background to his unique prophetic style. Elisha is ploughing with the twelfth pair of oxen in a field when Elija finds him, "and threw his mantle over him. He left the oxen, ran after Elijah, and said, 'let me kiss my father and my mother, and I will follow you.' Then he [Elijah] said to him, 'go back again; for what have I done to you?' He [Elisha] returned from following him, took the yoke of oxen, and slaughtered them; using the equipment from the oxen [plough, harness, etc.] he boiled their flesh, and gave it to the people, and they ate. Then he followed Elijah, and became his servant."

Elisha was denied the opportunity to depart from his parents with an emotionally fulfilling farewell, and from that moment on he is often portrayed as a tough, unsentimental, indeed emotionally immune prophet. He immediately understood Elijah's non-verbal gesture of throwing his mantle over him, as being called to serve the older, well-known prophet. In reaction to Elijah's words, implying "if you don't understand the gesture, no words will convince you", Elisha made his first crucial and life-long decision to dedicate himself to God and to Elijah. He then performed his first reported strong-willed act and sacrificed his past life, burning all the bridges behind him, symbolizing that he was now fully committed to his new mission. He gave the flesh of the oxen to the people, now ready to feed them instead with the spirit of God.

The books of *Kings* also tell of the special relationships Elisha has with his master. For example, he does not need the company of prophets to tell him that "today the Lord will take your master away from (over your head) you". He knows it by himself. On the way to Beth-El Elijah tells Elisha not follow him, but the absolutely dedicated disciple says: "As the God lives, and as you yourself live, I will not leave you." A similar situation recurs twice more on the way Jericho and to Jordan. "Then Elijah took his mantle and rolled it up, and struck the water; the water was parted to the one side and to the other, until the two of them crossed on dry ground" (2:8). Parting the water is not only reminiscent of Moses's parting the sea for the Israelites to cross on dry land. This symbolic deed is also an esoteric sign for the supremacy of spirit over matter, of faith over emotions, which will henceforth characterize Elisha's activity. The most meaningful words between Elisha and his master are exchanged at the beginning and at the end of their relationship:

> "When they crossed, Elijah said to Elisha:
> 'Tell me what I may do for you, before I am taken from you.'
> Elisha said, 'Please let me inherit a double share of your spirit.'"

Perfectly in line with his initial decision to join Elijah, Elisha's request is, nevertheless, a proof of his enormous spiritual aspirations.

> "He responded, 'You have asked a hard thing; yet if you see me as I am being taken away from you, it will be granted you; if not, it will not.'"

> "As they continued walking and talking, a chariot of fire and horses of fire separated the two of them, and Elijah ascended in a whirlwind into heaven. Elisha kept watching and crying out, 'my father, my father! The chariot of Israel and its horsemen!' But when he could no longer see him, he grasped his own clothes and tore them in two pieces. He picked up the mantle of Elijah that had fallen from him, and went back and stood on the bank of the Jordan. He took the mantle of Elijah that had fallen from him, and struck the water saying, 'Where is the Lord, the God of Elijah?' When he had struck the water, the water was parted to the one side and to the other, and Elisha went over. When the company of prophets who were at Jericho saw him at a distance, they declared, 'The spirit of Elijah rests in Elisha.'"

Already at the beginning of his prophetic path, Elisha's portrait reveals two outstanding qualities. He is utterly dedicated to his master and to God, and at the same time he is spiritually ambitious and fully aware (and proud) of his capability. In Chapters Elisha, like Elijah, is often described as deeply involved in political matters, in constant touch with the kings and high-ranking officers in Israel and in Aram. However, he does develop a 'style' of his own.[1] Having indeed seen Elijah's ascent into heaven, as proof of his passive spiritual ability, Elisha, following his master's miraculous ascent, first rents his own clothes in two possibly signifying that he and Elijah were one. Then, immediately, he tests God as to whether he too has now been endowed with the active ability to perform miracles. He uses his master's physical as well as symbolic mantle – the same mantle thrown over him at the beginning – and successfully parts the waters of the Jordan. He is recognized by the company of prophets as one on whom the spirit of Elijah now rests, and his next miracle is the curing of the water in Jericho (2:19–22). However, no prophet before Elisha or after him ordered forty-two children to be killed by two bears, just for jeering at him "come up, bald-head, come up bald-head!" Whereas Elijah too had revived a child (II *Kings* 17:17–24), Elisha has a profound personal reason from now on to revive dead children.

The book of *Kings* describes Elisha as a particularly hard and zealous prophet of great spiritual powers. The religious point of view is often expressed more extremely in *Kings*, to counterweight the political aspects presented by the kings, who were dedicated to various matters of ruling and not only to messages preached by the prophets. *Kings* describes Elisha as an aggressive, often unpleasantly sniping, perhaps even spiritually conceited man of God, as reflected, for example in his communication with the company of prophets, when looking for Elijah's body (2:16–18) or with king Jehoshafat (3:13). Elisha is involved in a number of national and international political affairs. He even has the commander Jehu anointed as king. He always represents a hard, imposingly religious line, and seems to love God more than human beings, but he has, nevertheless, a soft spot for children and women. His exceptional power to perform miracles is effective even posthumously: "As a man was being buried, a marauding band was seen and the man was thrown into the grave of Elisha; as soon as the man touched the bones of Elisha, he came to life and stood on his feet" (13:21).

This chapter concentrates on the dramatic clash between text and subtext in the story of Elisha and the Shunamite woman[2] (4:8–37). The series of events reveals an almost singular tension in a biblical prophet's life: the tension between Elisha's spiritual halo, his public image and his miracles on the one hand, and his private, emotional demeanour and responsibility, on the other.

Analyzing the story as a play, the program could offer the following items:

Speaking parts:	Elisha
	Gehazi
	The Shunammite Woman
	Her Husband
Silent roles:	A Boy (servant)
	Another Boy (servant)

	A group of Servants
	Reapers
Locations:	The Shunammite's House
	Elisha's Room (in the Shunammite's House)
	A wheatfield
	The Road to Mount Carmel (and back!)
	Elisha's (unspecified) Place on Mount Carmel
Stage Properties:	One Staff
	One Bed
	One Table
	One Chair
	One Lamp
	One Door

Exposition (Elisha and the Shunammite)

"One day Elisha was passing through Shunem, where a great woman lived, who [held him, grabbed him] urged him to eat bread [have a meal]. So whenever he passed that way, he would stop there to eat bread [have a meal]." The expression a 'great' (gedola) may have meant big, wealthy, important, etc., and draws our attention. Was this woman, who remains nameless throughout the story, of high social status, large in spirit and/or in body? Realizing that Elisha is passing through town, she invites him for a meal, but the question is whether '*vatahezek bo*' means she physically held him, or was just insistent. Both the adjective 'great' and the verb 'to hold' indicate that she was a dominant woman, who almost or actually imposed her hospitality on the prophet. Her strength of character will be contrasted with the prophet's. The exposition serves as an interesting anticipation to the peculiarly ambiguous attitude Elisha shows towards her, a mixture of 'rough and tender'. After this first 'holding' out for three more, Elisha made it a habit to have a meal at her house, whenever he happened to 'pass that way'. The playwright establishes an on-going relationship, a single visit that becomes a standing tradition.

Act 1, Scene i: At the Shunammite's home – The Shunammite woman and her husband

"And she said to her husband: 'I know that this is a holy to God man, who regularly passes our way. Let us make a small roof chamber, and put there for him a bed, and a table, and a chair and a lamp, so that whenever he comes to us he can stay there'." Now the text reveals the important information that she is married, and her initial 'holding' of Elisha becomes, retrospectively, more meaningful. Being married to an elderly husband, as the text will only later disclose, the women carefully prepares her request to host the prophet, first telling her husband about Elisha's holiness. It would appear that she wants to establish her relationship with him as founded upon the (holy) man's (physical) comfort. The husband's answer, and perhaps also further questions are not reported. But the attic becomes Elisha's permanent hotel in Shunem. The detailed, simple yet cosy pieces of furniture turn the room into a small intimate lodging. Like most theatrical props, these pieces will be filled with people and significance, physically and metaphorically. In the meantime they wait, like the famous pistol, to be activated in due course.

Elisha will sleep in the bed, but the text never specifies whether the woman ever joined him there. The still unborn child will be laid dead on this same bed, and there be revived. One may assume that Elisha received his meals sitting on the chair by the table, snugly lit by the yellowish oil-lamp. Whereas the dialogical text carefully avoids any erotic insinuations regarding the Elisha–Shunammite relationship, the stage instructions and the overall interpersonal attitudes may be understood as highly emotional, albeit explicit, in this respect.

Act I, Scene ii: At the Shunammite's home – Elisha, Gehazi and the woman

"One day when he came there, he went up to the chamber and lay down there." Elisha accepted the woman's offer and on his next visit in Shunem he goes straight to the room and lies down to rest. The text does not specify whether Gehazi shared the room with him, or stayed in the servants' quarters. Resting in his room, Elisha must have pondered what the woman could want from him in return for her generous hospitality. He was not so naïve as to believe that the sheer fame of his holiness had won him a free bed and meals. "He said to his servant Gehazi, 'Call that Shunammite woman'." The almost careless address "that Shunammite" becomes Elisha's normal way of relating to her verbally. It does not excel in tenderness. Elisha behaves like an aloof master in the Shunammite's own home. Calling her through the servant implies that Elisha's status was high, and that he readily accepted the mental distance between himself and the world. Retrospectively, especially from a dramatic point of view, it also emphasizes the difference between the woman's distance-breaking 'holding' him, and his own present distance-establishing, once he is firmly settled in her house.

"When he (Gehazi) called her, she stood before him (Elisha)." Either still lying down, or perhaps sitting up upon her entrance (this is left for the director of the scene to decide), Elisha's posture, though physically lower, radiates a patronizing authority toward the lady of the house, now standing in front of him. However, his attitude is tinged with an interesting reservation. He does not turn to the woman; rather, despite her actual presence, he speaks to her only through his servant Gehazi. Receptive to this unique situation, Talmudic scholars have interpreted it as a sign of Elisha's sexual propriety. The non-verbal language in the scene may be read: "I want no exclusive intimacy with you, hence not only do I avoid being alone with you in the same room, but I also do not address you directly." Modern readers might easily see a sign here that 'something had already happened between the prophet and the woman'. The actual verbal text, however, says something different: "He said to him, 'Say to her, since you have taken all this trouble for us, what may be done for you? Would you have a word spoken on your behalf to the king or to the commander of the army?'" Sternberg notes: "Before Gehazi divulges the Shunamite's misfortunes, it would no more occur to the reader to wonder whether she was childless than whether she was handsome or popular with the neighbors. Not that the question is not important to her, but that the tale has thus far done nothing to make it so for us – to force open a gap – and therefore it simply fails to arise."[3]

Elisha, either in true innocence or as a means to find out what the woman really wants, makes his political connections available to her. She may need some strings pulling in higher places. Later in *Kings* it is reported that he not only indeed had such influence, but actually used it for her benefit (8:1–6). As a distinguished guest, Elisha is clearly condescending – an essential tactic no doubt if the possibility that the two had a physical relationship is considered (it would be in neither Elisha nor the Bible's interest to be explicit about it). It is for this reason, perhaps, that her full name is never given. While recognizing 'all her trouble for us', firstly he doesn't thank her, and secondly he speaks using the real or royal plural 'we'. Perhaps including Gehazi in the hospitality provided a cover-up? Or perhaps he truly meant only his grand self. In both cases, however, he deliberately avoids a no-nonsense I–You encounter with the woman. Rather than plainly thanking her for the hospitality, he presents it as a deal, albeit unspecified as such by her. The woman's reply sounds, perhaps naturally, slightly irritated. "She answered. 'I have lived among my people'." This idiomatic line is a vague and evasive. Translated, its subtext may mean a variety of possibilities, such as: 'No, thanks, I am well situated socially, independently rich, I have my own ties, I get along fine by myself . . .' – or else: 'it's not what you've just mentioned that I really need.' If indeed they had slept together, she may have meant that she was not satisfied with sex alone. At this point she leaves the room, an exquisite theatrical exit.

———

The dialogue indicates a definite emotional tension between a famous, self-confident man of God, and a big, assertive and proud woman who wants something of him, but dares not express her true wish. Elisha's avoidance of talking to her directly suggests a certain embarrassment. Is he attracted to her? What is Gehazi's real role in the scene and in the complex relationship with both his master and with the woman?

Act 1, Scene iii

Left with the impression of her answer still echoing after her exit, Elisha, in her absence and after a theatrical little 'pause', asks Gehazi: "What then may be done to her?" Obviously he has perceived the discrepancy between her vague text and her precise body language. Elisha might have been taken aback by the woman's laconic, stand-offish retort, which in fact was no less than an invitation for further inquiries. He addresses his question in the passive voice, rather than 'what can I, or even we, do for her?' The so-far passive third person in the scene, Gehazi, is now given the opportunity to play a more active part. Bluntly, he indeed provides the answer. Being markedly less holy than his master, and also having apparently spent time with the servants of the house, as well as being overall more worldly, he has learnt what the woman's real plight is: "But (or 'well . . . ') she has no son, and her husband is old." In other words, 'You, too holy a man to understand the basics of life, don't you know? . . .' In the Shunammite womans' presence, Gehazi could not have afforded the gall implied in his response.

Together with body language – lying, standing – the exits and entrances in the entire scene also carry the overall message, independent of but commensurate with the text. Certain things cannot be uttered in the presence of certain characters, or else said in their presence, but only indirectly. Moreover, from a dramatic-theatrical angle, whereas the text is diplomatic, evasive and indirect, the body-language is straight and clear. Elisha does not understand the woman, perhaps because he is paying attention to her words alone. Perhaps too he receives his subtexts from divine sources only, as later indicated, and is deaf to human subtexts. In this respect Elisha will change. Perhaps he knows things subconsciously, but is not emotionally open.

It is Gehazi who now links the verbal dramatic mode with the non-verbal. He knows that the woman's real unspoken request, and consequently her bitterness, are easily explainable. By telling Elisha that 'her husband is old', Gehazi reveals an important informational gap in the events, namely, who will be the father of the woman's future child. Nevertheless, Gehazi refrains from saying to Elisha directly 'she wants a child from you', though this is exactly what she does want. The question, never to be fully posed, is not whether Elisha will give the woman a child. He will, in his way. The deliberately concealed issue is that of the child's natural father. His identity hovers unsolved between Elisha's miracles, stature and piety on the one hand, and the woman's childlessness – emotionally and biologically – on the other. Even Gehazi does not fully reveal the issue; but he does serve as an excellent and dramatically efficient go-between. Could he be the father? Did he "perform the miracle" that Elisha had prophesied?

Act 1, Scene iv

From Gehazi's words, Elisha realizes that he has failed to understand the woman's agony. "He said: 'Call her'." Exit Gehazi, and Elisha is for a short while alone on stage – the only time. "When he (Gehazi) had called her, she stood at the door-step ('opening', 'threshold')."

Physical distances and movement on stage (proxemics) are typical theatrical indices of the relationships among the dramatic personae, which complement the purely verbal messages through the non-verbal behavior in the dramatic space. A sensitive theatrical picture is revealed in the Shunammite woman's (silent) standing on the threshold. The opening to this special room connects as well as separates between inside and outside. Out there is her husband; in here is the prophet. The threshold is the narrow space between her secure but barren public stature ("I live among my people") and the intimacy of this little room with the bed, the table, the chair and the lamp. It is the borderline between light and darkness – mental and physical, beyond which her personal agony of barrenness has been exposed. Will the sanctity (or perhaps can the body too) of the prophet redeem her from her physical, social and personal agony? Or is it possible that she is already pregnant, and needs a post-factum blessing so as to explain the baby as a miracle rather than the result of adultery?

Elisha uses a direct as well as much gentler appeal than before toward the woman, because now he knows what her problem is (or because he is the father), and too because she is standing at a distance from him. "At this season, in a year's time, you shall embrace a son." There is no mention whatsoever or from whom she will receive the child. "She said: 'No my lord, O man of God, do not deceive your servant'."[4] This answer opens up further possible interpretations concerning the real meaning. Whereas she has already given Elisha a comfortable home, he has made 'only' a promise. Her answer indicates how dear and important a child is to her, but nevertheless expresses spiritual doubts in the prophet's ability. Is she now hinting a little more clearly that she is pregnant? Or is she subtly suggesting, if she is not pregnant, a more concrete action, and her words mean 'let's see you do it, not just say it'?

In an interlude between the scenes, "The woman conceived and bore a son at that season, in due time, as Elisha has declared to her." Whoever the real father was, the text ascribes paternity to the old man, the Shunammite's husband: "When the child was older, he went out one day to his father among the reapers." A number of scholars do not ascribe the fatherhood of this child to the Shunammite's old husband, assuming that the old man was no longer able to procreate. They rely partially on the husband's strange reaction later in the scene. Elisha, as a man of God, should not have been the father, since sexual relations with a married woman, being highly inappropriate behavior, indeed a deadly sin, would gravely besmirch his image. This possibility was absolutely ruled out by Talmudic scholars, who considered Gehazi to be the actual father, leaving the prophet with unsullied reputation. Moreover, this version can be substantiated by Gehazi's demeanor later on in this particular story, and by his behavior in other affairs as well. (If this is the case, does it imply that Elisha covered-up for Gehazi, or that Gehazi could be reasonably considered as one who would translate his master's words into physical contact with the woman?)

Act 2, Scene i: Wheatfield, sunlight; the child, the old father (?), servant (or boy), reapers

Out in the field, the child must be already weaned, at least three or four years old, and able to talk. He says, "My head, my head", clearly complaining of a strong headache. It may be asked why the twice-mentioned father had not thought about putting a hat on the child's head, but his reaction sounds natural enough: "The father said to his servant: 'Carry him home to his mother'." The reader may still remember the words of the company of prophets to Elisha: "Today the Lord will take your master [literally, in Hebrew] from over your head." Elisha is often associated with "head": Elijah was indeed Elisha's "head"; children jeered at his bald head; the king of Israel (Jehoram) swore: "So may God do to me, and more, if the head of Elisha son of Shaphat stays on his shoulders today" (6:31). Elisha took the threat seriously, and asked to be protected: "Are you aware that this murderer has sent someone to take off my head?" (6:32). Elisha seems to work mainly with his head. It is therefore reasonable to assume that the biblical sources related the child's headache directly to Elisha.

Act 2, Scene ii: Carrying the sick child home

"He carried him and brought him to his mother . . ." – the intermediary scene, created through movement alone, moves from outdoors to indoors, from an uncertain father to the real mother.

Act 2, Scene iii:, At home, in Elisha's room: the child and his mother

" . . . the child sat on her knees until noon", from which it is to be deduced
that the event happened in the morning hours, "and died. She went up
and laid him on the bed of the man of God, closed the door on him and
left." The line, hiding hours of hope finally deferred, and all the thoughts
the Shunammite woman must have had about her years of childlessness,
concentrates on facts, not on feelings. Biblical texts usually tend not to
invade the privacy of their grieving characters. Unless used as prophetic
warnings and national-religious admonitions, biblical narrators are
tactful in regard to images of dead children in their mother's lap. The
woman, knowing Elisha, certainly knew of his ability to revive the dead,
and definitely ascribed to him a responsibility ensuing from his earlier
promise that the child would be born. She takes the body of her lifeless
son up to the only spiritually, emotionally (for her, at least), and potentially safe space in the house, the prophet's room. Avoiding any
sentimental speeches about the child's death, which in any case will, retrospectively, be proven wrong, the scene focuses on her silent action. The
most touching gesture is the closing of the door.

Act 2, Scene iv: Field, woman, her husband, servant (boy)

Having left the child at home, she goes out to her husband in the field:
"Then she called to her husband, and said, 'send me ('give me,' or 'make
available for me,' in this context) one of the servants, and one of the
(female) donkeys, so that I may quickly go ('run') to the man of God and
come back again'." Her one sentence of thirteen words (in Hebrew) is duly
compact, but subtextually not completely clear, certainly not to her
husband. True, she is in great hurry to try and save the boy. She nevertheless does not give her husband the one reason for her demand that
might naturally convince him immediately. In fact, she does not give him
any reason at all why, in the middle of harvest, she suddenly needs an
indispensable worker as well as a means of transportation. She only says
"I will run to the man of God and come back again."

In contradistinction to her by now well established clarity of attitude,
her words themselves raise a number of questions. Does she believe that
Elisha would revive the child and prefers not to worry her (old) husband
unnecessarily? Does she want to avoid wasting time on irrelevant explanations? Why does she mention "and [I] come back again?" Is it in order
to reassure him that she will not use the working-power of the servant and
the donkey more than absolutely necessary? If the child is not in fact her
husband's, does she think that if he too suspects this, he will not give her
the servant and the donkey? The action now picks up speed, reflecting the
woman's situation. Elisha too will make Gehazi run towards her.

"He said: 'Why do you go to him today, it is neither new moon nor sabbath'." The man knows of his wife's special relationship with Elisha, and may assume she wants to go to the prophet for some kind of consultation. But why on a week-day, rather than on the days regularly allocated for the prophet's normal office-hours? His text suggests that she has continued to visit Elisha after the child was born. But why does the husband not realize her distress? Or does he, but ignore it? Does he suspect that there is anything beyond religious consultation involved in his wife's hurried visit to the prophet, miles away?

Her reply is as typical to her as it is surprising: "She said, 'Shalom'", the briefest possible 'goodbye', which could mean 'don't get on my nerves right now with your requests for explanations', and off she goes; or else 'everything will be "in peace", don't worry'.

Act 3, Scene i: The road to Mount Carmel, woman, servant (donkey)

"She saddled the donkey" – a phrase reminiscent of Abraham who saddled the donkey before binding Isaac (*Genesis* 22) – since it is not the servant who does this job. She is in a great hurry and does it herself to make sure all is done right. The playwright does not neglect to depict her, once more, as a proud commanding woman: "Urge on, do not stop riding unless I tell you." The ride itself is no doubt charged with her hopes and fears, in a way echoing the scene in which the sick child was carried home by the same or another servant. The text refrains from indicating whether the anonymous servant knew of the purpose of the journey. He is just the driver; she and the child's emergency are the focus. "So she set out, and came to the man of God at Mount Carmel."

Act 3, Scene ii: Elisha's place, the Shunammite, Elisha, Gehazi, servant with donkey in the background

"When the man of God saw her coming", he identified her. Was he surprised, happy to see her? His next words to Gehazi show that he, unlike her husband, realizes the emergency of her unexpected visit. Warmly (the unwritten stage instruction may add), " . . . he said to Gehazi his servant: [with a slight sniping undertone, to hide his joy] 'Look, there is that Shunammite woman; [now compassionately] (please) run to meet her, and say to her, Are you all right (*Shalom* is the Hebrew word repeatedly used for 'all right')? Is your husband all right? Is the child all right?" Judging by the order in which Elisha wishes Gehazi to question the woman who in just a few moments will come to him anyway, he is primarily interested in the woman's 'peace'. Then, tactfully, he asks for her husband's 'peace', and last but not least, he asks for the child's peace, without, however, using any personal pronouns, just 'the child' – not '*yaldech*' (your child),

or 'yaldo' ('his child'). If the child is indeed Elisha's, his present lesser
interest in him reflects different emotional subtext than if he is Gehazi's
child. In this case, Gehazi's later reaction to the woman falling at Elisha's
feet is, again, explicable in quite different terms.

There is a small discrepancy between Elisha's habitual offhand 'that
Shunammite woman' and his expression of true interest in her, in her
husband and in the child. The change in tone can be explained by the short
time lapse that occurs between his recognizing her, and realizing that it is
an emergency that has brought her, without yet knowing its exact nature.
Moreover, the realism of the scene can be further substantiated if the time
lapse is also due to the actual distance between them. Elisha is likely to be
higher up on the mountain, but not very far; close enough to immediately
recognize her, but allowing a few moments to pass before she has climbed
the steep path up to him. Another time-gap opens up between Gehazi's
meeting the hurriedly approaching woman and delivering Elisha's warm
welcome to her, and her own brief 'Shalom'. Perhaps she does not want
to waste any time on Gehazi, whether he is or is not the biological father
of the (dead, so she believes) child. As an answer to the question about
the child's 'Shalom', namely health, she gives a general non-committal
'Shalom'. Her impolite 'Shalom' to Gehazi may have angered him, and
triggered his pushing her. Does the Shunammite treat Gehazi as a servant?
This 'Shalom', however, marks the end of her journey, as a brilliantly
dramatic echo to her hurried 'Shalom' to her husband at the beginning of
the journey. With a few other 'Shaloms' strewn along the way, the entire
journey has been stretched between her first and last 'Shaloms'.

Exhausted, she finally reaches Elisha himself. "Then she came to the
man of God at the mountain, she caught hold of his feet." The woman
and Gehazi approach Elisha. The servant who has brought both the
woman and the donkey are left behind and never appear again in the text.
As soon as the woman comes near, she, this time physically, 'caught hold'
(*vatahazek*) of Elisha's feet. "Gehazi approached to push her away. But
the man of God said: 'Let her alone, for she is in bitter distress; the Lord
has hidden it from me and has not told me'." The scene builds up Elisha's
relationship with the Shunammite in three steps: recognition, joy, realization of her situation – and then a fourth: finding out what the matter
really is. It also creates a fine, complementary relationship between
Elisha's words and the woman's silent deeds. She clings to his feet, but he
will follow her; she speaks harshly, he – softly. This time it is Gehazi who
is unable to interpret the woman's real needs, whereas Elisha sees her
distress. The dramatic triangle of Elisha, Gehazi and the Shunammite
constantly seethes with tensions that rarely erupt.

In pushing the woman away, Gehazi, the faithful servant, wants to

protect his master from the woman's 'assault' – if this is how he has interpreted her clinging to Elisha's feet; or perhaps he wants to protect his
master's aura of modesty. If the former is the case, it surely ensues from
the woman's excitable and hasty behaviour, the reason for which Gehazi
does not know, ergo his violent reaction. If the latter interpretation is
correct, we can still wonder what brought it about. Were prophets not
allowed to touch married women, in general? Be touched by them? Or is
Gehazi jealous of 'his' woman? From a psychoanalytical perspective, this
is a 'projection'. Dramatically, however, the Shunammite speaks to Elisha
as if Gehazi does not exist, just as Elisha spoke to Gehazi in her presence
but not to her. It is this technique that creates the triple tension.

Elisha, though kind and gentle to the woman in a way never described
elsewhere about him, is nevertheless somewhat irritated that God has not
'told him' anything about the child. Assuming, by force of his previous
experience or presumption, that God always tells him things, Elisha has
certainly learnt something about human behavior since he last saw the
Shunammite.

"She said: 'Did I ask my lord for a son? Did I not say, Do not mislead
[give me the illusion] me?'" She reminds Elisha that she had never asked
for the child in the first place, and that already then, in the attic, she had
said "do not deceive your servant". Throughout the play, an intricate
relation of alternating dominance develops between the Shunammite
woman and Elisha. Their emotional–spiritual see-saw is expressed in their
texts and body-language alike. Within the changing balance of the intimacy between them, she now feels free to use emotional blackmail as well
as to lay upon him the spiritual responsibility for the child's situation. It
is not enough, she implies, to prophesy the child's life, Elisha must also
keep him alive. She is about to collect the debt-of-life he owes her. If Elisha
is the biological father, her speech and his response are theatrically doubly
effective.

"He said to Gehazi: 'Gird your loins, and take my staff in your hand,
and go . . . '." Elijah's main prop was the mantle. The more aggressive
Elisha uses a staff, like Moses (who, incidentally, was much more
humble). The staff, Elisha believes, endowed with his own powers, even
in the hands of Gehazi, will revive the child. But knowing Gehazi's character, especially after pushing the woman, he warns him severely to
concentrate fully on his mission and make haste: "If you meet anyone,
give no greeting, and if anyone greets you, do not answer." Elisha may
also know that Gehazi is not altogether a reliable servant, which the
biblical text confirms in the Naaman affair, when Elisha curses Gehazi
with leprosy for taking money he himself had refused.

Elisha instructs him: "and lay my staff on the face of the child." The

Shunammite woman understands that Elisha does not intend to try and save the child himself, and is instead sending Gehazi. "Then the mother of the child said: 'As the Lord lives, and as you yourself live, I will not leave without you'." These words are yet another way of 'holding on' to Elisha. From her point of view, she must be present at the child's side. But rather than going to him with Gehazi, she compels Elisha to come with her by saying that she will not leave him. She does not want a paramedic; she needs a real doctor. The Shunammite woman does not, however, say 'don't send this blunt Gehazi, who, moreover, must be specially warned against chattering to people on his way to save my child, as you, man of God, have just said yourself'. She is more diplomatic than that. The biblical text puts in her mouth almost the same words Elisha had said to Elijah before the latter was taken from over his head. And she succeeded. "So he rose up and followed her", almost like following Elijah. At this point we do not know who used the 'ambulance'. It could have been Gehazi, in order to get to the child as fast as possible, or perhaps Gehazi could have run on foot while the older, more distinguished prophet rode there on the (female) donkey's back. On the other hand, it is more likely to assume that Gehazi used the donkey, because he came back with it after he had failed to revive the child. In this latter case, Elisha and the Shunammite woman were, for the one and only time, left to walk alone. "And he rose up and followed her." The geographical road she took to Elisha was the same; the emotional path was not.

Road and House: Act 4, Scene i – Gehazi, the child
"Gehazi went on ahead before them, and laid the staff on the face of the child, but there was no sound or sign of life." The plot is here divided into a main plot, in which Gehazi is engaged in an unsuccessful resuscitation, and a subplot of the approaching Elisha and mother, who has chosen to stay with what she believes to be the only real help. These two actions meet up when Gehazi returns, on the same road, to report his failure.

Road: Act 4, Scene i – Gehazi, Elisha, the Shunammite woman
"He (Gehazi) came back to meet him (Elisha) and told him, 'The child has not awakened'." Elisha then takes over. The spectator need not be surprised that Gehazi has failed. The text demands that Elisha revive the child, thus admitting at least his spiritual fatherhood.

Act 5, Scene i: House, Elisha, the child
"When Elisha came into the house, he saw the child lying dead on his bed." His emotional reaction can only be guessed at, but Elisha certainly understood that it was his ultimate task to do something. "So he went in

and closed the door on the two of them"; the same door that the mother had closed on her child, hiding the secrets of life and death. The mother and Gehazi remain outside, together or alone. "And (Elisha) prayed to the Lord. Then he got up (on the bed) and lay upon the child, putting his mouth upon his mouth, his eyes upon his eyes, and his hands upon his hands; and while he lay bent over him, the flesh of the child became warm." This most important scene in the play is performed through an unreported prayer, and a series of gestures and movements. Whereas Elisha's staff did not work in Gehazi's hands, Elisha, as a 'staff' in God's hand, does indeed work. The text implies that certain things cannot be performed by proxy. He, no other, is expected to fulfil his promise to the woman, as well as to justify the insinuation "the Lord has hidden it from me . . .".

The actual resuscitation is performed as a striking, perhaps unprecedented mixture of intensely physical activity, and spiritual power. Indeed, it is described as an act of spiritual intercourse, of true 'animation'. Through it, Elisha earns his fatherhood of the child, regardless of whether this had initially also been a physical one. Interestingly, the priest Eli had also nominated Samuel, his spiritual disciple, as his son, rather than Hophni or Pinehas, his real but sinful offspring. Gehazi too has not proven to be a particularly successful 'son' to Elisha.

"He got down, walked once to and fro in the room, then got up again and bent over him; the child sneezed seven times, and the child opened his eyes." The director of the scene may use various forms of breathing as the vocal–visual leitmotif for the action. Elisha may now sigh with relief.

Act 5, Scene ii – House, Elisha, the child, the Shunammite woman, Gehazi

"Elisha summoned Gehazi and said: 'Call that Shunammite woman'." With the child alive once more, Elisha's habitually offhand address to the woman now sounds considerably kinder than before. "So he called her. When she came in to him, he said, 'Take your son'." Outwardly, the text suggests 'I have done what you wanted, now leave me alone'. The subtext, however, is quite different. Elisha avoids sentimentality. The power of the deed itself needs no unnecessary emotion. "Take your son" means in fact 'Have I deceived you?'; or else: 'Having witnessed God's intervention, neither I nor you can say anything further.'

"She came and fell at his feet, bowing to the ground; then she took her son and went out."

The end of the drama retrospectively rectifies its beginning. Biological procreation and child-bearing, with all their emotional ramifications, are elucidated *vis-à-vis* God's providence and his prophet's miracles. The potential 'gossip' in regard to the biological fatherhood is rendered a trifle when compared with the life-giving force in the end. The happy end is in God's hands, as this drama clearly states.

9

Jonah: a Quest Play

───────

The shortest prophesy in the Bible is an absolutely decisive prophesy of wrath: "Another forty days, and Nineveh shall be overthrown" (*Jonah* 3:4), is extorted by means of divine and violent irony from Jonah son of Amitai, a prophet who is no prophet[1]; Jonah, the fugitive prophet, yet God-fearing, claims later that he had known in advance that the prophesy would not be fulfilled. The four chapters of this short book reveal an intensive, conflictual plot in the highly dramatic and totally uneven relationships between God's will and a man who chose to escape it. The 'play' begins with a categorical decree: "Arise, go to Nineveh, that great city, and cry against it; for their wickedness is come up before me"; then rapidly develops over seas and deserts, and ends with a huge question mark that hovers over an enigmatic conclusion. Every reader, it seems, is invited to fill in this final gap with a psychological, religious, moral, literary or, in this case, a dramatic and theatrical interpretation.

This chapter examines the dramatic elements in the 'fantastic' text of the *Book of Jonah*, and the theatrical potential of actually staging it. I assume that structure, characters, locations and even the relationships between the biblical 'dialogical text' and the 'stage instructions' are metonymous to the overall 'meaning' of this biblical drama.

Had Jonah originally been intended for theatre, it would have been written as a voyage or a quest play. In such plays, the hero goes through 'stations' on a road to self-discovery. Each station is an encounter, a crisis and a shedding of one more layer until finally revealing the most profound inner layer of the personality. For example, in the late fifteenth-century Morality play *Everyman*, the title character is asked to deliver up his soul but nevertheless wants to keep his body, and sequentially begs Friendship, Gold, Desire, etc. to accompany him on his last pilgrimage. The personi-fied characteristics, the Seven Deadly Sins, are primarily an inventory list for Everyman, who 'owns' them and who must learn not to depend on wordly qualities: they are evil both in themselves and as traits belonging to this world. Peer Gynt, in Ibsen's late nineteenth-century drama, who travels over dales and hills in the oceans and deserts of the world, walks through the psycho-geographical landscapes of his own soul. Only on his final encounter with Solvej, does he realize that though 'lost to himself', he has always been 'there' in the (Pauline sense of) Hope, Faith and Love of Solvej *qua* Maria, mother of Christ. Faust, too, in both Marlow's and Goethe's play, sells his soul to Mephistopheles, and he also roves among many and varied states of Being and consciousness, both 'realistic' and imaginary. In Hebrew drama this theme is quite well known as well, as in Zaccuto's *Tofte Aruch* ['Hell Prepared'] (not unlike Dante's *Divina Commedia*), in which the nameless protagonist 'enjoys' a guided tour in the seven circles of Hell; a highly educational trip on the one hand, and actually a series of innitiation rites on the other, through which he is meant to learn about his soul.

Jonah, similar to these and many other heroes of quest plays, passes through a number of stations on his escape-route as the unwilling, rebellious prophet who refuses to utter a simple five words. Unlike Everyman, Jonah neither wants nor needs anybody to escort him. Unlike Peer Gynt, he seems to be well aware of his peculiar situation. Quite different from Faust, too, Jonah does not sell his soul to the Devil. Rather, and paradoxically, like Job, he keeps believing in God. But like many heroes of plays, myths, fairytales and picaresque novels,[2] Jonah must visit different sorts of Hell, and is then tested in such classical initiation rites as water, darkness, heat and great misery. Must he endure all these difficulties simply because he refuses to be 'a mere vehicle' of God's will?

In comparison to some other heroes who escape their inner and/or divine calling, Jonah is presented in a state of conflict right from the word 'Arise'. As we soon learn, he believes in God, fears God and admits God's enormous might; yet despite his knowledge he tries to escape. From a Socratic point of view, it may be argued that Jonah's knowledge, though great, was incomplete; or else he would have acted 'properly'. Following Marmeladov's more modern argument in Dostoevski's *Crime and Punishment*, however, though he knows very well that it is bad to drink, he still keeps on drinking. One tends to identify the biblical Jonah with a very modern, Albert Camus-like rebel, a Sisyphus carrying his rock yet again up the hill, and always completely conscious of the futility of the task. One may also claim that Jonah's rebellion and refusal to prophesy bears a certain resemblance to hubris. Either way, Jonah 'throws' himself (rather than being thrust by the observing, slightly ironical God) into a state Heidegger would call *Geworfenheit*. Does he indeed know, as he later claims, what God's real intention is in demanding of him to cry out his prophesy? Does he really guess what result his words will cause? (A prophesy with an expiry date as its tag!)

Was Jonah perhaps simply afraid to prophesy an apocalyptic End in a major city? Was it, perhaps, his human pride that made him run? If so, were his reasons to escape just a poor excuse (as the Bible seems to imply) or (and at the same time?) an honorable if anthropocentric attitude which the Bible is promoting in an almost subversive drama? In other words, can we defend the view that both the book and personality of Jonah represent an existentalist–Sisyphean philosophy, whereby the protagonist must yield to divine commands, but at the same time maintain an inner freedom? Throughout the course of the drama, Jonah is often shown as appearing willing to pay with his life. Or is he?

Jonah's drama is presented as a physically unsuccessful escape, because it is an impossible one. Since God's omnipotence is clearly stated in the Hebrew Bible, 'drama' in the sense of genuine conflict cannot be classically 'tragic'. A drama, nonetheless, the book can be read as a modern quest play *because* of the plot-structure and the deliberately unbalanced powers (of God on the one hand, Man on the other), and the many ironies that ensue from the behavior of the two main protagonists. The dramatic balance is achieved by Jonah's persistent sense of personal integrity, in that he strangely refuses to be God's messenger of wrath but only a vehicle of His Grace.[3] Jonah's particular hubris may be interpreted as his wish to participate in God's forgiveness rather than anger. The real conflict in this (almost) mono-drama lies in the discrepancy between one man's sheer belief in God and his determination actively and willingly, to serve that will of God.

Jonah, despite – or even because of – his flight, touches the reader's heart with his frank, uncompromising integrity toward the sailors on the ship, and his willingness to sacrifice his own life so that they will not perish. At the same time he is also passive: he goes to sleep in the middle of a great storm and behaves like a typical Yiddish 'nebech' (simpleton). He and all the other human beings in the story behave with amazing (almost absurd) propriety – logically, emotionally and morally. These positive human qualities are nevertheless ironically juxtaposed with God's might.

The reader's mind is inescapably drawn to the conclusion that things happen in an overly 'right and nice' way. Even the King and inhabitants of Nineveh undergo an immediate, grotesque conversion whereas, on the other hand, God chases Jonah relentlessly. In the midst of the storm Jonah is asked a number of questions by the sailors, raising some curiosity as to how they had the leisure to ask them in the first place – when the ship was about to be wrecked! Why does God bother to pursue the 'conscientious objector' prophet, through all the elements of nature? Is this drama focused on the mode in which Jonah, and then the sailors and the people of Nineveh, are obliged to perform willingly, humanly, that which is anyway objective, divine and therefore inevitable? May we not conclude therefore that God demands a crisis, while Jonah prefers great physical hardships and even death, as long as he can 'enjoy' existential or religious comfort? The drama in the *Book of Jonah* can, accordingly, be regarded in the main as a conflict between the theocentric and the anthropocentric approach.

God's 'expressive means' constitute some of the theatrical elements in this play, including nature's forces, the casting of lots and even the various human discourses. They are designed to draw the blind observer into the story as well as the outside readers to the inevitable conclusion about God's infinite might – except over Man's free will.

Meir Sternberg mentions a few reasons why the *Book of Jonah* deserves special attention: (1):"It is the only biblical instance where a surprise gap controls the readers over a whole book . . ."; (2) "the narrative . . . misleading the reader . . . about the relations between God and prophet . . ."; (3) ". . . both the false impression produced at the start and its ultimate reversal work in two directions at once . . ."; (4) "the whole tortuous process of interpretation bears on the nature not of the agents only but also of the framework . . . in which they operate."[4]

Robert Alter emphasizes that the *Book of Jonah*, "with its satiric and fantastic exaggerations, looks like a parabolic illustration of the prophetic calling and of God's universality".[5]

Structure

The dramatic plot of the book can be divided into seven scenes, based on 'entrances and exits'.

Act 1, Scenes i–ii: God's word to Jonah

"Arise, go to Nineveh, that great city, and cry against it; for their wickedness is come up before me." The opening is immediate, describes no background, almost surprising. Jonah's reaction is equally surprising, especially since the verb 'Arise' (*kum*), is used for both the divine command and for the escape: "And Jonah rose up to flee to Tarshish from the presence of God . . ." There is an obvious conflict between God's will and Jonah's. God's 'dramatic *presence*' (according to some English translations) is not yet felt, but the text soon proves that His presence is everywhere. The dramatic shift of scenes serves as an ironic device, subtly suggesting that Jonah's escape will become increasingly futile throughout the plot. While knowing that God is 'there' and believing in Him, Jonah still tries to ignore – perhaps his own – true knowledge of God's word, God's word, as (*davar*) – implies action.

Act 1, Scenes iii–xvi: The escape, Jonah in the ship

Jonah's escape is characterized by the key (or 'Leit')-verb (following Martin Buber) *yarad*, 'to go down' or 'descend', which dominates the scenic images on board the ship. Does Jonah try to find refuge – tentative and poor as it soon proves to be – in naval technology, in nature or among the company of fellow human beings? Aboard the ship, the dramatic presentation divides between the sailors' actions during the great storm: it is they who cry to their respective gods; and Jonah's passivity; it is the prophet who remains silent. The sailors' actions may be taken as ironic *imitatio dei*: for like God who 'hurled' a great wind, the sailors throw articles of cargo overboard. The Hebrew uses the same verb *hatel*. Other modulations of similar action follow with *hapel* ('let fall' or 'throw' and 'cast') concerning the cashing of lots, which the sailors use to find out whom they should blame for their misfortune. Soon they will cast Jonah himself into the sea.

While the sailors are hyper-active, the dramatic tension is enhanced by the contrast of Jonah's inactivity. He goes down to the recesses of the ship and falls asleep. His way down is both realistic and metaphoric. Using the Hebrew *vayered*, Jonah first 'goes down' to Jaffa, then 'down into a ship', then further down into the 'recesses' of the ship. Finally he seems to 'go down' into himself by falling asleep. Not only does he try to flee from God, but from his own consciousness. As the only person on board who knows the reason for the storm, he tries to find in forgetfulness the very eye of the storm. This homeopathic 'no other choice' solution is dramatically coherent in spatial terms, since indeed he has nowhere else to turn. At this stage, Jonah can no longer escape in space; therefore he escapes consciousness. The biblical dramatist juxtaposes not just the raging storm and the appropriate human reactions of the sailors, but also Jonah's introverted consciousness and the frenzied external activity surrounding him.

The different dialogues in this scene are dramatically developed on the basis of relying on discrepancies between text, subtext and context and on a meta-dialogical level between the dialogues themselves. The first dialogue takes place between crying sailors and their silent gods. Rather than belittling these deities, the text makes it clear that their silence is the real answer. This dialogue 'merely' reports that each of the sailors cries to his own god.

The second dialogue is one-sided and takes place between a silent Jonah and the worried ship's captain: " – What meanest thou, O sleeper? Arise, call upon thy God, perhaps God will think upon us, that we perish not."

Now it is Jonah who does not answer! Is he still half asleep? Spellbound? In such one-sided conversations, the reader (and even more so the spectator in a theatre) is invited to provide the answer.

The next dialogue is again given as a report, but its content nevertheless is clearly stated: "And they said everyone to his fellow, Come and let us cast lots, that we may know for whose cause this evil is upon us." We may assume that these verbal exchanges were part of a general conversation near Jonah's sleeping-place. It is just as valid to asssume they took placed at different times during the storm. If they were connected, as part of one long conversation, the comic effect would be enhanced – because of the gap between the urgency of their situation and the length of the theological enquiry! If these snippets of talk were disconnected, on the other hand, then the scene would appear more realistic, given the fear felt and the hard task all the participants (except for Jonah) had before them.

Once the lots are cast, however, and not only Nature's and Jonah's behavior indicate who the culprit is, God's guided 'chance' joins in as well and the lot 'falls' (again) on Jonah.

In this first two-sided full dialogue the sailors flood the prophet with five questions: "Tell us, pray thee, (1) for whose cause this evil is upon us; (2) what is thy occupation?; (3) and where dost thou come from?; (4) what is thy country?; (5) and of what people art thou?" The first question is the most pressing, and requires Jonah to accept responsibility. Though Jonah's answer is purely informative, it still carries a performative charge for his listeners: "the men were exceedingly afraid." This is a foreshadowing of the effect that God's word will have on the Ninevites.

Jonah answers: "I am a Hebrew, and I fear the Lord, the God of heaven," who made the sea and the dry land." He ignores some of the questions and responds to some un-asked ones. He does not refer to 'occupation' or profession. In saying 'Hebrew', he refers to both country and people. However, as a runaway, he does not tell the sailors where he has come from. His response expresses his 'fear' of God, and the dramatic irony here lies in the double meaning of Jonah's 'fear' which is both general and quite specific.

The 'stage instruction' tells the reader of the fear (in both meanings, again!) the sailors felt. While Jonah hides his immediate fear under the more general sense of a 'God-fearing man', the opposite is true for the sailors. They immediately recognize that which Jonah realized at the very beginning of the storm: it is a mighty God who has indeed created sea and storm and all. At this point, the narrator supplies an indirect piece of information: "For the men knew that he had fled from the presence of the Lord, because he had told them . . ."

The sailors say: "What shall we do to thee, that the sea may be calm for us?" And the following stage instruction furnishes the proper context for the rising danger: "For the sea grew more and more tempestuous." Jonah tells them to throw him into the sea, confessing matter-of-factly that he is the reason for the great storm. Again the narrator intervenes with a note on the growing tempest and describes how the sailors tried in vain to reach land, in an attempt to save his life. In the next 'one-sided' dialogue they pray to God – the 'real' and mighty one – not to be blamed for innocent blood, but they are finally forced to cast Jonah into the sea. It is the cumulative value of stage directions that links Jonah's fate (*goral*) to his 'fortune' as an 'object'. Although God does not answer, His presence is nevertheless strongly felt – unlike the gods' silent response to the sailors. No two silences of God/gods are the same: God's verbal silence is well compensated by His deeds with winds and waves.

Most of the dialogues held between Jonah, the captain, the sailors, their gods and the Lord God, are fragments in which the other interlocutor is implied. Nonetheless, the reader or potential spectator to this play can easily discern the level of reality ascribable both to the present human partners and to the hovering presence of God.

Parallel to the dialogues in the ship scene we can observe the main sequence of action:

The storm breaks out: Sailors cry while Jonah sleeps.
The captain speaks to Jonah while the sailors cast lots.
The sailors pray – Jonah is silent.
The sailors cast Jonah into the sea.
The sailors offer sacrifice and make vows.

Act 2, Scenes i–xi: Jonah's prayer

Jonah's prayer in the belly of the fish is a typical monodramatic scene. As in many monodramas, the audience may have a notion about who the silent partner is, yet the protagonist must create his stage-partner. Being swallowed by the fish, in great distress and at the lowest depths possible, in this scene with lonely Jonah there is a fantastic image and a realization of a metaphor. In fact, by casting him down to this narrow, dark and awful place, the dramatic author proves that Jonah no longer has any means of escape, not even into his unconscious. If the epitome of drama is a maximal condensation of time, space and plot, the belly of the fish proves an ideal stage. Realistically, of course, the space is inconceivable; but as an image – there is no better. Between the physical impossibility and the artistic fictionality, the fish's belly becomes a dramatic space that combines the 'architectonic' theatre space with the only inner, 'designed' space possible for such a situation. In the theatrical 'here and now' Jonah has no other option but to face the inevitable. Nevertheless, he does not seem to undergo the expected process of *anagnorisis*, of a sudden realization of the truth. He has, after all, known the truth all along but refused to act upon his knowledge, an absurd cognitive discrepancy.

Jonah's words: "They that guard lying vanities forsake their loyalty" (a weak translation, especially of *khasdam* (grace) which implies 'God'!) may serve as his half-hearted *anagnorisis*. Jonah's faith and fear of God have certainly increased under his present circumstances, and even his gratitude for his life being saved sounds authentic. Does "They that guard lying vanities forsake their loyalty" mean that Jonah now sees that his own escape was 'vanity'? and therefore is it he who 'left' God? Dramatically, this mono-dialogue is a perfect evocation of God's grace. And yet there is not the slightest mention of the mission Jonah is still required to carry out, i.e., his prophesy.

The author of this beautiful (but strangely amusing in this context) prayer *qua* monodrama, inserts in Jonah's speech a number of expressions that disclose his (the author's!) awareness of the metaphoric significance the situation should have for Jonah, and the lesson he ought to have learnt. But Jonah does not learn. His obstinacy, the main obstacle in the plot and therefore its motivating (or blocking . . .) force, does not break. Jonah prays "out of the belly of She'ol . . ." and "all thy billows and thy waves passed over me". He refers to his actual situation and says something to the effect of 'thanks for saving me' but not one word is uttered about regret for his escape or about his willingness finally to go to Nineveh. Jonah has been swallowed by the darkness of his own blindness. Although he is now re-born, indeed vomitted on to dry land, he has not yet gained insight. The fish is God's vehicle, as the opening and last lines clearly indicate.

Act 3, Scenes, i–ii: The second calling

In the second calling of God to Jonah the word *davar* (word) is repeated twice. This time, after the word 'arise', Jonah does arise and go to Nineveh. It is not only in this context that the word ãáøis linked in biblical Hebrew with *doing*, usually connecting God's words with the need to act upon them (in a way similar to the Greek *dran*). Jonah, compelled again by God's Word, enters "the city of a day's journey", a place that takes him three days to walk. For Jonah marches slowly and without enthusiasm through the streets of this alien metropolis, a fantastic stranger in a mythically evil city. Had Nineveh been as huge as described, it would have been as big as Los Angeles. One may conclude that Jonah is still reluctant, and his prophesy has to be squeezed out of him in the shortest possible five-word phrasing – "In forty days Nineveh's overthrown."

Act 3, Scenes, iii–x: The overthrowing of the prophesy

Like the sailors at sea, the people of Nineveh react first and the king (or the captain) a little later. In a swift series of activities they all repent their evil deeds. They proclaim a fast and put on sackcloth; then the king 'arose' (note again the cumulative and dramatically varied tensions in the verbs 'rising' and 'falling') "from his throne, and he laid his robe from him, and covered himself with sackcloth, and sat in ashes". He then proclaims a royal decree that "neither man or beast, herd nor flock, taste anything", etc. Whereas the tumult on board the ship is described as at least partially restrained and moreover justified because of the storm, the reaction in Nineveh seems deliberately exaggerated. Jonah's prophesy functions here like the storm at sea.

The redundancy effect achieves a comic result. This collective repentence is built on the hope that "Who can tell? God may turn and relent, and turn away from his fierce anger, so that we perish not." While the sailors throw Jonah the sinner overboard, the Ninevites throw their own sins away. Again, the physical level and the metaphoric correspond.

Not only are nature and fate (or chance) meant to be Jonah's teachers, but the social order of Nineveh too is supposed to draw his attention to the inevitable: captain of the ship, king of a city, storm at sea and fish in the sea – all obey God's orders, even those who do so unknowingly. Only Jonah who does know, does not obey, or obeys reluctantly, unconvinced.

Act 4, Scenes i–iv: The second prayer

Jonah is 'exceedingly displeased', and presents in prayer his 'word' against God's. He explains why he fled: "for I knew that thou art a gracious God, and merciful, slow to anger, and great in love, and repentest of the evil." This second prayer parallels his previous prayer from the belly of the fish, as though his earlier lack of remorse (and therefore want of *anagnorisis*!) are a common and known subtext in his conversation with God. Jonah, however, again begs God "to take my life from me". The reader is invited to decide whether Jonah really means this, since a willingness to give up his life has become Jonah's *leitmotif*. God responds with a laconic, ironic and open question, reminiscent of a patient father or teacher: "Art thou so greatly vexed?" God demonstrates sovereignity, since Jonah's 'quest' hovers between the two meanings of God's word, – knowing and doing.

Act 4, Scenes v–xi: East of Nineveh

The next and final station in Jonah's voyage is out of the city, where he makes himself a shelter "till he might see what would come to pass in the city". Despite the hut Jonah has made for himself, God provides him with additional shade, that of the castor oil plant. Interestingly, this plant has hallucinogenic and other therapeutic qualities. It is also noteworthy that God does not depend on the shade Jonah has prepared for himself. It is an indirect 'stage-instruction', auctorial text-modulation, through which God will teach Jonah yet another lesson. This station in the prophet's quest is the site of a trial by heat. Perhaps the divine shade God gives Jonah is a foreshadowing of the shade of destruction that hovered above Nineveh. Taking the shade away from Jonah on a scorching day suggests, by way of contrast, the removal of the threat to destroy Nineveh: because it was Jonah who would rather see an entire city eclipsed than face the retraction of his (or God's) word.

Jonah is 'exceeding glad' of the shady plant, only to realize soon after that a gnawing worm has caused his plant to wither. The worm, another image and non-image at the same time, devours the plant from within, while the 'silent east wind' beats at the plant from the outside. Metaphorically, Jonah is invited to identify himself with all of these elements: plant, wind and worm. This multi-focal metaphor depends on the particular point of view for interpretation. The worm is like Jonah in the belly of the fish. The plant grows and dies, like Jonah himself, likened also to the city of Nineveh, according to God's explanation. Is Jonah likened also to the east wind that makes the plant – the city – wither? What happened to the shelter that Jonah had made and that is now tacitly presented as a futile gesture, like all of man's efforts.

Quest plays are often an initiation process, laden with spiritual messages. Jonah, like many protagonists in fairy tales, novels and plays, has already suffered storm and water, and is now doomed to great heat, dryness and excessive light. As Lord of the Land, God proves his omnipotence through this element too. Hardships and calamities are supposed to forge and finally enhance the hero's biography, personality and consciousness. Following the deep structure of quest-plots, a calamity primarily invites redemption coming from both divine grace *and* the hero's preparedness. There is hardly a classical quest or initiation drama that does not rely on the protagonist's activation of his or her own independent free will. This explains why even after Jonah has carried out His word, the Lord God keeps right on educating him. Initiation is not a *result*, but an endless process. It cannot 'happen' without the active participation of the hierophant, the prophet.

Jonah undergoes trial by the four elements – earth, water, air and fire. The parallel realms of the inanimate world (to follow Lovejoy), the plants and the animals, also show him the right road to take. The various 'punishments' can therefore be conceived of as means to save him from his own real 'plight' (*ra'ato*). The fish, in a typical biblical homeopathic punishment, which is usually commensurate with the crime, makes Jonah suffer and yet saves him from drowning in a stormy sea. It also carries him to where he should have gone in the first place.

From a theatrical point of view, the common denominator of most images in the text constituting the 'Stations', ship, fish, city and the shade of the castor oil plant eaten by the worm – is the *being inside*. The dramatic significance is quite obvious: Evil is inside, not "out there". Whereas Norman Simms claims that "Fish, and city are figuratively all the same place: the living world of God's obedient nature . . .", we may also see these 'locations' as spatial theatrical images that invite Jonah, his readers and spectators to examine their own inner spaces. Jonah is thrown out of the ship, vomited by the fish, reluctantly enters Nineveh, and finally gnaws at the plant. Within Jonah gnaws the refusal to perform willingly what he is obliged to do according to God's word. These images of space are organically connected with Jonah's soul as dramatically presented here.

Simms has noted the interesting dramatic quality in the book of Jonah: "It requires only a mouthpiece, a persona, an actor, willing or not, understanding or not"[6] – and, as I show – Jonah is not *willing* to be 'a mouthpiece, a persona, an actor' of a text written and directed by anyone else, God included. In this respect Jonah, an actor in a divine show, refuses to act a text with which he does not identify.

It is also interesting to observe how the dramatist describes Jonah's plight in the fish's belly with watery poetry while his trouble under the scorching sky is delivered in dry prose, leading to the final full dialogue:

> Art thou so greatly vexed on account of the castor oil plant?
> I am greatly vexed to death.
> Thou art concerned [lit. "have pity"] about the castor oil plant, for which thou hast not laboured, and which thou didst not rear, which came up at night, and perished in a night . . .

Jonah's depiction, in the direct text as well as the stage instructions, is of a man who knows the truth quite well, but refuses to act upon a conviction which is not 'his'. What first seems like a demanding theocentric stance is clarified at the end of the drama as a better understanding by God himself of the anthropocentric stance represented by Jonah. In this sense Jonah indeed does not identify himself with his prophesy, and is therefore a prophet only in the superficial meaning of carrying the word of God, a prophet of a single message. The play gives him a number of chances to experience inwardly what he is relentlessly required to do from the the 'outside'. Jonah is a prophet who refuses to be initiated.

Props, Costumes and Lighting

In an unabridged and unchanged performance-text, the director can draw up a list of props. The first is the money paid for the voyage, soon to prove quite damaging to all the other travellers (if there are any) and sailors. The ship itself is full of 'props' thrown into the sea. Dramatically, they function as images for Jonah. On the ship the sailors cast 'lots' – probably little sticks or stones. The fish itself is a prop, a space, a natural power. In Nineveh we find sack cloths (to wear), the King's robe, the king's sacks, ashes and more sacks, even for the beasts. One wonders about 'the evil on their hands' – is it real or metaphoric? Out of Nineveh Jonah builds a shelter, and there are also the castor oil plant, the worm. All the props are both 'real' things on stage and heavily charged images.

The potential (partially implicit) lighting pattern of the play ranges through the scenes from half-light of clouds and storm to the darkness of the fish's belly, then to the extreme light of the hot day east of Nineveh. Both extremes of light and darkness are quite explicit in the auctorial text. The darkness is made almost palpable in Jonah's prayer while the light and heat seem to ensue from God. In the last very bright scene in particular, the text mentions the rising, scorching sun. As in other parts of this drama, the expressive theatrical means are both a 'realistic' set design and metaphorically charged.

In conclusion, the mode of theatrical qua existential presentation of God is probably the most relevant point to be made in this drama: God is undoubtedly present here, in his words and deeds. It may be said that inasmuch as Jonah flees God, God is in pursuit of Man. From a Kabbalistic point of view, God needs man's willing participation. For the spectator/reader, this crucial issue remains unanswered at the end of Jonah's drama.

10

Ezekiel: the Holy Actor

An Introductory Note on Sacred Spaces in *Daniel*

Some books in the Old Testament are more dramatic than others, but the enigmatic *Daniel* is certainly one of the most theatrical biblical scriptures. The text is imbued with richly developed monologues and dialogues, and its theatricality lies, primarily, in the performative nature of the language and its messages. The theatricality can also be found in its 'stage instructions', which relate to the organization of the dramatic space, to the rich and variegated decor of the plot, and to a number of stage-props. *Daniel*, written partly in Hebrew and partly in Aramaic, narrates the history of Daniel, a child abducted together with three other children from conquered Jerusalem to the court of the Babylonian king (Chapters 1–6). There, with God's help, Daniel is able to interpret the King's dreams and he becomes a powerful figure at court. The second half of the text tells of Daniel's mystical apocalyptic visions (Chapters 7–12) – such as the vision of the four beasts; the vision of the ram and the goat; the visions with the man clothed in linen; and the vision with Michael.

Daniel excels in being a "true perception of the present and the immediate future".[1] Daniel must be regarded as highly theatrical not only in its unique spatial tensions that will be treated here, but in the temporal sense as well, because it hovers between the plights of time present and the prophesies of time future. Traditional Jewish scholars have explicated Daniel's visions as an historical, immediately relevant 'apocalypse soon', whereas Christian exegesis has tended to present the text as a messianic pre-figuration of Christ, an 'apocalypse now and always'. Since the predominant themes in the book are the dreams and apocalyptic visions of Daniel and the kings of Babylon, the book can be examined as a series of temporalized spaces. Observed theatrically, the various times, spaces and plots of *Daniel*, are 'temporarily' suspended in order to reveal a somber, prophetic future. The protagonist Daniel is the main actor, the shifter of realities in this apocalyptic drama. He hovers between the affluent but frail material reality of the present, and the absolute confidence of what is bound to happen in the future. The main spatial elements in *Daniel* are presented as dialectically opposing complementary pairs:

- Real, as opposed to dreamed and visionary spaces.
- Babylon versus Jerusalem. These compose the proposed stage design, in which the physically absent, invaded and looted Jerusalem nonetheless still has the upper hand.
- The once holy vessels at the Temple, now defiled, are important spatial 'props' in the show's first part. Poetically, they also suggest that the children too are pure and undefilable 'Holy Vessels' (as the Hebrew term of later periods implies).
- Jerusalem, vanquished on the physical level, is represented through the person of Daniel, the protagonist of this religious play, through whom God keeps working.
- Daniel's visions which take place in a most personal but also totally universal space.

Acknowledging the actual drama and the theatrical potential of the text, *Daniel* has indeed often been adapted for drama and performed on European stages from the thirteenth century on.[2] In the Catholic context of harnessing theatricality to the educational and religious purposes of the Church, the many productions of the *Daniel* text may be ascribed to the performers' particular understanding of this complex text and its theological and propagandist effectiveness. However, they were surely also able to appreciate the intrinsic theatricality of the play within the text.

The theatrical element under scrutiny here is dramatic space, and some of its physical, psychological and spiritual notions in the text. Seen as a metaphor to the meaning of the entire text, *Daniel*'s space provides a certain clue to an otherwise much more obscure text. Written not earlier than 300 BCE in Palestine, *Daniel* was probably composed while the Jewish population was suffering the persecutions of Antioch Epiphanes (168/7 BCE). The book deals with the numerous personal, national and profoundly religious extremities of exile. The text treats the Palestinian 'here and now' of the actual time and space of writing, from an assumed literary perspective of 'there', in Babylon. This unique perspective, seldom used in other Old Testament texts, endows the 'exile' of the Jews in Babylon with an additional emotional, historic and religious charge. As a result, the dramatic space described, becomes both '(t)here' and 'not (t)here' at one and the same time. *Daniel* is rooted in an ardently consistent rejection of exile, and in attempts to compensate for the Jewish uprootedness. The theatrical experience too is a form of consciously (or 'inlusively') being 'there' and 'not there' at the same time. Exile, in mythopoetic space-related terms, implies being bereft of the 'proper' location. Persons in exile find and feel themselves in the wrong place. Exile is always 'the other' location or 'the others' space'. In this respect, this concept invites a comparison between *Daniel* and the typically theatrical suspension of disbelief, concerning the degree of reality of the performed stage-space. The modern Hebrew term for space, 'Halal', though etymologically stemming from a different origin, is nevertheless associated with 'hilul', to defile or secularize. Following Gaston Bachelard's *The Poetics of Space*, we observe that already at the beginning of *Daniel* an intricate hierarchical system of holy and secular spaces is presented. This system links physical–geographical, psychological and spiritual 'locations', which together constitute the internal as well as external structure of the book.

The first chapter in *Daniel* reveals most of the important spaces in the entire book. It opens with a brief report on King Nebuchadnezzar's siege of Jerusalem, which God, as the text carefully reminds us, 'gave into his hands'. As the non-spatial, unseen and omnipresent protagonist of the entire Old Testament, God constantly hovers above the Book of *Daniel*. Theatrically, Babylon is the dramatic space present in the play and most of the events happen there. Nevertheless, as the text meticulously emphasizes, the 'offstage' yearned-for Jerusalem is just as powerfully re/presented in its physical absence. Within the glorious space of the victorious city, a number of smaller spaces are also mentioned: the king's room and bed, the city gates, etc. The main notion in the exposition, later explored in detail by the text itself, is the invasion of the Jerusalem Temple, the most sacred space of the Hebrews.

The second type of space revealed at the beginning relates to stage properties, namely the Temple vessels, a few of which were taken by the king. As ritual objects, the vessels, containers for the sanctified food and drink, are themselves contained within the holiest space of the Temple. The very transfer of the vessels from their place to Babylon defiles them, even without filling them with the sacrilegious contents in the king's court. Nebuchadnezzar, obviously conscious of their national and religious value in the eyes of the vanquished Jews, removes the vessels "to the land of Shinar, to the house of his god and the vessels he brought into the treasure house of his god" (1:2).

What Queen Esther achieves in the court of the Persian king, Daniel does in Babylon. As almost a religious version of *Esther*, *Daniel* too is written about Exile. But whereas God is not mentioned even once in *Esther*, He is constantly present in *Daniel*, although His presence may arouse conflicting notions of divinity. On the one hand, the Jewish God is not place-bound. On the other, He still chose Jerusalem as a particular space to build His Temple. Between the evidently more space-centered and national aspect of the Jewish religion, and the more universal and certainly more mystical perspective, *Daniel* plays a particularly theatrical role. Like a play which is 'there' on stage, but not 'really' there, God in *Daniel* is both local and universal. For example, and since the significance of a change of place in theater and ritual is well known, Nebuchadnezzar employs the theatricality of space in this victorious parade of the temple vessels to the house of his god. In a way, he empties the vessels of their religious content, and fills them with the victorious theatricality of the conqueror. *Daniel* deals with this national-religious dialectic in a sophisticated way in using 'space' on three levels: The real space, the dreamed space and the visionary space.

A fascinating third kind of space is created in metaphorically yoking the holy temple vessels with the children Daniel, Hananiah, Mishael and Azariah. Like the attempt to change the function of the vessels, the children too are given new, Babylonian, names. Unlike the inanimate vessels, though, they refuse to consume unholy food to be contained in the inner spaces of their bodies: "But Daniel purposed in his heart that he would not defile himself with the king's food, nor with the wine which he drank." This fine image, moreover, supplies indirect information regarding the treatment of the vessels, never explicitly mentioned in the text.

The second half of the book takes place in the prophetic space of Daniel's further visions. Dramatically, these visions are presented on a higher and clearer spiritual level than the king's dreams, since the text makes a clear distinction between dreams and visions. Nebuchadnezzar, already in the beginning of the book, has a dream he cannot solve by himself, nor can his advisors penetrate its meaning. They are unable to distinguish the subjective-psychological elements from the objective (mystical and/or historic) ones. Another metamorphosis of this particular notion of dramatic space is found in the psychological and spiritual 'inner worlds' of both the king and Daniel. The latter 'had understanding in all visions and dreams'. As Daniel's 'inner space' is not defiled by the king's food and drink, he remains pure and his insight is holy. The king, however, is not, and therefore he suffers from the haunting dream. Ironically, Daniel will soon be invited to 'invade' this inner dream-world of Nebuchadnezzar with his own correct interpretations of doom. Daniel, like the king's advisors, must find out what the dream itself is all about. In the now common 'dream-space' created between Daniel and the king, in the presence of the entire court in the king's palace, Daniel transcends space and deals with Time. It is God who gives Daniel the ability to "know what lies in darkness because the light is with Him" (2:22).

In the Old Testament, as we have already seen in many other examples, we find a recurrent pattern, according to which crime and punishment are commensurate. Often they are presented as inseparably linked. The punishment ensues from the crime itself. This 'homeopathic' rule is easily discerned through the active, dramatic and theatrical employment of space in *Daniel*. He who invades (the space of the holiness of Jerusalem), shall be invaded by one from 'there'. Physical invasion invites retribution with a different kind of invasion, while those who have been invaded physically, remain spiritually untouched.

Additional extraordinary dramatic spaces can be observed in *Daniel*. One of the most remembered is the 'Writing on the Wall' scene: "King Belshazzar made a great feast for a thousand of his lords", and under the influence of the wine, he "commanded that they bring in the vessels of gold and silver that his father Nebuchadnezzar had taken out from the temple in Jerusalem, so that the king and his lords, his wives and his concubines might drink from them" (5:1–2). There appear the fingers of an independent bodiless human hand, invading what is erroneously believed to be the safe space of the king's palace, writing a mysterious message on the wall, near the lamp. As a *Leitmotif* in *Daniel*, commensurate with the sacrilegious usage of the vessels, a 'holy' hand enters the king's unholy palace.

The Fiery Furnace and the Lions' Den in *Daniel* are particularly dramatic spaces. As often occurs in myths and fairy-tales, they may represent two stages of initiation. In this context, the lion is a symbol of faith and courage, though more from an emotional perspective. Those confronted with a lion, are 'invited' to harness the 'lion' within themselves. The furnace of fire, into which the three men are thrown, and a fourth is seen amongst them, is also closely linked with ancient initiation rites. Fire is the dialectical element, which gives light and warmth, but also destroys and consumes. Fire is associated with the more spiritual stage in the initiate's way. In this sense too, these traditionally esoteric locations are, like theater, both an actual space and an image at the same time.

In *Daniel* 3, a special place is designed for the Babylonian "image of gold, whose height was threescore cubits, and the breadth thereof six cubits; he set it up in the plain of Dura . . ." (3:1). There exists a deliberate discrepancy between the depiction of this idol's set-design, and the almost offstage design meant for what the biblical dramatist believed to be truly divine. The physicality of the idol's structure suggests that the material itself totally undermines any spirituality. Here again the material affluence of Babel is shrewdly counter-balanced with the poor Hebrew exiles who are nevertheless spiritually rich.

Chapter 10 describes one of Daniel's several visions: "And in the four and twentieth day of the first month, as I was by the side of the great river, which is Tigris, I lifted up mine eyes, and looked, and behold a man clothed in linen, whose loins were girded with fine gold of Uphaz; his body also was like the beryl, and his face as the appearance of lightning, and his eyes as torches of fire . . ." (10:4–6). The description is commensurate with classical analyses of a typical numinous experience (to follow William James or Rudolf Otto, for example). While Chapter 10 is primarily dedicated to a first-person description of the enormous impact the revelation had on the speaker, other chapters and visions specify the content of the divine Word: an apocalyptic prophecy regarding world politics, the decline of Persia and Mede and the vrise of other powers, together with a mixed prophecy about the Hebrews (Chapter 12). Theatrically, the space of the vision is a unique combination between the real space in which the vision occurs: the banks of the river Tigris; the overwhelmed inner space of the prophet, and the entire world to which the words of the Man clad in linen relate. This particular vision, similar to the ones in Chapters 11 and 12, are dramatically opposed to the Babylonian idol in Chapter 3. Daniel "alone saw the vision; for the men that were with me saw not the vision; howbeit a great trembling fell upon them, and they fled to hide themselves" (10:7). In his innermost 'space' the most private and the utterly universal are (temporarily) united.

Ezekiel

Like other biblical prophets, the priest Ezekiel too is commanded by God to deliver His Word to the people of Israel, which he does in a variety of speeches, sermons, proverbs, fables and visions. Ezekiel, moreover, was one of the few prophets (like Daniel) who had to carry out his mission in the Babylonian exile, far away from the land of Israel. This chapter analyzes the uniquely theatrical quality of some of this particular prophet's public performances. The theatrical elements in Ezekiel's prophecies can certainly be ascribed to his individual approach, and perhaps also to the fact that as a priest he was experienced in public communication. However, the peculiarly theatrical nature of Ezekiel's prophecy also ensues from the potentially greater efficacy of exploiting a number of non-verbal, performative techniques, under the specific socio-religious circumstances of exile.

The unique theatricality displayed by Ezekiel arises from the immense tension between the mystic character of some of his major visions, and the specifically national-religious interpretation they are given in the book itself. The esoteric, verbally inexpressible element in some of the visions, demands their presentation in a variety of non-verbal (i.e., theatrical) means, in order to ensure their reception by the audience. In contradistinction to the time-less and space-less nature of some of his visions, Ezekiel is often ordered to perform his one-man shows in precisely specified times and locations (probably the street or market-place). He can thus be conceived of as a live human link between God on the one hand and the exiled people of Israel on the other.

As an actor, he is required to embody the divine message and present it to the people through his own body and soul, in order to connect between the spiritually objective truth ascribed to the divine message and its visionary manifestations, and the subjective, suffering and sinful Israelites, his audience. Though not always completely willing, Ezekiel is always a fully committed holy actor, playing in the service of a highly demanding director.

Many of Ezekiel's always 'dramatic' but frequently also explicitly theatrical prophesies employ a single central metaphor. Among these single-metaphor messages of God, are the vision of the great eagle (17:1–4), the fable of the vine (17:5–10), and the proverb of the lioness (19). More directly theatrical, namely intended by the text itself for actual performance, are images like 'the tree' (37:15–20), and 'the metal-smelter' (22:17), in which the prophet is commanded to do things, not only to talk. The span of Ezekiel's daring images is rich and vast. He moves from angels to faeces, from the Glory of God and holy 'animals' to building materials, pots and pans. He harnesses strong body metaphors, food, sewing, prostitutes and swords, "ceiling-wax and cabbages and kings" (with due respect to Lewis Caroll), exclusively to God's messages. Some of the images re-appear in different contexts in the book. Reshuffled and reused, the images intertwine into a larger framework of reference and create a distinct prophetic oral–aural style. Such, for example, are the images of the sword, the wall and the hole in it. The following discussion, however, focuses on the most overtly theatrical prophesy that opens the entire book with five interrelated chapters. But before developing the theatrical analysis of the first vision (the eating of the scroll, the brick-model 'show' and the sword), I briefly describe Ezekiel's rival performers: the False Prophets. Also, I propose an outline of three of the main theatrical modalities found in the whole book:

1 The Erotic Theatre (Sex)
2 Kitchen Sink Theatre (Food)
3 Theatre of the Living Dead (Life)

False Prophets

God and Ezekiel are well aware of the danger of the false visionaries, the prophets of deceit, of "flattering divination" and "envisioned lies" (12:24), who try to console the miserable people in vain. Ezekiel must have been conscious of competitors in the field of educational, religious or quasi-religious entertainment, who drew the masses to their sessions of false promises, uttering prophesies not based on the absolute necessity for repentance. A number of sections in *Ezekiel* are dedicated to false prophesies that may be understood as rival performances, presenting mystical, moral and generally 'prophetic' shows. Like Ezekiel's they are performed in the quarters of the exiled Israeli community in Babylon. Chapters 12–13, for instance, deal with "there shall no longer be any false vision or flattering divination within the house of Israel". As experienced in other times, places and cultures, periods of financial hardship and political suppression provide an excellent background for the development of escapist prophets, entertaining street visionaries and other theatrical vendors of fast, cheap and consoling spiritual junk-food. Ezekiel is very harsh in his approach to 'other' shows given by public figures, consoling charlatans and the like. He attacks the "prophets of Israel . . . who prophesy out of their own imagination" (13:1–6) and not in God's name. He ridicules "the daughters of your nation . . . who sew bands [or "gloves"?] on all wrists ["hands"] and make veils for the heads of persons of every height, in the hunt for human lives!" (13:18). Ezekiel addresses various female soothsayers and enchantresses who "tie knots on people's hands". He accuses them of catering to the people's fears and hopes, rather than telling them the truth, which they themselves do not know. The true prophet verbally slashes the ready-made, commercial approach of these men and women, who "misled my people saying 'peace,' when there is no peace; and because when He builds a dividing-wall, these prophets smear whitewash on it" (13:10). In dire straits between an uncompromising God and the oppressed, hope-thirsty but religiously 'rebellious' audience, Ezekiel is presented as fully involved, utterly committed to his prophetic theatre.

The Erotic Theatre

The Biblical prophets often compare the people of Israel and the city of Jerusalem to various personal phases and social aspects in a woman's life. In *Lamentations*, for instance, Jerusalem is described as a widow, a virgin and a whore. Jeremiah says "I remember the devotion of your youth, your love as a bride, how you followed me in the wilderness, in a land not sown" (2:2). As a realization of a metaphor, the prophet Hosea was even ordered to take a "wife of whoredom and have children of whoredom" (1:2), so as to be a walking 'ridiculous' educational example of God's wrath. However, none of the prophets was as erotically explicit as Ezekiel in comparing Jerusalem and Samaria, metonyms for the people of Israel and of Judah, to abominable prostitutes. His images develop from tender pictures of a helpless baby-girl, into a blatantly sexual, often deliberately pornographic language, in the attempt to fulfil his mission and make his main point: the infidelity of the Israelites to their once loving, now betrayed and wrathful God, who nevertheless wants his bride to repent and return to Him.

Chapter 16 is a developmental (melo-)drama with distinct acts and scenes.

Exposition,	16:1–2	Declarative opening: The Abominations of Jerusalem
Act 1 Sc. i	16:3–7	A dirty baby, wallowing in blood
Sc. ii	16:8–14	Beautifying a young girl, ready for love
Act 2	16:15–35	Crime: The whoring woman
Sc. i	(15–19)	Giving away God's gifts
Sc. ii	(20–23)	Killing the children and another reminder
Sc. iii	(24–29)	Whoring with Egyptians, Philistines, Assyrians, Babylonians . . .
Sc. iv	(30–35)	The unsuccessful whore
Act 3	16:36–43	Punishment commensurate with the crime
Act 4 16:44–58		Crimes + punishments: Jerusalem, Sodom + Samaria
Act 5	6:59–63	Ashamed reconciliation

In the first scene (16:1–7) Ezekiel describes, most sensuously, the birth and early childhood of a baby girl who, under God's tender loving care, grows up to be a beautiful young woman. Despite the constantly negative depiction, a positive picture is nevertheless drawn: "As for your birth, on the day you were born your navel cord was not cut, nor were you washed with water to cleanse you, nor rubbed with salt, nor wrapped in cloths. No eye pitied you, to do any of these things for you out of compassion for you; but you were thrown out in the open field, for you were abhorred on the day you were born." The poor baby is then found by God: "I passed by you, and saw you flailing about in your blood. As you lay in your blood, I said to you 'Live! and grow up like a plant of the field'."

Interestingly in the context of *Ezekiel*, but typically biblical, life is given
to the baby by God's word. "You grew up and became tall and arrived at
full womanhood"; and at this point the erotic insinuations, likely to catch
the audience's attention better than compassion, become more explicit:
"your breasts were formed, and your hair had grown; yet you were naked
and bare."

Except for the still mildly erotic overtone to the scene, the emotionally
most suggestive and rhetorically efficient image is that of blood. The
prophet uses it in a repeated and ambiguous sense of life and death: "Live
in your blood . . . live in your blood." Blood connotes life and death, both
of which God holds in His hands.

As Israel the girl grows older, the erotic images are intensified. In scene
ii (16:8–14) she has come of age, and the prophet, representing and
playing God by speaking His word in the first person, engages in a tender-
loving, more intimate contact with her, though no physical intercourse is
mentioned. "I passed by you again and looked on you, you were at the
age for love. I spread the edge of my cloak over you, and covered your
nakedness . . ." Though realizing this young woman's ripeness, the
speaker is tactful and considerate. But the tension between the potential
onslaught on this blooming body and the modest "I spread the edge of
my cloak over you", can only enhance the audience's curiosity. The
elderly Ezekiel says: "I pledged myself to you and entered into a covenant
with you, says the Lord God, and you became mine."

The main sensual appeal made in this scene is tactile, etymologically
connected with tactfulness, to portray the exclusive intimacy of a husband
touching his young wife. The scene describes past events, depicting God
as a deeply disappointed lover who is remembering the olden days. At the
same time, His relationship toward the woman is utterly possessive, as
clearly implied and probably understood by the audience: the Hebrew
word 'Baal' means both owner and husband.

The intense theatricality of this text comes across best by being experienced through the spoken words rather than being acted-out, especially
in the patriarchal society of the Hebrews of that time. It is inconceivable
that this suggestive theatrical text could possibly be fully played with an
actress. It is, on the other hand, equally reasonable to assume that this so
far mild verbal eroticism is likely to be even more effective than an actual
live show. Due to the imaginative power of the words themselves, the
theatre in the minds of the listeners was surely activated in complementing
the picture. In the intimate recesses of their imaginations, while the
prophet was talking, the audience might have envisioned him in their
mind's eye taking a shy but consenting, young and good-looking woman,
and slowly washing her, anointing her, and so on:

"Then I bathed you with water and washed off the blood from you, and anointed you with oil. I clothed you with embroidered cloth and with sandals of fine leather . . ." The present-in-absentia offstage-positioned God as playwright, the prophet–actor, the reader and the live audience alike, are all aware that there is a clear difference between washing a baby-girl and washing a young woman and anointing her with oil. "I bound you in fine linen and covered you with rich fabric. I put bracelets on your arms, a chain on your neck, a ring on your nose, earrings in your ears, and a beautiful crown upon your head." In a male-dominated society these deeds may be considered to be signs of tender-loving-care. Under a more feminist scrutiny, however, it is easy to identify in this text a series of chains and locks put on the young woman. One may wonder, more-over, to what extent the audience was already able, by this stage in the show, to recognize the hidden spiritual meaning through the sensuous and erotic mask. The repetition of certain words should be understood here, and in many other originally aural deliveries, as a rhetorical device.

"You were adorned with gold and silver, while your clothing was of fine linen, rich fabric and embroidered cloth. You had choice flour and oil for food. You grew exceedingly beautiful, fit to be a queen. Your fame spread among the nations on account of your beauty, for it was perfect because of my splendour that I had bestowed on you, says the Lord God."

In scene iii (16:15–19) a major (not unexpected) shift occurs in the plot, ensuing from the girl's hubris. Good plays often deliver the expected in an unexpected way, and indeed, despite being rich, beloved and beautiful, instead of everlasting fidelity, she betrays her God–husband and engages in a series of atrocious sexual–religious betrayals. In his sophisticated (often anti-feminist) rhetoric, Ezekiel describes how the young woman uses the very same objects she was given by her lover, to turn to 'any passer-by'.

"But you trusted in your beauty" – failing, in your pride to grasp that I (God) gave it to you – "and played the whore because of your fame" – which I gave to you, etc.; so goes the subtext expected from the audience, "and lavished your whorings on any passer-by. You took some of your garments, and made for yourself colorful shrines, and on them [played the] whore[d]; nothing like this has ever been or ever shall be. You also took your beautiful jewels of my gold and my silver that I had given to you, and made for yourself male images, and with them played the whore; and you took your embroidered garments to cover them, and set my oil and my incense before them. Also my bread that I gave you – I fed you with choice flour and oil and honey – you set it before them as a pleasing odour; and so it was, says the Lord God."

In scene iv (16:20–35) the language becomes more aggressive and explicitly sexual, perfectly commensurate with God's wrath and jealousy. The audience are not aware that the couple (God and the 'woman') had children together, and that in fact they themselves are those very children; but now they learn of it through a particularly strong image: "You took your sons and your daughters, whom you had borne to me, and these you sacrificed to them to be devoured. As if your whorings were not enough! You slaughtered my children and delivered them up as offering to them." For the audience of exiles, this metaphor was well understood. This extended metaphor also implies that the fault lies with mom, not with dad.

Then come a series of sexual images such as "you spread-out your legs to all passers by", "you whored with the lustful sons of ['big-fleshed' in the original Hebrew, which connotes 'big-phallused'] the lustful Egyptians", "you played the whore with the Assyrians because you were insatiable . . .". In order to humiliate her further, God adds: "Gifts are given to all whores, but you gave your gifts to all your lovers . . .", which relate to the assumption that this particular whore, on top of everything, paid rather than was paid for her services. In these few verses (21–35) the verb "to whore" is used eleven times in its different Hebrew conjugations, not to mention a few other highly sexually charged terms.

Whereas the previous scene described the crimes in detail, the following scene (16:36–43) is dedicated primarily to the punishment. God will "gather all your lovers . . . against you from all around and will uncover your nakedness . . . they shall strip you . . . they shall stone you and cut you to pieces with their swords . . . ". God's anger will subside only after the lovers "shall execute judgements on you" and "my jealousy shall turn away" because "I have returned your deed upon your head". The scene ends with the nostalgic, emotionally binding reminder "because you have not remembered the days of your youth", linking the later years of the woman with the days when God had found her. Here again the crime of betrayal is commensurate with the punishment of inflicting pain and humiliation on a woman's body and spirit. While such usage (even metaphorical) of a woman may be quite horrifying to the modern reader, one is nevertheless obliged to admit that the *Ezekiel* text concentrates not on sheer sexuality but, rather, focuses on the (spiritual!) 'how' of the sexual metaphor.

In the next scene (16:44–59) Ezekiel compares Jerusalem to Sodom and to Samaria, her two sinning sisters. Family metaphors are readily received by any audience. Samaria, together with Jerusalem, will be treated in a similarly cruel and even more detailed and sexually explicit way in Chapter 23. Sodom, nonetheless, is deeply engraved in the biblical listener's mind as the epitome of sin, for which the city was destroyed. The prophet subtly alludes to the story in which the evil inhabitants of

Sodom wanted to rape Lot's two angelic guests (*Genesis* 19:1–12). In this way, sexuality is re-connected to the present show through a rhetorical linkage between morality, sexuality and religiosity: "you acted more abominably than they, they are more in the right than you . . ." and therefore "I will restore their fortunes . . . in order that you may bear your disgrace and be ashamed of all that you have done". The text (compare 23:43) implies that Jerusalem is a worn old prostitute, thus completing the life-cycle of the sinful woman, that started with her birth.

The last scene in this sexual–national–religious drama (16:59–63) is an amazing finale. After all the people have heard from the actor and visualized in the privacy of their imaginations, God will "establish with you an everlasting covenant. Then you will remember your ways and be ashamed . . . when I forgive you all that you have done, says the Lord God". This is clearly not a happy end to a gruesome play, but it nevertheless leaves some hope of fixing the marriage if, of course, we abide by the exclusive conditions specified by the husband.

Kitchen Sink Theatre: The Meat-pot

The fable of the cooking-pot relates to two sophisticatedly juxtaposed activities well familiar to the audience: cooking in general (usually done by women) and the ritual offerings in the Jerusalem temple. The central theatrical element in God's command to the prophet cannot be identified for certain, since the words 'set the pot, set it on' etc., may relate to a purely verbal, rather than to an actual performative act. Nevertheless, we may assume that Ezekiel indeed used a pot and performed the whole act prior to explaining his deeds, as is later implied. The Cooking-pot show employs, like some of Ezekiel's other performances, a device to alienate the familiar.

Cooking meat, even if considered a luxury, is nonetheless a familiar household activity. Many of the exiled Jews were also well acquainted with the rituals of the sacrifice. Employing both potential levels of known experiences, this fable inverts the meaning of this ready-made, basically pleasant memory. But in preparing the scene (spoken or performed) with the actor as a chef-cook, God first establishes the dramatic time as the very present:

"In the ninth year, in the tenth month, on the tenth day of the month, the word of the Lord came to me: 'Son of man, write down the name of this day [present tense]. The king of Babylon has laid siege to Jerusalem this very day. And utter an allegory to the rebellious house and say to them'." Now come the precise instructions, with which Ezekiel, as a priest in Jerusalem, was probably quite familiar, recognizing a good piece of meat when he saw one: "Set on the pot, set it on, pour in water also; put in it the pieces, all the good pieces, the thigh, and the shoulder; fill it with choice bones. Take the choicest one of the flock, pile the log under it; boil its pieces, seethe also its bones in it." Cooking in public was perhaps an unusual thing to do in the Babylonian exile, but the other allusion, namely to ritual sacrifices in exile, was an absolute impossibility. The estrangement of the theatrical act therefore ensues from the vast gap between the familiar content and the unsuitable circumstances under which the action was performed.

Having witnessed the visual, auditory, olfactory act of cooking, likely to arouse the audience's appetites, the properly disappointing explanation arrives, not a moment too late: "Therefore thus says the Lord God: Woe to the bloody city, the pot whose rust [filth . . .] is in it, whose rust has not gone out of it! Empty it piece by piece, make no choice at all. For the blood she shed is inside it; she placed it on a bare rock; she did not pour it out on the ground, to cover it with earth. To rouse my wrath, to take vengeance, I have placed the blood she shed on a bare rock, so that it may not be covered."

The pot turns to be the whole of Jerusalem, the pieces of 'choice' meat are none other than the inhabitants of the city, now in exile, as suggested by 'empty it piece by piece'. Instead of the potential eaters, the onlookers turn out to be the eaten. Instead of enjoying a good meal, the cook (instigated by the divine chef) turns the attention of the hungry audience to filth and to the overflowing blood. The blood itself is further used for moral purposes.

"Therefore thus says the Lord God: Woe to the bloody city! I will even make the pile great. Heap up the logs, kindle the fire; boil the meat well, mix in the spices, let the bones be burned. Stand it empty upon the coals, so that it may become hot, its copper glow, its filth melt in it, its rust [filth, impurity . . .] be consumed. In vain I wearied myself [or: in vain you have wearied the prophets who warned you . . .] its thick rust [filth . . .] does not depart. To the fire with the rust [filth . . .]!"

This parable, especially if really performed, is a multi-sensual experience, which, typical to Ezekiel's prophecies, enlists the senses and the emotions to the moral–spiritual service. However, rather than 'a willing suspension of disbelief', Ezekiel's theatre attempts to impose belief on the unwilling – more often than not, through the senses. Typical too is the 'homeopathic' treatment of the crimes and the punishment, and their intimate relationships:

"Yet when I cleansed you in your filthy lewdness, you did not become clean from your filth; you shall not again be cleansed until I have satisfied my fury upon you. I the Lord have spoken; the time is coming, I will act. I will not refrain, I will not spare, I will not relent. According to your ways and your doings I will judge you, says the Lord God."

In this fable-play, Ezekiel in fact describes the unities of time, space and plot: the time is given in advance, the dramatic space is a pot, the dramatis personae are the onlookers inside it, and the fire beneath motivates the whole 'action', especially once the onlookers finally understand that the play is about them. This Boyle's (or boil) law of condensed time, a narrow space and a heated action, results in a relatively short, intensive, inescapable plot.

The Theatre of the Living Dead
(Cooking the Audience)

The Vision of the Dry Bones is a complex combination of a carrier-monologue and inserted dialogical texts. This unique alternation between two modes of speech serves to narrow the distance between the divine source of this vision, according to the speaker at least, and the audience. The poetic vision begins with a report in the first person singular: "The hand of the Lord came upon me, and he brought me out by the spirit of the Lord and set me down in the middle of the valley; it was full of bones. He led me all around them; there were very many lying in the valley, and they were very dry." This apocalyptic scene looks like the very end of the world, but the speaker is careful to describe, not evaluate. It is an object-sight, unadulterated by emotions, and may therefore allow the listeners to form their own opinions and reactions. The depiction of the scene places Ezekiel in the same bewildered situation as his audience.
The opening is followed by a short (reported) dialogue:

> "He said to me, – son of man, can these bones live?
> I answered, – O Lord God, you know."

The question can be understood as a riddle. The obvious response would be 'of course the bones cannot live'. But once asked at all, Ezekiel can well image that 'of course they'll live, otherwise why did you bring me here in the first place?' The answer is therefore both diplomatic and perfectly sincere. The dialogue becomes a quoted monologue, addressed to the bones, which only later will be presented as 'The entire House of Israel'. At this stage they are mere bone:

> "Then he said to me – Prophecy to these bones, and say to them:
> O dry bones, hear the word of the Lord
> Thus says the Lord God to these dry bones:

I will bring spirit into you, and you shall live.
I will lay sinews on you, and will cause flesh to come upon you,
And cover you with skin, and bring spirit into you, and you shall live;
And you shall know that I am the Lord."

Ezekiel says "So I prophesied as I had been commanded" – turning the text he heard into a text spoken by himself. It becomes clear that the prophet's actual speech is the motivating force that makes the bones gather, and he becomes a vice-creator, though no spirit is in them yet: "and as I prophesied, suddenly there was a noise, a rattling, and the bones came together, bone to its bone. I looked and there were sinews on them, and flesh had come upon them, and skin had covered them; but there was no spirit in them".

Ezekiel's creative words were given him by God, but he can create only under God's directly followed instructions, stage by stunning stage. Within an already reported speech the listeners find yet another speech, in which the prophet is ordered to talk to the spirit, or wind: "Then he said to me, prophesy to the spirit, prophesy son of man, and say to the spirit: Thus says the Lord God, Come from the four winds, spirit, and blow [breath] upon these slain, that they may live."

The previous pattern is repeated: "I prophesied as he had commanded me, and the spirit came into them, and they lived, and stood on their feet, as a vast multitude." Significantly, it is not the words alone that gave life to the dry-dead bones, but 'Ru'ach' (spirit). Whereas the previous words alone could create lifeless zombies, but not living people, the wind, or spirit, is presented as an independent element, without which no life is possible.

Having succeeded in endowing life to the bones, God explains the meaning of this vision, or actual event, or poetic metaphor, in a continuation of a reported speech: "Then he said to me: son of man, these bones are the whole house of Israel." Again there is an inserted report in this one: "They say, our bones are dried up, and our hoe is lost; we are cut off completely." God foresees the reaction of the audience, expected to understand that the bones they see are their own: "Therefore prophesy, and say to them: Thus says the Lord God, I am going to open your graves, and bring you up from your graves, O my people; and I will bring you back to the land of Israel. And you shall know that I am the Lord, when I open your graves, O my people. I will put my spirit within you, and you shall live, and I will place you on your own soil; then you shall know that I, the Lord, have spoken and will act, says the Lord."

Time present and time past are both present here in time future. The Vision of the Dry Bones is a wonderfully ominous yet comforting text for a Holy Theatre. It is necessary, nevertheless, to reflect upon its possible mode of delivery, as already implied in Ezekiel's self-effacing monologue, which presents itself as subservient to God's delivered dialogues and monologues. One possibility is that Ezekiel, in absolute seclusion, has a vision that he later presents to his audience. In this case, the audience was not present when the bones came alive. Consequently, the divine verifying source of the vision is kept secret, and the theatrical mode of presentation employs a stronger rhetorical and potentially more influential element.

Another possibility is that the event takes place as an inner (real or made-up) vision Ezekiel is having while talking to the audience, present, so to speak, when the bones come alive in his mind. In this case the theatrical effectiveness of the event is greatly enhanced. From a less mystical, more materialistic point of view, one can even imagine a real valley nearby, in which there were many bones lying around. I contend that, in relating to the written text in the Bible, these two interpretations offer two mutually complementary readings. The difference between the interpretations lies in their relative degree of realism, esoteric or theatrical. However, in both cases the text itself makes it evident that the bones spoken about, those of the spectators and listeners, are the very same bones.

Following the blatantly sexual imagery in Chapter 16 and the bloody imagery of meat in Chapter 24, the Vision of the Dry Bones employs another inescapably personal and thus inevitably suggestive use of something we all carry inside: bones. Pursuing his theatrical strategy of re-contextualizing the known and familiar and presenting it as shockingly new, Ezekiel first reveals his non-verbal images as non-metaphoric, and only later does he verbally make them into metaphors. On the first, simple level, all people carry their bones in their bodies, but when found scattered in the field, it is clear that their ex-carriers are dead. As parts of the body, bones may readily symbolize the hardest, most 'material' element in the human anatomy. Bones, notably, are the most 'living' reminder of death, since they remain long after all flesh, blood, sinews and skin have decomposed. Furthermore, the bones signify the socially dispersed, scattered situation of the Israelites, and the national death of the hopeless exiles. It would appear that God alone can come to the rescue and breathe spirit into both the body personal and the national body.

The Vision of the Dry Bones is constructed, to a great extent, as an allusion to the biblical stories of Creation, probably well known to Ezekiel's listeners. The device of alienating familiar situations applies to texts too, since the audience is invited to re-interpret an already known story in a new light. This device, moreover, is highly commensurate with the overall message itself: the renewal of God's ancient covenant with the people of

Israel. However, the text is specifically directed toward the second Creation story: "then the Lord God formed man from the dust of the ground and breathed into his nostrils the breath of life" (*Genesis* 2:7). As the audience of Ezekiel's vision may realize, the bones return to life rather than are created afresh. God hence does not 'create' the bones as in the first Creation story, but 'brings spirit into them', more like the second Creation of Man story in *Genesis*, and even that is done indirectly, through the wind, or spirit. It is noteworthy, particularly in this context, that Ezekiel is constantly addressed by God as 'Ben Adam', Son of Man.

The theatricality of this text is based on the profound similarity between the performative function of words spoken on-stage, and the utmost importance of speech as a creative force in biblical Judaism. Ezekiel's vision hovers between the performative mode and the descriptive, depending on how the mode of presentation is interpreted. Instead of creating one Man, this vision is a re-creation of an entire people. Taken literally, the Vision of the Dry Bones is a miracle. But poetically and theatrically, it is also a wonder-full scene. Considering that the bones represent the audience, the audience is invited to accept God's spirit, now through the theatrical event. In this sense, the spirit, or wind, is far more than just the life-giving power, as is obvious from the content. It is, moreover, the performative usage, as well as possible mode of delivery, which gives the Vision of the Dry Bones its uniquely impressive character.

The First Vision: the Scroll, the Brick and the Sword

The first verse of *Ezekiel* reveals, as in classical drama, the speaker, the time and the place of the events about to happen, and the general nature of the subject matter. The exact time given is "the thirtieth year, in the fourth month, on the fifth day", the fifth of Tamuz, which is believed to be 587 BCE. The year indicates the thirtieth anniversary of finding the Torah scroll in the Jerusalem Temple, an event whose importance is primarily an inner religious–Jewish matter. Although the personal pronoun 'I' is relatively rare in the books of prophets, the book of *Ezekiel* is indeed presented as a personal account. The precise mentioning of the place "I was among the exiles by the river Chebar . . . in the land of the Chaldeans", establishes the fact that this account is one of the only collections of prophecies reported from Exile, rather than from within the borders of the homeland, Eretz-Israel.

The dramatic character of Ezekiel's messages is nourished by the tensions between the 'here, in exile' and the notion of 'there, in Jerusalem'. The first verse also includes "the heavens were opened, and I saw visions of God". The book of *Ezekiel* reflects a polarization between the subjective specificity of the speaker, the precision of the time and the place on the one hand, and the expected objective truth of the divine and thus implicitly time-and-spaceless visions. The next verse is a third-person expanded repetition of the details, functioning as an objective verification: "On the fifth day of the month, it was the fifth year of the exile of King Jehoiachim, the word of the Lord came to the priest Ezekiel son of Buzi, in the land of the Chaldeans by the river Chebar; and the hand of the Lord was on him there."

Having established the concrete realistic basis, the narration returns to the first-person singular: "As I looked, a stormy wind came out of the north: a great cloud with brightness around it and fire flashing forth continually, and in the middle of the fire, something like gleaming amber. In the middle of it was something like four living creatures. This was their appearance: they were of human form" (1:4–5). Whether indeed mystical, or imaginary or fictitious in any other sense, this amazing first vision (*Ma'ase Merkava*), which has received numerous Cabalistic interpretations because of its esoteric and mysterious content, transposes the reader (or listener and spectator) to a different realm of reality. In this context it may be regarded as a private, highly 'theatrical' celestial vision, which the prophet tries to reconstruct and tell. The vision, as scholars have shown, may be regarded as a poetic rendition of the Jerusalem Temple. From a dramatic point of view, the vision is characterized mainly by the least material theatrical elements: wind (the Hebrew 'Ruach' refers to both wind and spirit!) and many light-effects. Images such as 'fire flashing', 'gleaming amber', 'sparkled', 'burning coals of fire', 'torches', 'bright' and 'lightning' suggest that the prophet was trying to express a basically inexpressibly bright sight. Religious theatre often attempts to manifest, indeed incarnate on the 'here and now' stage, notions that are neither from here, nor from now. In mystical terms, light and spirit (or wind) are both an expressive theatrical means and the religious target to be achieved through them. The text of Ezekiel's vision indicates that these two elements are also an attempted bridge between the mystical vision, by definition almost inexpressible, and the prophet's duty to deliver it nevertheless.

Many prophets had been ordered to deliver God's words, and employed various non-verbal elements in their attempts to do so. As already noted, the 'word' of God (in Hebrew '*davar*'), means both 'a spoken thing' and a 'thing', because God's performative words do rather than describe events. *Ezekiel* is particularly replete with sights and visions that the priest–prophet is ordered to pass on to his audience by means of a theatrical presentation. Consequently, the most basic theatrical tension ensues between the self-evident truth of the visions, and the extreme difficulty of transmitting that same truth to the audience. This tension between the message, the expressive means and the incredulous audience, is typical to the endeavours of other biblical prophets too, but in *Ezekiel* special theatrical devices are enlisted. Moreover, *Ezekiel* reflects two additional sorts of tensions: the first is between the universal–mystical nature of many of the visions and their particular national–historic Jewish inter-pretations, as given by the prophet himself, though often quoting God as the verifying source; the second is between the message, once given to the people, and their own reluctance if not outright objection to whatever Ezekiel has to say. Employing theatrical means can therefore be seen as both an intrinsic component in the prophet's mission, and a necessary tactic to reach his audience. Ezekiel describes numerous attempts to mani-fest through verbal and non-verbal means of presentation what he has experienced spiritually in his visions. He is trying to turn his inner 'theatre of visions' into an external, publicly communicable theatre.

The first vision motivates the entire book. Once it is over, the prophet describes himself as crushed under its impact: "When I saw it I fell on my face, and I heard the voice speaking . . . : Son of Man, stand on your feet and I will speak to you" (1:28–2:1). The divine voice tells the prophet of his mission and of his prospective tough audience: "I am sending you to the people of Israel, to a nation of rebels who have rebelled against me, they and their ancestors have transgressed against me to this very day. The descendants are impudent and stubborn. I am sending you to them, and you will say to them, 'Thus says the Lord God.' Whether they hear or refuse to hear, for they are a rebellious house, they shall know that there has been a prophet among them."

As an actor, the prophet is assigned an (almost?) impossible mission. He learns in advance that the text given to him will be received by a partic-ularly hostile crowd, as clearly stated by repetition, for example, of the term 'rebellious house'. Ezekiel's task is hence to perform, regardless of his audience's response. His words, in expressing the divine–performative word of God, are important as such, and as a warning to the people.

Ezekiel is strengthened by God's words "do not be afraid of their words" and warned "do not be rebellious like that rebellious house". In this process of choosing and training the actor for his presentation, God himself resorts to non-verbal means: "open your mouth and eat what I give you." This actor surely found it difficult to swallow God's words, which, as both a real act and as a realization of a metaphor, he must now do, but is nonetheless compelled to internalize the text (or perhaps all of his future texts) for his coming show: "I looked, and a hand was stretched out to me, and a written scroll was in it. He spread it before me; it had writing on the front and on the back, and written on it were words of lamentation and mourning and woe. He said to me: 'Son of Man, eat what is offered to you, eat this scroll, and go, speak to the house of Israel.' So I opened my mouth, and he gave me the scroll to eat." The text makes a subtle allusion to the opening words of the book "In the thirtieth year", relating, as noted, to the anniversary of finding the ancient Torah scroll. The idea involved in this allusion is that the discovered holy text is not simply an archaeological event or material for good reading, but that the *content* of the book must be accepted, followed, internalised. Considering the content (and material) of the scroll, one can only interpret Ezekiel's reaction "Then I ate it; and in my mouth it was as sweet as honey" as full acceptance, body and soul, of God's mission. Or was it that God coated the bitter pill with sugar?

Having made the actor swallow, 'materialize' and internalize the text, the divine director then has more to say about the audience. It is an audience Ezekiel already knows well, but God re-emphasizes how difficult the coming mission will be. The crowd will understand the language, but reject the message. "For you are not sent to a people of obscure speech and difficult language, but to the house of Israel – not to many peoples of obscure speech and difficult language, whose words you cannot understand." Again God explains, now based on the already semi-digested text, "I will make your face hard against their faces and your forehead hard against their foreheads. Like the hardest stone, harder than flint . . . " God continues to prepare his actor by encouraging Ezekiel not to fear and "all my words that I shall speak to you receive in your heart and hear with your ears . . .". Having received God's written and spoken words, the prophet must now "go to the exiles, to your people (!!), and speak to them . . . whether they hear or refuse". The divine playwright–director is well aware of the effectiveness of this up-coming show, which is anything but entertaining. The chances of changing the people's hearts are known in advance to be slim, but the very utterance counts.

The characteristics of the theatre show about to begin and its prospective communicative parameters are hence: a highly demanding semi-offstage playwright–director, an unpopular harsh message ('lamentation, mourning and woe'), a lonely actor who has fully embodied the 'word', and an extremely hostile audience. This show is prophesied to become a flop even before its premiere.

Ezekiel's theatre is out to transmit a religious-educational message, and as such, it is a perfect example of 'Enlisted Theatre', a means rather than an end. This kind of theatre is bound to rely heavily on the discrepancy between presentation and representation. Theatre, as a medium, can exist only in any given 'present'. But Ezekiel's planned presentation is harnessed to extra-theatrical purposes. Its specific times and spaces therefore serve an ulterior motivation. The message is not meant to consecrate the present, but rather to use 'show-time' as an opportunity for the spectators to repent their evil deeds. Relying on the collective memory of the 'good old times' the people of Israel had had with their God, the present theatrical time in and of the show is harnessed to future (apocalyptic) time. Future hopes and past memories will receive a short, tentative, highly precarious 'show-present'. It has been observed that biblical Hebrew does not have a real grammatical present tense. The period between past and future can be described as an 'in-between' (*benoni*), a tightly stretched situation which indicates a doing of some kind. Thus 'I see' is written (and sometimes understood) as 'A Seer'. In this show, the future of the people of Israel is projected upon its past. The fundamental notion of the show is no less than the present possibility of correcting the sins of the past. Therefore the theatrically necessary fictionality of the event serves well the shifts between past and future.

The space of the show too is typically both 'here' and 'not here'. The actual playing space is a precisely designed model around which Ezekiel performs. The model of Jerusalem is located in a more vaguely depicted street or market place, probably in the Jewish exiles' neighborhood, somewhere in or near Babylon, in a place called Tel Aviv, on the banks of the River Chebar. The space 'from which' the actor plays is the mystical or poetic space of his vision. The space of the model Jerusalem represents a remote place, and relates to both the past and the future. It is, at the same time, imbued with the spiritual 'Merkava' notions. The actual geography and the visionary and imaginative are superimposed on the theatrical space. In theatrical terms, God as the playwright–director and Ezekiel as His actor, yoke together the actual location, the dramatic space and the designed stage-space through spiritual violence.

The entire 'plot' is supposed to dissolve as soon as the audience not only 'get the message', but indeed internalize it, like the actor, and follow it. Therefore, all the other expressive theatrical means such as props, costume, movement etc., must also be regarded as totally harnessed to the divine message. None of the theatrical means is ascribed a value of its own, they are all parts of a Holy Theatre that calls for complete dedication from both the actor and his audience, though only the actor's dedication can be expected. The 'plot-text' is heavily based on motifs of rebellion and infidelity – both time-related factors in the people's religious behaviour. Ezekiel, for example, is required to lie 390 days on his left side and 40 days on his right side. The days stand for years and generations. The present of the exiled people of Israel is a period of great distress, and the fictitious theatrical present in particular is a narrow bridge between their glorious past and – depending on them – a promising future.

The beginning of the scene is highly theatrical, connecting the mystical visionary space to the actual performance space: "Then the spirit [wind] lifted me up, and as the glory of the Lord rose from its place [!!], I heard behind me the sound of loud rumbling; it was the sound of the wings of the living creatures brushing against one another, and the sound of the wheels beside them, that sounded like a loud rumbling" (3:12–13). It is hard to imagine a more dramatically effective 'entrance' than an actor being wind-borne on-stage. An interesting dialectic, moreover, is created in the next verse: "The spirit [wind] lifted me up and bore me away; I went in bitterness in the heat of my spirit, the hand of the Lord being strong upon me" (3:14). And now he arrives: "I came to the exiles at Tel Aviv, who lived by the river Chebar . . ." The text of Ezekiel opens with " . . . as I was among the exiles . . ." and thus we may conclude that Ezekiel's wind (or spirit) voyage was a quality, rather than geographic, change of space – a quantum-leap.

"And I sat there among them, stunned, for seven days", perhaps silent. These highly theatrical seven days of being 'stunned', are not only the psychologically understandable reaction of the actor, crushed under the weight of both the vision itself and his charge to deliver it, but also a brilliant theatrical device and a wonderful preparation for the coming show – from the audience's point of view as well. The actor is now speechlessly situated in the midst of his audience. This period of the 'stunned' Ezekiel is likely to intensify the audience's expectations, while giving the actor more time to concentrate on his mission. However, spending time with the audience prior to the presentation necessarily narrows the real and the theatrical distance between the parties.

Having already received general instructions to speak to the audience, Ezekiel now waits for particular stage instructions for his debut, while digesting (virtually? metaphorically?) the scroll. At the end of this week, the word of God comes: "Son of man, I have made you a sentinel (Hebrew '*Tzofe*'), or a seer; an expression which appears again in Ezekiel, a leit-motif indeed] to the house of Israel" (3:16). He is ordered to give the people a warning from God: "But if you warn the wicked, and they do not turn from their wickedness, or from their wicked way, they shall die for their iniquity; but you will have saved your life" (3:19). Other than commanding Ezekiel to act, God is very specific in explaining to the actor his exclusive responsibility for his audience's lives. In modern Hebrew the word '*Tzofe*' also means a theatre spectator.

Following the text, at the end of God's speech about the actor's responsibility there is yet another shift to a different space: "Then the hand of the Lord was upon me there; and he said to me, Rise up, go out into the valley, and there I will speak with you. So I rose up and went out into the valley; and the glory of the Lord stood there, like the glory that I had seen by the river Chebar; and I fell on my face. The spirit entered into me, and set me on my feet; and he spoke with me and said to me: 'Go, shut yourself inside your house. As for you, son of man, cords shall be placed on you, and you shall be bound with them, so that you cannot go out among the people, and I will make your tongue cling to the roof of your mouth, so that you shall be speechless and unable to reprove them . . ." (3:22–27). Whereas the first seven-day period of silence is merely indicated, the next required silence, side by side with active inactivity, is clearly specified here.

In Chapter 4 God gives the actor the long expected exact instructions for the show: "take a brick and set it before you. On it portray ("carve") a city, Jerusalem."[3] It is important to note that Jerusalem plays a major role in *Ezekiel*. From a later passage (8:3) we learn that in the sixth year Ezekiel is transferred to Jerusalem where he is shown all the "great abominations" of Jaazaniah son of Shaphan and seventy of the elders of Israel. In Chapter 40, moreover, Ezekiel is brought by the hand of God to the land of Israel, "and set me down upon a very high mountain, on which was a structure like a city to the south" (40:2), and a man with "a measuring reed in his hand" (an angelic architect?) then gives the prophet a long and technically very detailed guided tour of yet another model of Jerusalem and the temple. In these chapters, Ezekiel's role as priest is important. When he built the brick model, he certainly relied on his minute knowledge of the actual measures and architectonic details of the place. The brick-model of the city encapsulates the real Jerusalem, the model in "a structure like a city" (Ch. 40), the vision as reflecting Jerusalem – and presents its holiness and its destruction as a leitmotif in the book of *Ezekiel*.

While Ezekiel was busy portraying or carving the city, many bystanders must have watched him: "and put siegeworks against it; and build a siege-wall against it, and cast up a ramp against it; set camps also against it, and plant battering rams against it all around" (4:1–2). This is a precise description of a maquette, a designer's model, the intended set-design for the show. God as architect is a well-known biblical image, but here God is also a master stage-designer. The Jerusalem model, in presenting their destroyed city right in front of their eyes, will most certainly draw their attention. The made-to-scale model will provide the audience with the necessary dramatic perspective. Furthermore, because of the relative size differences, the model transforms Ezekiel and presents him as a looming mini-god, executing absolute control: first over the building and later in maneuvering the city. In the same way that God maintains His providence over the holy city in real life, so too does the prophet in the performance, representing God.

"Then take an iron plate and place it as an iron wall between you and the city; set your face toward it, and let it be in a state of siege, and press the siege against it. This is a sign for the house of Israel." The iron plate (or pan, '*Mahvat*') is a familiar cooking utensil for the audience, which (aside from its material metallic quality of iron, also used for weapons), Ezekiel employs as a device of deliberate estrangement. Like the iron-pot (Ch. 11), the plate may also allude to the people's preference for meat. Under God's guidance as master of stage-properties, Ezekiel uses the pan as an object that is a metaphor and not-a-metaphor at the same time. It is suggested that the audience must change not only their moral-religious attitudes, but their everyday behavior as well. Thus, through the props too, the audience is invited to a process of 'inlusion', namely of perceiving their own perception of the event as theatrical. They are invited to be fully conscious of the gap between the theatrical illusion, and the message this illusion is intended to deliver.

The preparations of the model, the building of siege-machines, and the pan, certainly evoke difficult past experiences in the audience, whose memories of the real events are still fresh and painful. Without uttering a single word, the silent acts performed by the prophet rekindle personal and national traumas. From the text we may conclude that Ezekiel was required first to act and only then to explain in words what he was doing.

Once the model and the siege-machines are ready, Ezekiel is ordered to "lie on your left side, and place the punishment of the house of Israel upon it; you shall bear their punishment for the number of the days that you lie there. For I assign to you a number of days, three hundred ninety days, equal to the number of the years of their punishment. When you have completed these, you shall lie down a second time, but on your right side, and bear the punishment of the house of Judah; forty days I assign you, one day for each year" (4:4–5). Similar to the diminution of space, so too does time shrink: each day in the show represents a year of Israel and Judah's sins against God. Ezekiel's performance therefore took at least 430 days, not including the time necessary to build the model. Lying on the left side represents the kingdom of Israel in the north, and the right side (*yemin, teman*) represents the southern kingdom of Judah.

God demands of the actor to lie inactive for 430 days and bear the collective symbolic punishment on his own body. In a Holy Theatre the actor is often a sacrifice, a truly willing social victim, an individual artist who serves his community's socio-religious needs. The actor Ezekiel will be tied with cords, forbidden to turn from side to side. His passive–aggressive behavior extends an invitation to the audience to reflect upon their own deeds. In lying there fettered, with his arm exposed as on the battlefield, Ezekiel takes upon himself, in a prolonged process of concentrated internalization, his people's sins. *Actor Dei qui tollis peccata Israel*.

During this long period the actor must eat, but his food too is enlisted to the service of total theatre. He is given a specific war-time diet, poor in quality and meagre in quantity, and very little water (during the intense heat of July, in today's Iraq . . .): "And you, take wheat and barley, beans and lentils, millet and spelt; put them into one vessel, and make bread for yourself . . . The food that you eat shall be twenty shekels a day by weight [about 300 gr.]; at fixed times you shall eat it. And you shall drink water by measure, one-sixth of a hin; at fixed times you shall drink" (4:9–10). The prophet's meals must be at fixed times, probably so that the audience will know when to come to see him eat and drink. Compare with "eat your bread with quaking [or 'loudly'] and drink your water with trembling and with fearfulness" (12:18).

So far Ezekiel seems to accept all the stage instructions, but when told "You shall eat it [your bread] as a barley-cake, baking it in their sight on human dung . . . thus shall the people of Israel eat their bread, unclean . . . " – he dares to rebel, albeit meekly, for the first time: "Then I said: Ah Lord God! I have never defiled myself; from my youth up until now I have never eaten what died of itself or was torn by animals (*Nevela, trefa*), nor has carrion flesh come into my mouth." Though not explicitly stated, it is possible to assume that Ezekiel was supposed to bake his food on his own faeces, thus indeed leaving absolutely no possible bodily element out of the show.

Though he had sat "bitter with the heat of my spirit" (3:14), he had never before verbally expressed his dismay in reaction to his director's demands. As an experienced director, God has shown his profound understanding of theatrical effects; just as he also knows that the different orifices of the human body provide the sensitively intimate biological communicative bridges between a person and the environment. It is interesting that Ezekiel does not express his natural disgust at baking his bread on (his own) human faeces, but tactfully conceals his opposition under a religious–dietary. The author of *Ezekiel* also seems to be enjoying playing a little joke concerning the limits of aesthetic and realistic acting in particular and theatricality in general. This time, it is implied, God really went too far. Ezekiel resorts to an argument whose sources, obviously, are deeply rooted in God's own given commandments, since He himself forbade eating defiled food. Whereas God is ready to sacrifice His dietary laws for the sake of an effective show, Ezekiel uses the same laws as an excuse to avoid performing the embarrassing act demanded. God the director is (apparently easily) convinced, and changes the fuel to "cow dung instead of human dung, on which you may prepare your bread" (4:15). This is the only explicit dialogue in the scene, followed, nevertheless, by an explanation: "I am going to break the staff of bread in Jerusalem; they shall eat bread by weight and with fearfulness; and they shall drink water by measure and in dismay. Lacking bread and water, they will look at one another in dismay, and waste away under their punishment." Alas, the extreme non-verbal metaphor of the people of Israel's sins as faeces has not worked, a fact which the verbal explanation attempts to rectify.

This scene is a perfect example of a total 'body-theatre', actually sacrificing the aesthetic theatrical materials to a religious and spiritual purpose. Employing the exits and entrances of the human body through watching, hearing, smelling – God makes sure the audience in the streets will get the message. Moreover, through Ezekiel's obedience as an actor, God makes a daring connection between His Word (*davar, dibbur*) – both material and spiritual, and sheer materiality, namely food (compare *Numbers* 11). He creates a homeopathic metaphor regarding the inevitable link between the people's crimes and His retribution. This connection is also seen in the particularly harsh rhetoric of the prophecy "Surely, parents shall eat their children in your midst, and children shall eat their parents . . ." (5:10). God is implicitly presented as the people of Israel's one and only real 'staff of bread'. Because they reject Him, they will suffer both physical and spiritual hunger. This process of mutual body–soul–spirit metaphorization is achieved through Ezekiel's complete commitment to his role.

In Chapter 5 the actor is given further directions for the next scene: "take a sharp sword; use it as a barber's razor and run it over your head and your beard; then take balances for weighing, and divide the hair. One third you shall burn in the fires inside the city, when the days of the siege are completed; one third you shall take and strike with the sword all around the city; and one third you shall scatter to the wind, and I will unsheathe the sword after them. Then you shall take from these a small number, and bind them in the skirts of your robe. From these, again, you shall take some, throw them into the fire and burn them up; from there a fire will come out against all the house of Israel" (5:1–4). After 430 days, Ezekiel's hair and beard have grown long, and as a finale to this longest show ever, yet another scene of body-theatre is performed. The House of Israel is likened to the prophet's hair. The people are part of the prophet.

Whatever has not been understood by the audience from the non-verbal actions, will now be very clearly stated in words (5:5–17). The final speech Ezekiel addresses to the audience opens with "This is Jerusalem", but instead of indulging in the military or historic meaning of the Babylonian siege on Jerusalem, the defeat is dealt with in primarily religious terms. The overall following message is absolutely clear: "I will make you a desolation and an object of mocking among the nations around you, in the sight of all that pass by. You shall be a mockery and a taunt, a warning and a horror, to the nations around you, when I execute judgements on you in anger and fury . . ." (5:14). However, as previously noted, this amazing text links the content with its modes of re/presentation. In a similar way that Ezekiel as actor was, most probably, ridiculed for his long strange acts in the street, so too will his onlookers be ridiculed in the extra-theatrical reality. Self-reflexively, God harnesses the actual conditions of the performance so that theatricality itself becomes a metaphor to the spiritual message.

The Case of the Real Motivation: A Dead Wife (24:15–27)

In the process of becoming God's one-man show, Ezekiel is spared nothing. As one of the cruellest devices of mixing 'real' truth with theatrical conviction when speaking to the people, Ezekiel's wife must die. Worse – he learns about it in advance: "The word of the Lord came to me: Son of man, with one blow I am about to take away from you the delight of your eyes . . ." Ezekiel, at the same time, is deprived of even the small consolation that may be found in mourning: "yet you shall not mourn or weep, nor shall your tears run down. Sigh but not aloud, make no mourning for the dead." On the contrary, he must behave as though it is a day of extra joy: "Bind on your best clothes and put your shoes on your feet; do not cover your moustache and do not eat the bread of mourners." Here the text is not quite clear. Is Ezekiel already bereft of his wife, or is he using a flash-back? "So I spoke to the people in the morning." He may have had his usual talks with the people, knowing what was about to happen: "and at evening my wife died, and on the next morning I did as I was commanded." In a relatively small place everybody knows what is going on in the neighbors' house, especially if it is a public figure like the prophet Ezekiel. "Then the people said to me, 'Will you not tell us what these things mean for us, that you are acting this way?'" The reported speech of the people is the epitome of tactlessness. Whereas they may wonder why, on his day of mourning, he is speaking to them at all, they do not offer a single word of consolation or sympathy. Rather, the people ask "what these things (!!) mean to us". Only the rhetorical, slightly excessive repetition of the (Hebrew) verb 'Amar' [say] in these few sentences, may perhaps signify the enormous emotional stress of the speaker, and the discrepancy between his personal mourning and his public duty: "Then the people said to me . . . tell us . . . then I said to them . . . the word of the Lord was said . . . (lemor) say to the house of Israel

. . . Thus says the Lord . . ." A furious God combines the personal and the public into one very true-to-life performance. God may have thought that no other theatrical means would have worked as efficiently as this one on the hard-necked audience. But it was Ezekiel who had to pay the price.

The text makes it clear that the prophet is making up his message as he goes along: "Then I said to them: The word of the Lord came to me: Say to the house of Israel, thus says the Lord God: I will profane my sanctuary, the pride of your power, the delight of your eyes, and your heart's desire; and your sons and your daughters whom you left behind shall fall by the sword." He uses the same expressions God used in previously talking to him. The theatrical device used here is the shocking similarity between the message and the carrier of the message: "And you shall do as I have done; You shall not cover your moustache, or eat the bread of mourners. Your turbans shall be on your heads and your shoes on your feet; you shall not mourn or weep, but you shall pine away in your iniquities and groan to one another." One can only surmise that Ezekiel himself, while delivering the Word, could but groan silently, as commanded. Therefore, he himself adds, as though talking of himself in the third person, "Thus Ezekiel shall be a sign to you; you shall do just as he has done."

There is no theatrical truth like the one deeply experienced by the actor, whether directly or indirectly related to any specific role. This is certainly a strange variation on 'Ridi, Pagliazzo'. One may wonder about the ethics of Ezekiel's speech and body-language – not of the content, rather his modes of delivering his words.[3] The dramatic irony is only hinted at in advance, but becomes explicit while the message is being delivered, creating a real live theatre-event about death. Only when actually talking will Ezekiel learn that what he might have thought to be a stage instruction . . . is in fact the text itself. As director, God certainly achieves spontaneity and (at least semi-) unrehearsed fresh feelings on-stage. Ezekiel's spouse herself is unimportant, except as a dramatic figure who dies no sooner than mentioned. God knows how effective personal sorrow can be when harnessed to a good role, and thus killing the wife is truly a wonderful emotional motivation for the actor to deliver a good speech on forbidden mourning.

"When this comes, then you shall know that I am the Lord God. And you, son of man, on the day when I take from them their stronghold, their joy and glory, the delight of their eyes and their heart's affection, and also their sons and their daughters . . . on that day, one who has escaped will come to you to report to you the news. On that day your mouth shall be opened to the one who has escaped, and you shall speak and no longer be silent. So you shall be a sign to them; and they shall know that I am the

Lord." God eliminates the borderlines between theatricality and life, and unites Ezekiel's text with his subtext.

After the successful show ('And otherwise, Mr Ben Buzi, how did you enjoy the show?') God turns again to the actor; but rather than complimenting him for a particularly good performance, which would be tactless under the given circumstances, or trying to comfort the newly widowed Ezekiel, He just says that the horrible vision will indeed happen: "Theatre can ground itself only when it uncovers its own limits – only when the artistic genre itself becomes tragic, beyond all the usual contrasts between tragedy and comedy."[4] The promised refugee arrives "on the twelfth year of our exile, in the tenth month, on the fifth day of the month" (33:21). The prophecy comes true. The only encouragement Ezekiel receives is "and you were a sign (*mofet*) to them", not without the final, much more important "and they shall know that I am the Lord God".

In a somewhat different context Derrida relates to Artaud's 'Theatre of Cruelty', which I believe is not too far from Ezekiel's show: "The public is not to exist outside, before or after the stage of cruelty, is not to await it, to contemplate it, or to survive it – it is not even to exist as a public at all." Ezekiel's public, exposed to a different kind of cruelty, are to behave exactly the opposite.[5]

This particular kind of Holy Theatre is predestined for self-destruction. Like Wittgenstein's ladder, it must be thrown down once the climber has reached the top. Its harsh symbolism, quite devoid of aesthetic or humanly–moral sublimation, is intended to impose the exclusively religious message.

Part V

Leaders:
A Theatrical Gaze

11

Moses in Flesh and Spirit

Chapter 11 in the *Book of Numbers* describes the complex attraction–rejection relationships between the Lord, the people of Israel, and Moses, the leader who 'referees' between a demanding God on the one hand, and the collective, variegated and socially stratified Israelites, on the other. The term 'dramatic' has often been used as an adjective accurately applied to the myth of the Exodus from Egypt, and the forty years of wandering in the desert, during which a free nation was supposed to be forged. The question presented in this chapter, however, is whether an approach using the more specific and medium-oriented tool of 'theatrical metaphor' in this indeed dramatic relationship will contribute to a better understanding of the text.

The plot in Chapter 11 is organized along two main axes: one is the administrative–political, characterized in the chapter itself as 'flesh'; and the other is the religious and spiritual, characterized as 'Ruach', (both 'spirit' and 'wind' in Hebrew). 'Flesh' is poetically closely associated with physical needs and includes social, economic and political issues. In the following reading, it refers to the administrative, secular matters of leading a great group of people. The other element, equally prevalent in Chapter 11 is Spirit, which is associated with faith in general and with the particular religious belief in the Lord God of the Hebrews. I contend that both axes behave like parallel lines which meet, as mathematicians claim, in infinity.

Chapter 11 in *Numbers* can hence be regarded as following the biblical line of Holy Performances, like Samuel's initiation, Ezekiel's 'shows', and Daniel's visions. In this chapter, God conceives, directs and partly participates in the 'performance', in order to bridge the abysmal gap between Flesh and Spirit. He creates a holy theatrical 'show', designed to help Moses in leading the Israelites. The climax of the conflict between Spirit and Flesh is the collective initiation scene, in which God takes "some of the spirit that was on him [Moses] and put it on the seventy elders" (11:25).

Treated and analyzed as an independent dramatic unit, the structure of the chapter, together with the characters' actions and the leitmotifs, are regarded as metaphoric to the overall meaning. This meaning, epitomized in Moses' wish, is expressed in the words "Would that all the Lord's people were prophets" (11:29). These words are spoken at the climax of the plot. Since the Lord's people are indeed not all prophets, one of the chapter's messages seems, consequently, to be to refrain from harnessing the Spiritual horses to the chariot of Flesh in the way that Joshua, for one, had erroneously proposed. A true spiritual experience, like the divine initiation of the seventy elders, must be considered self-evident, and does not need any external proof beyond itself (and the faith in God). Nevertheless, a crucial problem in this text still remains: namely, whether the divine spirit can at all ever be harnessed to the everyday, non-spiritual issues of life.

Theatre often tries to link 'Spirit' and 'Flesh', and this particular kind of Holy Theatre attempts to bridge these two different aspects of reality. The chapter can conveniently be considered 'theatrical', because it uses space, characters, special effects and dialogues as well as dramatic structure to enhance its meaning. At the same time, it presents its own theatrical devices as means to an end, not as the end itself. The Israelite audience, however, does not appear to fully comprehend the message, or perhaps is unable to sustain its practical ramifications for very long. Neither does Joshua. Only Moses is presented as undergoing a major change.

As in the previous chapters of *Numbers*, here too Moses the leader is stuck between the sinning, complaining people, and God who punishes them.[1] In the conflictual dramatic circumstances of this chapter, Moses serves as the human bridge between the Spirit and the Flesh, performing his duties and beliefs in a theatrical balancing act. He can be regarded as the human stage in/on which the conflict is performed, and the only character to undergo a change.

Structure

The opening verses (11:1–3) describe a condensed series of events that serve as a model not only for the more detailed story to come, but also for the interrelationships between God, Moses and the Israelites during the 40 years in the desert. The opening contains elements of plot and the nucleus of structure and characters, which will be fully developed later on in the people's voyage from physical and spiritual slavery in Egypt to freedom and independence in the Promised Land. The exposition is divided into five distinct parts and anticipates the events of the whole chapter, setting-up the typical dynamics of:

Sin → Punishment → Mediation → Forgiveness → Summary

1 The (Israelites') Sin: "Now when the people were (as though), complaining in the hearing of the Lord."
2 The (Lord's) Punishment: "The Lord heard it and his anger was kindled. Then the fire of the Lord burned against them, and consumed some outlying parts of the camp."
3 (Moses') Mediation: "But the people cried out to Moses, and Moses prayed to the Lord . . ."
4 Lifting the Punishment: " . . . and the fire abated."
5 Summary: "So that place was called Taberah [Fire], because the fire of the Lord burnt against them."

The opening of the main plot (11:4–5) differs from the exposition in two points. Now not only 'the people' express a general complaint, but 'the rabble' among the people (*bekirbo*) have a 'strong craving' too. The complaint is perceived by the writer as sinful, albeit unspecified, but the explanation follows immediately. It is the sin of craving for meat (or 'Flesh'), which enhances the dramatic tension. Such a craving is a vice, worse than sheer complaining, as it is associated with slavery and materialism. As explicitly stated only toward the end, it is indeed a double sin: that of craving for meat as well as that of rejecting manna, the 'divine' food.

The Israelite people join the rabble, and they "wept again and said, 'who will feed us meat?' (the Hebrew for both 'flesh' and 'meat' is '*Bassar*'). We remember the fish we used to eat in Egypt for nothing, the cucumbers, the melons, the leeks, the onions, and the garlic; but now our soul (strength) is dried up, and there is nothing at all but this manna to look at." With the "As though complaining" of the exposition having been punished severely with fire, one wonders what punishment will follow this sin.

Meat, mentioned here for the first time, will gain in its metaphoric suggestiveness. It is gradually perceived not only as food from living animals, but a metonym for the food they maintain they had been given 'free' in Egypt. The text supplies an excessively long list of food the Israelites claimed to have eaten there. Such an overly detailed list of trifles is often indicative of the typically biblical ironic literary device of redundancy. Lists are based on material quantity, and here the lists function as a negative corrective to the desired qualitative element – the spirit.

Moreover, in claiming that food was given free in Egypt, the complaining Israelites forget that they had earned their food by working as slaves. Meat is therefore the price for both physical and spiritual slavery. Manna, on the other hand, is God's food, given to a people released from slavery.

Since manna is mockingly rejected in the people's direct speech (11:6) the playwright makes a special effort to correct the wrong impression and explain the real facts to the people: "Now the manna was like coriander seed, and its color was like the color of gum resin. The people went around and gathered it, ground it in mills or beat it on mortars, then boiled it in pots and made cakes of it; and the taste of it was like the taste of cakes baked with oil. When the dew fell on the camp in the night, the manna would fall with it."

The surprisingly long description of manna serves a number of purposes. It serves as a dramatic 'ritardando', slowing the pace of the action the (expected) next emotional eruption. The previous false impression of manna as "we have nothing save this manna to look to", is rectified with a qualitative rather than quantitative description. Whereas the people make a list of the kinds of (trivial) foods they had had in Egypt, the author, siding with, and indded creating, the spiritual approach in the text, indulges in a truly poetic repartee, turning the manna, like 'meat', into a metaphor. The manna is depicted with a richly imaginative language, as having great visual beauty (like coriander, gum resin, or crystal). It is collected in an idyllic way (*shatu*, for instance, means 'floated around'). Moreover, the culinary possibilities of preparing manna are varied, tasty and (should be) satisfying. The Hebrew emphasizes even the musical quality of this food through the soft alliterative L sound in "*ha'tall 'al . . . laila . . . 'alav*", drawing attention to freshness, softness, etc. ("When the dew fell on the camp in the night, the manna would fall with it.") 'Spiritual' food is presented as a qualitative, refined pleasure for all the senses (not necessarily a paradox in this context), a slow, conscious way of consuming it; rather than the indistinct craving, of grabbing quantities of meat.

Interestingly, when recalling the kinds of food they had had in Egypt, the Israelites do not mention meat. The depiction of manna is inserted in the text as an independent scene, reinforcing the spiritual, elevated meaning of manna versus fish, melons, onions, etc., and proving that the complainers were doubly wrong. The people, as the text clarifies, prefer large quantities of their slavery's bad quality fast-food, and reject the carefully prepared quality of the good food of freedom. The text moves from 'as though complaining' to 'craving', then to 'crying' before undergoing a change in ambience with one of the most ironic and longest descriptions of food in the Bible, which must be understood as referring to something much more than simply physical food. Regarded as offstage stage-properties, both manna and meat are highly effective.

In the next scene, "Moses heard the people weeping throughout their families, each one at the entrance of the tent". The tension, built upon the pattern of the opening exposition lines, is rising, and soon expressed: "Then the Lord became very angry, and Moses was displeased." God's anger can be understood from the previous verses. His chosen people have rejected his gift of manna. The term used is *'va'yihar appo'*. The Hebrew *'aff'* (literally – nose) is often connected with emotions like anger and disgust; especially in this particular text. It was also 'bad' in the eyes of Moses (or 'he was displeased'). God is presented as unequivocally angry, but Moses' task is more complicated. He too is grieved with the religious as well as social implications of the people's complaints. But as a human, he probably understood (without justifying them) why the people were sick and tired of manna. Knowing God's ways, he is also profoundly worried about the expected punishment his people will receive. The repeated expression used to describe the Israelites is 'crying', which is suggestive of a childish demeanour. The drama in/of the text is portrayed as a family affair, with the typical mix of intimacy and intensity such relations imply. The family metaphor will soon become explicit in the text.

> "So Moses said to the Lord:
> 'Why have you treated your servant so badly? [Same verb as in "In Moses' eyes it was bad"!] Why have I not found favour in your eyes, ["Eyes," too, have just been used – Moses' eyes] that you lay the burden of all this people on me? Did I conceive all this people? Did I give birth to them, that you should say to me, 'Carry them in your bosom, as a nurse carries a sucking baby on the land that you promised on oath to their ancestors? Where am I to get meat to give to all this people? For they come weeping to me and say, 'give us meat to eat!' I am not able to carry all those people alone, for they are too heavy for me. If this is the way you are going to treat me, put me to death at once – if I have found favour in your eyes – and do not let me see my misery."

As verse 10 says, Moses 'heard' and it was bad in his 'eyes'. The text uses two senses, suggesting that all of Moses' senses were offended. His entire speech is a monologue of a profoundly hurt person, exquisitely substantiated with a masterfully sensual, very physical body-metaphor rhetoric. He appears totally honest in being torn between the materiality of the people and the spirituality of God, between the people's humanly understandable (and half-justified, from their point-of-view, at least) needs, complaints, weeping and crying; and God's acknowledged absolute justice and still restrained wrath. The theatricality of this text ensues not only from this highly dramatic conflict. It is also prevalent in Moses' excruciating situation of utterly identifying with what he says, and at the same time 'playing it out' to God.

Moses begins his monologue with a series of questions, rhetorically intended to place God, the listening partner, on the defensive. Emotional statements like "Why have you treated your servant so badly?" or "Why have I not found favor in your eyes?" are sophisticatedly aimed at transforming the feared divine wrath into a purely personal matter, primarily concerning the speaker Moses himself. At the same time, Moses takes upon himself the sins of the people. In fact, he attempts to neutralize God's punishment by shifting the matter onto himself, by internalizing the issue at stake and presenting it as his own (perfectly justified!) axe to grind with God. Rhetorically, it is not the people's sinful complaints that must be dealt with, but Moses' own situation of being crushed down under the weight of leading the Israelites, against his initial wishes, but nonetheless complying with God's command to serve as leader. Truthfully, painfully but smartly too, Moses changes the (still unmentioned!) real subject.

However, in his speech even Moses is caught up in the sin of being overly 'fleshly'. His superbly theatrical images are primarily body-metaphors. After God and Moses' ears and eyes have been mentioned, Moses continues with his whole body breaking under "the burden of all this people on me". The images become not only more daring, but replete with a beautifully feminine mixture of softness and suffering: "Did I conceive all this people? Did I give birth to them, that you should say to me, 'Carry them in your bosom, as a (male!) nurse carries a sucking baby . . .'" It is relatively rare to find in the Bible such images spoken by a man, and not as a public prophesy, but in exclusive intimacy with God. Having exhausted the womanly metaphors, Moses adds: "on the land that you promised on oath to their ancestors?" 'Fathers' is the word used in the original, as though Moses is taken aback by his own imaginative daring. However, the female metaphor receives an added suggestive power because it is stated in the interrogative, verging on the negative implications. Nevertheless, because of this particular phrasing, Moses is felt to be closer to the people he wants, metaphorically, to push away from his womb and his breasts. On the other hand, he is felt to be more estranged from them, when he uses the male image of the nurse, in the masculine form, and especially the term 'their fathers'. He emphasizes 'their' rather than 'our' fathers. This rhetoric device reinforces the spiritual–material rift in Moses' situation, who uses a highly physical imagery to express the plights of soul and spirit.

He now turns to the issue at stake, meat, also expressed in a question form: "Where am I to get meat to give to all this people? For they come weeping to me and say, 'give us meat to eat!'" Moses suffers from not being able to supply the people's demand for material, administrative, political 'meat', and real simple meat too; not yet realizing (or too modest to realize, as the text tells of him in 12:3) that there is still something that he is able to give. It is God who must tell him so.

"I am not able to carry all this people alone, for they are too heavy for me. If this is the way you are going to treat me, put me to death at once – if I have found favor in your eyes – and do not let me see my misery." His final words express his utter misery, but also present a superb, because true, emotional blackmail. God has no better leader for His people than Moses. And both seem to know it. Moses' speech begins with "bad" and ends with 'bad' – "Why have you treated your servant so badly", and "do not let me see my misery" – literally 'my "badness".' The monologue is an authentic, yet well-designed outburst of an exhausted leader, torn between the burden of his impossible mission, and his responsibility for it. As a resignation speech it is masterful.

God does not reprimand Moses for threatening to resign. In the dialogue between them (11:16–20), God too becomes very emotional. The subject of discussion is the people, dramatically a third, problematic party, quoted by both God and Moses and thus made vicariously present in their absence. In his divine wisdom, God gives a two-step solution to the problem. The first is primarily designed to help Moses with his problems of leadership; while the second step will solve the people's desire for meat. The two steps are tightly interrelated, but it is only in the second solution, which directly concerns the people, that God expresses his so-far hidden wrath with pointed sarcasm.

"Gather for me seventy of the elders of Israel, whom you know to be the elders of the people and officers over them; take them to the tent of meeting, and let them present themselves there with you. I will come down and talk with you there; and I will take from the spirit that is on you and put it on them; and they shall bear the burden of the people along with you so that you will not bear it all by yourself."

From a secular perspective, God is using a nowadays familiar technique of business and leadership management: delegation of authority, for the sake of greater efficiency. Indeed, God is convinced that one man alone cannot carry the heavy weight of responsibility and intense emotion. But this profoundly religious text is best served and explicated according to its own intentions. Instead of giving to Moses, God seems to be taking something away from him – his spirit. From a spiritual perspective, however, spirit is not of course quantifiable, whereas meat is. In taking from Moses 'from the spirit that is on' him, Moses himself will not suffer any loss of spirit, though the elders shall have 'more'. The laws of the spirit are categorically different from the laws of material 'meat'. God plans a

Holy Theatre show in the tent of meeting, a public act of spiritual initiation, intended for the chosen seventy elders. Moses will be the leading
actor, while God, in his typical semi-offstage appearance as the director
and the designer, will cause Moses' spirit to emanate upon the elders.

The link between the spiritual and the material is found in God's next
words: "And say to the people: 'Consecrate yourselves for tomorrow, and
you shall eat meat'." Even the Almighty admits (ironically?) that the
people need meat. However, God raises the eating of meat to His level. If
the people of Israel had been as spiritually advanced as God wants them
to be, the whole issue would not have come up in the first place. The
planned show is hence intended as a bridge between Flesh and Spirit.
Moses will later relate to this crucially important issue by saying, "Would
that all the Lord's people were prophets".

The next step in the Lord's plan concerns the people directly: "for you
have wailed in the hearing [ears] of the Lord, saying, 'Who will feed us
meat to eat! Surely it was better for us in Egypt'." Any unbiased reading
of this text discloses God's truly personal sense of insult, his disappoint-
ment and anger too. Dramatically (at least), He too, like Moses before
him, indulges in a highly emotional repartee. Having rightly diagnosed
the problem, he continues to use sarcastic redundancy: "Therefore the
Lord will give you meat, and you shall eat. You shall eat not only one day,
or two days, or five days, or ten days, or twenty days, but for a whole
month—until it comes out of your nose and becomes loathsome to you –
because you have rejected the Lord who is among you, and have wailed
before him, saying, 'Why did we ever leave Egypt?'" Realizing that the
masses (in contradistinction to the elders, who will be endowed with
spirit) cannot be made more spiritual (i.e., 'free') than they already are,
God decides to re-apply his characteristic educational methods: "If indeed
you want meat, meat it is you shall be given." The word 'meat' appears
once when it is mentioned for the first time by the people in 11:4. It
appears twice in Moses' speech, once as quoting the people and once in
his own name, in 11:13. Meat appears for the third time three times in
God's speech, in 11:18. The repetitive accelerated accumulation endows
the word with extra significance. And the divine frustration is expressed
in the deliberately fatiguing repetition of how long the people shall eat
meat, as a means of ridiculing the quantitative aspect.

Only the original Hebrew style fully expresses God's profoundly
sarcastic monologue. For example, the idiomatic expression 'comes out
of your nose' is synonymous with 'rejecting God' (*me'astem et . . .*) Hence
the punishment is not only commensurate with the sin but indeed will
prove to ensue from it, and be almost identical with it. God recognizes the
limitations of his own omnipotence, since true freedom cannot be imposed

without being destroyed. It must come from within. In shifting the responsibility back to the complainers, God forces the people to learn the consequences of their rejections of Him – from within. By the same exegetical token the word '*bekirbechem*' (in your midst, or in your entrails), which frequently appears in different contexts, also links the spiritual with the material, 'fleshly' and bodily connotation.

Moses is not convinced: "The people I am with number six hundred thousand on foot; and you say, 'I will give them meat, that they may eat for a whole month!' Are there enough flock and herds to slaughter for them? Are there enough fish in the sea to catch for them?" Genuinely despairing or still playing hard to appease, Moses nevertheless commits the sin of material quantification, in re-mentioning fish and meat, though to a lesser degree than the people. Here again Moses, inadvertently perhaps, admits how closely he is related to his people, in whose midst he sees himself (*bekirbo*), In this sense, he may be even closer to the people than the nominal value of the previous parent-metaphor suggests. Moreover, in doubting God's ability to feed the people, Moses in fact sins. The dialogue elaborately presents the main standpoints of Moses and God in longish monologues, while toward the end the lines allocated to each speaker become shorter. God finishes the bitter discussion with a promise that deeds, not words, are finally what counts: 'Is the Lord's power limited?' (literally: "Is the Lord's hand too short?") "Now you shall see whether my word will come true for you or not."

The sensitive reader may detect a slight impatience in God's words, but dramatically these words push the plot forwards to the initiation performance: "So Moses went out (which suggests that his conversation with God took place in the meeting tent) and told the people the words of the Lord; and he gathered seventy elders of the people, and placed them all around the tent. Then the Lord came down in a (very impressive) cloud and spoke to him, and took of the spirit that was on him and put it on the seventy elders; and when the spirit rested upon them, they prophesied. But they did not do so again." This effective public, collective initiation is first reported to the people, then performed out of their sight, in the tent (or, perhaps, as other interpreters suggest 'around the tent' and outside). In matters of spirit, there seems to be an economy, untypical in comparison with disgusting abundance of meat.

The Eldad and Medad scene (11:26–29), focuses on the religious–political ramifications of the Spirit–Flesh issue in a condensed, dramatically most effective way. These two men "were among those registered, but they had not gone out to the tent, but prophesied in the camp", at some distance from the seventy. However, the text specifies that the Lord's spirit rested on them too. A question arises regarding the numbers 70 and 2.

Were Eldad and Medad among the 70 chosen elders, or would the elders, with them, number 72, a number which divides well into the 12 tribes, six men representing each. However, this point is left vague, whereas the out of boundaries prophesy of these two men most certainly lies at the center of the plot.

"And a young man ran and told Moses, 'Eldad and Medad are prophesying in the camp'." The young man's running rather than walking indicates that he (like Joshua) considered the event highly suspicious, if not outrageous. Though he reports only the facts alone, the implication is 'Mutiny'. Hurrying to report Eldad and Medad to Moses, the text indulges in another 'riterdando' in explaining that "Joshua son of Nun, the assistant of Moses, one of his chosen men", is also there with Moses, as his most faithful follower. Without giving Moses time to react, as at least a token of respect for his leader, the alarmed younger leader Joshua immediately intervenes. Obviously shocked by the news, he abruptly says: "My Lord Moses, lock'em up!" His reaction clearly explains that the elders (represented by Joshua) as well as the people (represented by the running young man) considered Eldad and Medad's prophesying as a political rebellion in religious disguise. Even if regarded as a purely religious affair, it is nonetheless totally improper, because it is only in the tent of meeting that one is, allegedly, allowed to prophesy.

The young man's report is a particularly tense theatrical moment. At the climax of the public initiation, a religious experience shared by the seventy chosen, charged with the numinous appearance of the Lord in the cloud, the lad breaks in, telling of a rival divine revelation. Eldad and Medad's prophesying has taken place elsewhere, and before people who, though registered, are 'not here,' 'not with us,' and 'not in the proper place'. At this moment, tense with the conflict between the religious experience and its political–administrative ramifications, Moses reveals his wisdom, his magnanimous character and his truly great leadership: "Are you jealous for my sake? Would that all the Lord's people were prophets, and that the Lord would put his spirit on them!"

His first words, "Are you jealous for my sake?", phrased as a rhetorical question, serve as an ironic answer to Joshua's advice to jail the rebels. The implication is clear that God's spirit must not be treated as a material, quantifiable element. Spirituality can, and indeed must, be shared. Moses thus gives an answer to two questions: is it forbidden to 'prophesy' without an authorization; and is it forbidden to prophesy in the 'wrong' space? Under the pressing circumstances of the Israelites' constant complaining, and the danger of losing control of leadership, Moses still claims that spiritual issues must not be harnessed to the political matters of secular administration, efficient as this may seem to be. Moses distinguishes the essential difference between the very revelation of the spiritual emanation, on the one hand, and the potential social function – or worse – manipulation of this revelation, on the other hand.[2] The initial relationships between administrative and religious issues are highly precarious in this, and other chapters. However, Moses draws a clear line between the intrinsic value of both elements. Nobody had suffered more than himself from the materialistic, 'fleshly' ramifications of the complaining people. He could have easily jailed Eldad and Medad, strengthened his control over the people and thus contributed to centralizing his exclusive rule. At that particularly dramatic moment, the *'peripeteia'* occurs, and the leader recognizes that the significance of God's revelation in a cloud and the emanation of spirit is not an emanation of power in the political sense alone.

Poetically, we discern the scenic space as the Tent of Meeting, but the real 'stage' and actual location of the theatrical shift between matter and spirit is Moses' soul. Hence, Eldad and Medad's 'private show' finally serves to enhance the true meaning of spirituality in this particularly complex context. Dialectically, the importance of the Meeting Tent – the holy location – is diminished as soon as the a-spatial nature of the spiritual message is correctly understood. The stage, theatrically and metaphorically, proves to be a means, not an end in itself. The initiation scene indicates that it is the offstage divine force that is the only essential element.

12

Jehu's Bloody Show

The history of Jehu's rise to power is portrayed in II *Kings* 9–10 in a series of ten scenes, replete with fascinating characters, witty dialogues, fast shifts and a bloody plot. Regarded as a play, the piece also contains a conflict between politics and religion, tinged with perceptible signs of the biblical playwright's discomfort. Part of the background for the coming events is revealed in the first chapters of II *Kings*, in the detailed description of the prophet Elisha's many miracles. Elisha is deeply involved in the political milieu of the period, ridden by wars and hunger. Jehu's character and rise to power develop from a mixture of actual deprivation and religious miracles. He receives Elisha's support in advance, and the Bible's Jahvistic blessing after the fact, in annihilating the House of Ahab together with the priests of Baal. Between the background supplied in the opening scene (II *Kings* 8:25–29) and the final remarks (10:31–36) are ten other distinct scenes of constant bloodshed, murder and deceit in a consistent, gradual take-over of power. The biblical play deals primarily with the first part of Jehu's 28 years of rule.

1 Background (Prologue, 8:25–29)
The text states the political background: Joram son of Ahab is king of Israel, Ahaziah, son of Jehoram and of Athaliah, herself a daughter of Omri, king of Israel are blood-related and political allies. The two kings wage war against Hazael king of Aram. Joram is wounded, returns to Jezreel to be healed, and Ahaziah comes to pay him a visit. Characteristic of *Kings*, in which political issues are always regarded as closely related to the kings' religious behavior, the text indicates that the Judean king Ahaziah "also walked in the way of the house of Ahab, doing what was evil in the sight of the Lord".

2 Elisha sends a messenger (9:1–3)
Elisha, who has already been frequently mentioned, summons one of the members of the company of prophets, gives him a flask of oil, and tells

him to 'gird up' his loins, suggesting that this man's task is a complicated and perhaps a dangerous mission. Instead of going himself, as Samuel had gone to anoint David, Elisha sends a messenger with a definite religious affiliation (a young prophet), to anoint Jehu, son of Nimshi, as the next king. In his instructions, Elisha adds: "Go in and get him to leave his companions ('raise him from among his brethren') and take him into an inner chamber (a 'chamber within a chamber'). Then take the flask of oil, pour it on his head, and say, 'Thus says the Lord: I anoint you king over Israel.' Then open the door and flee; do not linger."

Elisha must have been aware of the political situation just described, in which the wounded and weak king of Israel and the king of Judah are together and (we assume) not far away from his own dwelling on Mount Carmel. Jehu, so far an unknown but high-ranking officer from Ramot-gilead, not too far to the east, is chosen by the prophet to be the usurper. He will, moreover, soon emerge as one of the most interesting biblical characters. Elisha plans, in fact directs, the forthcoming usurpation in a highly dramatic way: abrupt, secretive and unexplained. His oral instructions emphasize the ritual deeds over the few explanatory words to be uttered. The young prophet messenger is supposed to enter, seek out Jehu, get him into an inside room and pour the oil on his head, saying (only?) "Thus says the Lord: I anoint you king over Israel", and then flee. Elisha chose to send a messenger rather than officiating over the anointment himself, as Samuel had done for David, thinking, perhaps, that if the coup failed he could then disclaim any responsibility. An anonymous messenger would draw less attention than he himself, as a famous public figure with contacts even with foreign kings (8:7–15; for example). However, the Hebrew is ambiguous: It can mean 'leave his companions' so that the messenger can perform the anointing in privacy, but it can also indicate 'raise him' or 'make him stand-up' from among his brothers, suggesting a well-planned revolution based and backed up by a whole clique of armed and powerful military people. In the Bible, messengers rarely do exactly what they are ordered to do, relating instead to the specificity of each situation. This messenger, too, carries out Elisha's orders, but in his own fashion. An added dramatic tension is revealed between the plan and its actual performance.

3 The messenger appoints Jehu (9:4–10)

Upon entering (the military headquarters?) the messenger sees a seated group of commanders. Not knowing who Jehu is, but fully justifying Elisha's faith in him, he cleverly addresses the entire group with the unfocused appeal: "I have a message for you, (The) commander." The unsuspecting Jehu is the one to reply with the question: "For which one of all of us?" The subtle tactic proves successful, and Jehu immediately reveals that he considers himself to be *The* commander, which he may or may not indeed have been, but modesty has clearly never been his main virtue. His "For which one of all of us?" shows a certain amount of caution nonetheless. The young prophet, now certain who his real addressee is, says: "For you, commander." Jehu "got up and went inside" where the young man "poured the oil on his head". However, instead of a twelve-word message, the messenger indulges in a relatively long and detailed monologue, addressed to an oil-dripping, perhaps slightly bewildered Jehu. The speech is a masterpiece of rhetorical religious–political incitement. It elaborates on Elisha's "I anoint you king over Israel" with "I anoint you king over the people of the Lord, over Israel". Jehu, at the very moment of this totally unexpected event, is in the same breath reminded of the divine power that is thus enthroning him. A religious motivation prevails in the next verses as well, including the messenger's own interests. Ahab had persecuted this young man's 'company of prophets'. Jehu is henceforth obliged to follow God's ways. Having obviously been oppressed by Ahab, a king who did his best not to follow God's ways, the messenger is quick to add: "You shall strike down the house of your master Ahab . . ." – really grinding the message into Jehu, who was serving under Ahab with the intention of provoking the desired vindictive effect. Master–slave relationships constitute an important motif in the drama. Jezebel is mentioned twice, Ahab – four times. Jehu is meant to become God's tool of vengeance in destroying their whole house. While Elisha is not physically present, it may be assumed that Jehu suspected who was pulling the string behind the scene. He thus treats the messenger too with due respect, especially since the message he has delivered is the greatest honor any Israelite is likely to ever receive. Nevertheless, between Jehu's possible ambition and his potential new status, there still lies a silence.

4 Jehu is crowned (9:11–13)

The young messenger of the 'company of prophets' (*bnei ha'nevi'im*) is not perceived as dangerous, either before or after speaking to Jehu. When Jehu comes out, the other officers, intentionally described as 'his master's servants', ask him: "Is everything all right? Why did that madman come to you?" The officers' attitude to the prophet as a madman is not untypical for military men toward religious fanatics.

They also use the natural term '*shalom*' in their question. This innocent term meaning 'peace', will gradually gain a superbly ironic significance throughout the drama, and become a subtle mode of criticizing Jehu's actions, which are anything but peaceful. After his encounter with the young prophet, Jehu might have first wiped away the oil from his head before rejoining the other officers. The text does not specify the purpose of the officers' meeting, which could even have been a conspiracy to begin with. However, the insert "his masters' servants" does not substantiate this assumption, despite Elisha possibly having suspected this to be the case. Perhaps some of the officers saw traces of oil on Jehu's face; but they all noticed a change in his demeanour. Jehu, nevertheless, is evasive, perhaps because they continue to behave as Ahab's servants. "He answered them: 'You know the sort and how they babble'." They remain unconvinced, which in this context means that there was a noticeable discrepancy between Jehu's response and his body language, and certainly *vis-à-vis* the strangeness of the initial situation. As Jehu's peers and buddies they allow themselves the rude soldierly: "(It is a) Lie! Come on, tell us!" (in modern colloquial English: 'Stop bullshitting!'). It is noteworthy that the biblical text here gets unusually close to ancient Hebrew slang, thus establishing through the style of language the cordial and friendly relationships between Jehu and his clique. Once they learn that he has been anointed, however, they will never again say 'Lie!' to him.

Unable to avoid his friends, Jehu must now tell them what had really happened: "This is just what he said to me: 'Thus says the Lord, I anoint you king over Israel'." Jehu uses the original words of Elisha, and does not repeat the more detailed speech of the messenger. The subtext may mean that Jehu relies on the divine calling ("Thus says the Lord . . ."), rather than on the political, totally explicit ramifications of the message. In this situation he continues to play safe, carefully examining his friends' next moves.

"Then hurriedly they all took their cloaks and spread them for him on the bare steps; and they blew the horn, and proclaimed, 'Jehu is king'." This splendidly theatrical act paves Jehu's first steps, literally and metaphorically. Costume, music and movement work together in Jehu's 'homecoming' crowning. However, since biblical texts must be regarded in their entirety, the perceptive observer is invited, in an assumed retrospective, to interpret Jehu's ascent with a touch of suspicion. At present he is treading only on clothes, later on he will tread on what is in them – human bodies. Jehu accepts his appointment without any hesitation or doubt; his friends are with him.

5 Coup d'Etat (9:14–28)

This scene elaborates on the prologue and explains that King Joram is indeed in the same place as Jehu, on guard in Ramot-gilead against Hazael's attack. As a usurper, made king by his peers, Jehu's conspiracy against Joram is already an actual fact, which, Joram, still recovering in

Jezreel from his injury, does not as yet know. Jehu must calculate his steps with extreme care if he is to ensure the mutiny's success and not lose his newly gained kingdom: "If this is your wish, then let no one slip out of the city to go and tell the news in Jezreel." Clearly implied in this message to his followers is: "if indeed you want me as king – not that I am necessarily interested – then . . . ." In this way, which Jehu will develop into an overall strategy, he forces all the other officers to actively collaborate and share the responsibility with him. Jehu's style is friendly, diplomatic and politically astute.

Jehu also knows that there are two, not just one, royal birds to be caught in Jezreel. Whereas the previous scene took place in a room, then in a 'room within a room', this one takes the rebellion out into the open field, geographically and publicly. The shift from the ritual act of crowning Jehu to the actual seizing of power is the focus of the scene, portrayed with great detail as well as with a wonderful sense of drama. The action not only takes place out in the open field, but employs the fast and aggressive 'location' of the war chariots. Resolutely sweeping movement will hence characterize Jehu's military and political strategy as well as his idiosyncratic and violent tactics in gaining power.

"Then Jehu rode ('mounted his chariot') and went to Jezreel . . ." The playwright rapidly shifts from the ominously advancing troops to King Joram and his camp. There, "a sentinel standing on the tower saw the multitude of Jehu's company arriving, and said: 'I see a multitude [of armies]'." The wounded Joram, obviously greatly disquieted, sends a horseman with the single (Hebrew) word "Is it peace?" as a message, perhaps as an early attempt to negotiate with the unknown intentions of the approaching multitude.

> "Horseman [once near Jehu]: 'Thus says the king: 'Is it peace?'"
> Jehu: What have you to do with peace? Fall in behind me."

The sentinel in Jezreel reports what he has seen from afar to Joram: "The messenger reached them, but he is not coming back." Tension is building up in the fast shifts between realization dawning upon the static Joram, and the swift assured approach of Jehu.[1] Jehu symbolically 'annexes' the Israeli king's horseman to his own forces, which, in turn, and through the highly theatrical report of the sentinel, not only threatens Joram but humiliates him too. The laconic *shalom* serves as the ironic key word. Jehu's command to the messenger, 'Fall in behind me' is yet another anticipatory remark, foreshadowing the many other people who will soon follow behind the new and relentless ruler (who is revealing a fair degree of dark and harsh military humor.)

A repeat performance occurs with the second horseman that Joram sends to Jehu; except that a recurrence of the 'same' event is never really the same. Now the sentinel adds: "It looks like the driving (in Hebrew also 'the habit') of Jehu son of Nimshi, for he drives like a maniac."[2] With exquisite irony, the biblical playwright allows himself for the second time to use the term 'mad' ('crazy,' 'maniac'); in relation to Jehu. The Hebrew (*shiga'on*) leaves the word ambiguously open, suggesting both a dare-devil mode of driving a chariot, and Jehu's general 'crazy' behavior. Both possible meanings, when reported by the sentinel, clearly have their impact on Joram. This supports Sternberg's notion on the complex nature of biblical modes of characterization.[3]

Back in Jezreel again, Joram commands "Get ready" (or 'harness!') – and "they got his chariot ready". Joram, perhaps afraid to meet Jehu alone, is joined by Ahaziah, king of Judah, "each in his chariot . . . they found him at the property of Naboth the Jezreelite". Whether it was Jehu himself who chose this most significant location, or whether it was the playwright who chose it as the killing field – from a political point of view there could have been no better place. The playwright maintains his omnisciently ironic and apparently objective superiority in indicating that King Ahaziah and King Joram 'found' Jehu – whereas it was clearly he who had trapped them.

Naboth's property is the epitome of King Ahab and his wife Jezebel's scene of horrendous social and religious crime. In planning to kill both kings (blood related to one another) there, Jehu will surely win the people's acclaim, at least that of those in the vicinity, who will support the rebellion.

King Joram addresses Jehu with the by now almost comic "Is it peace, Jehu?" Jehu replies: "What peace can there be, so long as the many whoredoms and sorceries of your mother Jezebel continue?" Jehu's characteristic style is to evade direct questions with his own questions, thus laying the responsibility for complete explicitness on his interlocuter(s). He, moreover, attacks Joram by insulting his mother. The political and religious ramifications of the insult may be the primary motivation, but Joram certainly takes the insult quite personally. Combining the personal with the political–religious aspects is yet another of Jehu's brilliant tactic.

Joram finally, but too late, fully understanding the situation, achieves *anagnorisis*; he "reined about and fled, saying to Ahaziah, 'Treason, Ahaziah!'" "Jehu drew his bow with all his strength, and shot Joram between the shoulders, so that the arrow pierced his heart; and he sank in his chariot", an exceptionally forceful and well-aimed shot indeed.

The action now focuses on Jehu, who characteristically turns to his adjutant Bidkar: "Lift him out and throw him on to the plot of ground belonging to Naboth the Jezreelite; for remember, when you and I rode side by side behind his father Ahab how the Lord uttered this oracle against him: 'For the blood of Naboth and for the blood of his children that I saw yesternight, says the Lord, I swear I will repay you on this very plot of ground.' Now therefore lift him out and throw him on the plot of ground, in accordance with the will of God."

This is Jehu's longest speech, and diplomatically a very revealing one, for Jehu's supporters and opponents alike. In the scene itself Bidkar is rightfully not given a single line. He is a silent listener in a political declaration of intent, thinly disguised as a conversation betgween old army buddies. The now silent Bidkar will, no doubt, deliver Jehu's words to all and sundry. In his words, uttered presumably over Joram's corpse, Jehu repeatedly links the (otherwise sinful) killing with the killed person's inherited crimes. Four times he emphasizes Naboth's property, and orders that the former king be thrown (rather than buried) on that very piece of land as a punishment commensurate with the crime. In this way he presents himself as simply carrying-out Elijah's prophesy (I *Kings* 21:17–26). Between the political and the religious aspects of the coup, Jehu maneuvers splendidly. He tells Bidkar of a vision he had last night, when he saw 'the blood of Naboth' and his children. This phrase ascribes to Jehu a somewhat unlikely (and retroactive!) capability of having visions. It is, under the circumstances, more feasible to assume that he concocts it as a moral (and biblically, perfectly acceptable) justification for his deeds, as ensuing from exclusively ethic–religious reasons. Equally smart is his comment to Bidkar: "Remember when you and I rode side by side behind his father . . ." The 'You and I' allude to the old soldiers' camaraderie that binds Jehu and Bidkar. It also reminds Bidkar of Elijah's words to Ahab, which they had both heard.

Jehu begins with the command to Bidkar to throw Joram's body on Naboth's ground, then he indulges in an explanation – perhaps because his adjutant was not too keen to perform the act, and finally, as a necessary QED, commands him again. Jehu, furthermore, uses the name of God three times, as a true or manipulated authorization: "The Lord uttered this oracle . . . I saw yesterday – by the name of the Lord . . . in accordance with the word of the Lord" (9:25–26). The speech may be regarded as Jehu's rapidly growing hubris, or else as that of a still weak man who is seeking divine justification for his deeds. Is he using the young prophet's words he had only recently heard? Is he using, ab- or mis-using a divine decree and divine visions for his own purposes; or is he truly a faithful (though bloody) servant of God? An interpretation favorable to Jehu would explain his speech as a gradual internalization of God's will. A less complimentary exegesis might rely on Jehu's own previous words about the young 'madman' prophet and explain his speech as a sophisticated manipulation, relying on the anticipated support he hopes to find in the religious centers of power, represented by the offstage Elisha.

At the end of this central scene (or in a separate one), Jehu pursues Ahaziah and has him killed too, although this time Jehu does not kill the king of Judah with his own hands. Unlike Joram, Ahaziah will at least be honored with a decent burial, in Jerusalem. The king of Judah is politically less important to Jehu, perhaps less 'unholy' than Joram and less associated with Ahab's crimes. Jehu, in fact, kills only one person with his own hands, becoming ever more successful in involving others in the long list of assassinations, and distributing the responsibility over as wide as possible a constituency. In other words, it is not God alone who will "put on him (Ahab's) this (moral) 'weight'" (9:25), but many less divine beings as well. This motif in Jehu's actions will soon become utterly explicit. In the meantime, however, there is another important personality to be disposed of – Queen Jezebel.

6 Killing Queen Jezebel (9:29–37)

Although Jehu is undoubtedly the protagonist of the drama, the play-wright pays full attention to secondary characters as well, like the young prophet messenger, and Joram, and especially to Jezebel, an exceptionally proud and powerful figure. Hearing that Jehu is about to come, Jezebel "painted her eyes, and adorned her head, and looked out of the window". Remembering Deborah's song "Out of the window she peered, the mother of Sisera gazed through the lattice", Jezebel's is a uniquely theatrical, costumed and made-up tour-de-force. Jezebel knows her son has been killed and that her fate will be no different. Rather than uselessly pleading for her life, the queen grandly prepares for her own inevitable death. Her behavior is strongly contrasted with that of many men in the play. Her arrogant presence of mind is truly impressive, even to Jehu himself, who is rendered speechless in response to her one resounding line "Is it peace, Zimri, murderer of his master?" This line, other than revealing Jezebel's character through the sheer nerve of the utterance itself, is at the same time a sophisticatedly complex allusion, designed to humiliate Jehu, as well as a wishful prophesy for his future regime. Like Jehu who (apparently) remembers Elijah's words to Ahab, an intertextual biblical allusion, Jezebel too refers to a known historical precedent. Elah, son of Baashah was murdered while drunk by Zimri his servant, who, furthermore, "destroyed all the house of Baashah" (I *Kings* 16:8–20). Zimri managed to reign for seven days only, because the people made Omri, commander of the army, king over Israel. Ahab himself was the son of Omri. Zimri, having watched Omri's army besiege his castle in Tirzah, entered the

citadel of the king's house, which he set alight with himself in it, and died."
All this and more is implied in Jezebel's sarcastic address to the
approaching Jehu. There is yet a further cynical allusion: the name of the
prophet who had delivered the message of doom to Baashah was also
Jehu. In her "Is it peace, Zimri, murderer of his master?" Jezebel is yet
one more person who uses '*shalom*' in addressing Jehu, this time in evident
derision. Her line makes comparison between Zimri and Jehu, in which
it is she who is besieged in the castle (like Zimri!) but suggesting an opposite interpretation, of which she seems also fully aware.

Jezebel's icy gall is cast down at the walking Jehu while she is (still
comfortably) sitting by the high window, far above him. Not only her
words, but the height difference between the interlocutors, not to mention
her womanhood, are a grievous insult to Jehu. Seen through her royal
eyes, he is no more than a rebellious lowly servant who might manage to
reign for a maximum of seven days. The castle window, moreover, constitutes the borderline between indoors and outdoors, representing the
enormous difference in status between the approaching man and the
seated woman.

Jehu "looked up to the window and said: 'Who is on my side?'" The
servants of the house, as knowledgeable as Jezebel concerning Jehu's latest
feats, and much more afraid than her, continue this scene with a mute,
short and intensely theatrical gaze, quite different from hers: "Two or
three eunuchs looked out at him." Laconically Jehu says one word:
"Drop'er," (or 'Throw her down') – and they do. Not only personally
satisfied because now she is literally down, Jehu has also begun to materialize Elijah's prophesy about the queen, "some of her blood spattered
on the wall and on the horses, which trampled her".

No further words spoil the stunningly effective non-verbal action. In
order to publicly manifest his unchallenged superiority, "Then he went
in, and ate and drank." Having made himself at home in his newly
conquered palace, Jehu can say "See to that cursed woman and bury her;
for she is a king's daughter." A ghastly contract is established between
Jehu's meal and Jezebel's torn corpse; as well as between her dismembered
skull, hands and feet and her careful make-up and coiffure. Jehu's words,
after his meal, perhaps pay his enemy a last minimal respect not given to
Joram, who was thrown on the field rather than buried. As the one and
only person in the entire story who had challenged him, at least verbally,
he probably respects her as a courageous, truly aristocratic enemy. His
gesture, however, comes too late, and the servants, highly impressed by
Jehu's handling of the queen, report that there is not much left of her to
be buried. He replies, with what could be seen as a steadily developing
sanctimoniousness: "This is the word of the Lord, which he spoke by his

servant Elijah the Tishbite, 'In the territory of Jezreel the dogs shall eat the flesh of Jezebel; the corpse of Jezebel shall be dung on the field in the territory of Jezreel, so that no one can say this is Jezebel'." Jehu, becoming ever more practised in the art of eulogizing over his enemies' bodies, again harnesses his deeds to religious motivations, according to which he himself is but an obedient tool in the hands of God and His prophets. He forgets to mention, or consciously ignores, Elisha's prophesy, delivered to him by the young prophet.

7   Jehu's letter to the elders of Ahab's House (10:1–6)

The next scene opens with the information that Ahab had seventy sons in Samaria. Jehu's next step is the letter he writes to the elders of the city, the guardians of the sons. Diplomatically he invites them, fairly, politely and in an almost friendly fashion to "select the son of your master who is the best qualified, set him on his father's throne, and fight for your master's house". As he also specifies, they have "chariots and horses, a fortified city and weapons". While appearing to admit his opponents' military superiority, Jehu could not have sent such a letter without being certain of his own greater chances. His evaluation of the situation is based upon the the fact that everybody knows he has already killed Joram, Jezebel and Ahaziah. It is also based on the clique of officers who support him, on the assured support of the religious Jahvistic establishment, and on a growing public support as well. The elders, 'utterly terrified', know that Jehu has already defeated two kings, and refuse to select a new king who will immediately have to enter upon a war with Jehu. They capitulate: "We are your servants; we will do anything you say. We will not make anyone king; do whatever you think right." Dramatically parallel to the two messengers Joram had sent him, Jehu sends a second letter, saying: "If you are on my side, and if you are ready to obey me, take the heads of your master's sons and come to me at Jezreel tomorrow at this time." Most of Jehu's direct orders have so far been clear: "Throw him on the plot", for Joram; "Shoot him too!" for Ahazia; and "Throw her down", for Jezebel/ All were perfectly unequivocal. But these were individual political assassinations. Later Jehu will give slightly euphemistic orders like "Take them alive!" about Ahaziah's "brethren" (or kin), only in order to have them slaughtered later. Seventy youngsters is yet another story.

Jehu had a peculiar sense of morbidly poetic humor. The letter contains a double ambiguity. Firstly, in stating that he is interested in the 'Heads', he may have meant the chief, most important aspirants to the throne. Secondly, Jehu did not mention the purpose for which he wants them "at the same time" on the next day. The elders may surely have guessed, yet nothing is explicit. The elders, hence, could have understood Jehu's letter as referring to a selected group of live princes, but 'utterly terrified' they chose to follow the vicious literal spirit, rather than the lenient and more poetic meaning of the diabolically ambiguous letter.

Before telling what the elders really do, the appalled playwright inserts a mock-naïve piece of information, the essence of which has already been given before, so that the repetition underscores to the elders' loyalty to their dead master and their enormous fear. Their deed, however, is an everlasting lesson in comparative atrocity – theirs and Jehu's: "Now the kings' sons, seventy persons, were with the leaders of the city, who were charged with their upbringing."

Once Jehu's letter reaches them, they do not waste a moment: "they took the king's sons and killed them, seventy persons [the author repeats again]; they put their heads in baskets and sent them to him at Jezreel."

The Jehu play excels in shifting its scenes between Jehu's space and location, and the spaces and locations of his opponents and victims. Scene shifts have included the killing of the kings, Jehu's entrance into Jezebel's palace, and now the shifts between the elders of Samaria and Jehu in Jezreel. The underlying motif, so well enhanced through the language of (theatrical . . .) space, is conquest and appropriation, of the living and the dead. Here Jehu turns the elders of Samaria into collaborators who, from the perspective of having actually slaughtered 'more', are bloodier than himself by far. Jehu killed an enemy. They have killed seventy innocent boys.

A messenger tells Jehu : "They have brought the heads of the king's sons", and he replies: "Lay them in two heaps at the entrance of the gate until the morning." Carefully he chooses the location, a place people must pass on their way in or out of town. Moreover, whoever passes there will not only see the seventy heads, but must indeed walk between them. Jehu hence proves to be not only theatrical, but a sophisticated director. In passing between two piles of decapitated heads, every passer-by becomes an accomplice-of-sorts to the crime, in sharing their space. One pile would have sufficed to make the townspeople see the heads. A pile on each side of the gate suggests very clearly that the way of and the way to Jehu is paved with 'heads'. But Jehu does not simply leave the heads to impress the onlookers without explanation. In the morning, once the main traffic has moved through the main gate, "he stood and said to the people: 'You are (just people) innocent. It was I who conspired against my master and killed him; but who struck down all these? Know then that there shall fall to the earth nothing of the word of the Lord, which the Lord spoke concerning the house of Ahab; for the Lord has done what he said through his servant Elijah'."

The opening of Jehu's speech is a verbal most unkindest cut of all, a brilliant rhetorical pseudo absolution of the people who have, in actual fact, already passed through seventy dead heads. The "You are just (or innocent)" can be both sincere and cynical. In the next line, Jehu openly, 'squarely' admits to his own responsibility for killing one person, King Joram. The third line is the most important, and presented as a (rhetorical) question: "Who struck down all these?" Questions demand answers, and invite the listeners to be more involved. Since Jehu's listeners had not killed the princes, the next reasonable step would be to ask who did. But Jehu does not elaborate. Instead he indulges again in the religious argument, and mentions Elijah's prophetic words regarding Ahab and his whole house. The bloodier Jehu's ascent to power, the more lucid his diplomatic tactics becomes. Not only has he frightened the elders of Ahab's house to the extent that they offer the princes' heads 'willingly' – he, moreover, rightly blames them, as willing accomplices to the deed. In other words: "What I did is morally much less blameworthy, both qualitatively and quantitatively."

Tyrants are always in dire need of collaborators, in fact they cannot rule without them, and Jehu is no exception. He began with making Bidkar an accomplice, moved on to the eunuchs who threw Jezebel down from the window, and has now smeared the Samaria elders' hands with blood. Henceforth they will not even squeak against him. Shakespeare may have learnt the rhetoric of Mark Antony's speech in *Julius Caesar* from II *Kings* 10:9–10.

The epilogue to this exceptionally gruesome scene is no comic relief either. "So Jehu killed all who were left of the house of Ahab in Jezreel" – showing that the playwright is still making him, not the elders, responsible – and adding a few more killings: "all his leaders, close friends, and priests, until he left no survivor." Broadening the cycle of obedient accomplices, who 'only carried out orders', Jehu not only purges his political enemies and any potential threat to his regime, at the same time he also establishes his rule upon a constantly widening circle of terrified murderers.

8 Jehu and the Heads of the Princes (10:7–11)

On his way to take over the main palace in Samaria, Jehu passes a place called Beth-Eked of the Shepherds (in Hebrew, "The House where Sheep are bound for Shearing"). The (incidental?) name of the location for this scene soon proves to be darkly ironic. Parallel to the annihilation of Ahab's entire house, Jehu, perhaps by pure chance, meets some people in Beth-Eked, and asks them: "Who are you?" They answer: "We are kin of Ahaziah, we have come down to visit the royal princes and the son of the queen mother." Obviously still unaware of their relatives' recent fate, they must have learned of Ahaziah's death. They do not mention the king himself or the queen – they may have heard of their deaths too. They probably do not recognize Jehu either. Perhaps they are on their way to pay their condolences at the late Joram's house, unsuspecting of the latest heads-in-the-baskets event. In addition to continuing the description of Jehu's path to absolute power, this scene functions to emphasize through contrast the difference between these 42 princes' innocence, and Jehu's mercilessly sophisticated conspiracy. This is substantiated by the princes' unsuspecting response to Jehu as well as by the place the playwright has chosen for their execution, like sheep.

Jehu said: "Take them alive." They take them and slaughter them at the pit of Beth-Eked, 42 in all, sparing none. Taking them alive prior to killing them can be interpreted as Jehu's tactics to avoid resistance until he can have them killed more safely.

9   Killing the Judean Princes (10:12–13)

"And he went from there" opens the next scene, suggesting that Jehu's drama is a political–religious (and personal) power-quest play. Each of the stations is marked with another heap of corpses, not just the officers' cloaks originally laid at Jehu's feet for him to ascend the stairs at Ramot-gilead. The way between the stations is the dramatically enhanced focus of this scene. Insofar as Jehu 'met' King Ahaziah's relatives, he now meets another person. Dramatically, again, the observer is curious to know whether this scene too will be as bloody as the others.

10   Jehu and Jehonadab on the chariot (10:14–17)

"When he left there, he met Jehonadab son of Rechab coming to meet him; he greeted him, and said to him: 'Is your heart as true to mine, as mine to yours?' He said, 'It is.' Jehu said, 'If it is, give me your hand.' So he gave him his hand. Jehu took him up with him into the chariot. He said, 'Come with me and see my zeal for the Lord.' So he had him ride in his chariot."

Jehonadab is one of the particularly zealous group of the Rechabites. They are a cast of extreme Nazirites who refrain from wine, do not have fields or seed, and live in tents (*Jeremiah* 35:6). Potentially they could well serve as an indispensable political aid to Jehu, supporting him from the ultra-religious sector. Jehonadab may even have made a special effort to meet Jehu, and offer his as yet unasked for help. We may assume that a new (and bloody) regime draws all kinds of extreme groups. Jehu, famous for his 'crazy driving', and/or general behavior, must prove to Jehonadab that he in fact is even crazier than supposed. The actual meeting takes place with Jehu on the chariot (driving fast as always), and Jehonadab walking. Jehu, as is his habit, gets straight to the point with his equally habitual questions. His (not surprisingly) cordial, even intimate appeal to Jehonadab can once again be explained as either premeditated emotional blackmail, or truly honest. For example, the word 'heart' appears three times in this highly political text. Murderers sometimes reveal a tendency to sentimentality, both because it is politically efficient, and because they may be devoid of real positive emotions. ('Heart' will be used again in God's praise to Jehu once the religious–political 'purification' is over.) Jehu's words seem to hit the zealous Jehonadab right between the eyes. Jehu has turned out to be an excellent sharpshooter, and not with his bow alone. His personal rhetoric often lets his partner's reply retrospectively illuminate the meaning of the initial appeal. Like in Chess, White moves first but Black determines the further development of the game. Placing both Jehu and Jehonadab on the same chariot is hence a charged metaphor.

The scene is methodically divided into a beautiful convergence of verbal and non-verbal acts. Jehonadab's answer agrees with Jehu's address, and the latter continues with "Give me your hand". The gesture is doubly functional. The giving of a hand was a well-known (performative–gestural) promise already in those days. It is, moreover, a practical, friendly means of lifting Jehonadab up to Jehu's physical and symbolic position on top of the chariot. The giving of the hand creates a bond of trust and a promise for the future. In the chariot, Jehu turns to his newly acquired ally, with a text befitting the religious zealot's own intentions. It means, subtextually, "I, Jehu, am at least as arduous in my zeal for the Lord." The stage instruction still leaves the spectator in the dark concerning the answer to the question who gave whom 'a lift'. The feasible reply is that, under the circumstances, the 'lift' was mutual.

This scene leads naturally to yet another series of political assassinations: "When he [note 'he' rather than 'they', which would have involved Jehonadab more actively in a killing in which he might have participated anyway!] came to Samaria, until he had wiped them out, according to the word of the Lord that he spoke to Elijah." The biblical text often hurries to stamp Jehu's action with the seal of religious authority. Whether this is ironical or not, depends on how often it is used. Since redundancy and excessive repetition is often a clear indication of biblical irony, an obviously deliberate gap is created here too between the overt sacred intention, and the subversive ironic one.

Jehu, having wiped out his political enemies, now turns to the religious opponents, in collaboration with Jehonadab. He assembles all the people and declares: "Ahab offered Baal small services; but Jehu will offer much more. Now therefore summon to me all the prophets of Baal, all his worshippers, and all his priests; let no one be missing, for I have a great sacrifice to offer to Baal; whoever is missing shall not live." In contradistinction to the readers, Jehu's listeners may not have been as well versed in his strategy, yet. Nevertheless, even if suspicious, they have no other option but to obey. Theatrically, at least dramatically, the following scene is not whether, but precisely how the next huge massacre will take place.

11   Killing the Baal worshipers (10:18–29)

The text specifies that "Jehu was acting with cunning in order to destroy the worshippers of Baal", and his plan works everywhere, "so that no one was left who did not come" to the promised feast, and "the temple of Baal was filled from wall to wall". Jehu commands the keeper of the wardrobe "Bring out the vestments for all the worshippers of Baal", which is done. Together with Jehonadab he tells the Baal worshippers to "search and see that there is no worshipper of the Lord here among you", pretending to show a pleasant degree of religious and ritual tact. Such careful selection between people doomed for death and those allowed to live has been equally meticulously employed in later history.

Eighty men are waiting outside, having been given the order that "Whoever allows any of those to escape who I deliver into your hands shall forfeit his life." Sonder-commando troops usually need no special encouragement to perform their jobs, but Jehu wants to be sure beyond any shadow of a doubt, in addition to reconfirming his characteristic tactics of letting others kill for him. Jehu remains in the house, not outside with the killers, thus managing to really deceive the Baal worshippers and calm them with his own presence at the ritual!) "As soon as he had finished presenting the burnt offering, Jehu said to the guards and to the officers [of Jehonadab's clan?]: 'Come in and kill them; let no one escape'."

The text uses many encompassing terms, typical to Jehu's previous assassinations, such as 'no one', 'all of them', etc. Furthermore, in this incident too, the sacrificers become sacrifices, according to Jehu's homeopathic methods: in a macabre way, the punishment is commensurate with the sin. Perhaps Jehu has learned the use of costume from his own first experience with the officers' cloaks. Theatrically, nevertheless, the motif of clothing is particularly effective in this killing scene. Once rid of the Baal worshippers, the temple itself can be demolished, burnt and made into a latrine 'to this day'.

12   Epilogue (10:30–36)

The playwright notes that Jehu "wiped out Baal from Israel", but "did

not turn aside from the sins of Jeroboam son of Nebat . . ."
Notwithstanding, Jehu receives an outstanding biblical badge of honor
and appreciation. "The Lord said to Jehu, 'Because you have done well in
carrying out what I consider right, and in accordance with all that was in
my heart have dealt with the house of Ahab, your sons of the fourth generation shall sit on the throne of Israel'." Before further developing this
issue, it must be added that the Canaanite Baal rituals were closely linked
with a political foreign influence, both totally abhorred by the predominantly religious perspective represented in the Old Testament. Killing even
Israelite Baal worshippers is therefore not considered a sin. However, the
horrendous ramifications of Jehu's systematic killings dor not escape the
playwright and his humanist point of view in regard to peoples' lives,
whether they worship Baal or the Lord God.

With more than a touch of irony, the text first describes the Lord's
praise to Jehu, but then specifies that even Jehu was no less holy than
might be expected from his zealous path to 28 years of kingship. This may
be explained by the political necessity for the relatively strong kingdom
of Israel to have its own local rituals, separate from the centralistic impact
of the weaker Judean kingdom. However, in this Jehu focused story, the
sensitive observer cannot possibly ignore the subtle criticism addressed
against Jehu. Since the commands of the Lord were Jehu's only possible
justification for his murders, even if such beliefs are rejected nowadays,
and Jehu did not follow the ways of the Lord "with all his heart" (!), this
particular insert discloses the text's own critique of its protagonist,
through its subtle choice of words. Moreover, the political situation did
not improve as a result of Jehu's regime, and "The Lord began to trim off
parts of Israel. Hazael defeated them throughout the territory of Isael" –
and a long list of other defeats is detailed. Ahab's regime, on the other
hand, was far from being morally pure, but in his and Jezebel's good old
days, at least, there was relative peace, prosperity and greater religious
freedom to worship Baal (except for the actions of Elijah, who slaughtered 400 Baal priests on Mount Carmel).

In conclusion, the text of Jehu's power-thirsty drama creates a deliberate
gap between his incessantly, exclusively bloody ascent, and his meager
achievements, politically and religiously. Jehu himself, nevertheless, is
depicted with careful attention to theatrical detail, verbal and non-verbal
alike. Each inevitable blood-bath soundly drowns the achievements of the
previous one, while more and more people are swept into ever widening
cycles of horror and collaboration.

Jehu's relationships are exclusively functional, albeit not without
enlisting pseudo personal undertones. So too are his conversations with

the the young prophet, with the officers, with Bidkar, with the elders of Samaria and with Jehonadab. The only exception would appear to be his terse comment over Jezebel's dismembered corpse. Jehu is often surrounded by officers, messengers, soldiers and special troops; but he really wallows in dead bodies, heads and feet and hands. It is worth examining the (non) burial places he chooses for his victims: on the open field, in the pit, in baskets and latrines. The authorial dramatic text discloses a unique, macabre stage syntax of the dead. Jehu seems to like the dead, who threaten him less, much more than the living. Perhaps he has developed a truly pure love for the dead.

Honest, tough and cruel generals have long been a favorite subject in world drama. Classical Greek drama presents generals in their struggle with hubris and the gods; the *commedia dell'arte* discloses the power-fooled desire of military force through humor; Shakespeare adds psychological factors. But in almost completely avoiding psychology, and yet depicting Jehu's motivations and actions so vividly, with the divine and the humorous factors built-in, the Bible presents one of the best and most blood-curdling plays ever written on this topic.

13

The (Unabridged) Play of David and Bathsheba

The ritual of finding heroes who later become leaders inspired by God, has always offered a special, surprising and dramatic event. After God has rejected Saul, he sends his prophet Samuel to anoint a king from the sons of Jesse of Bethlehem. Samuel errs in choosing Eliab, the eldest, and God tells him that "man sees to the eyes and God sees into the heart" (I *Sam.* 16:7). After none of Jesse's seven older sons are found fit, the youngest son is brought in from tending the sheep and is described in his own presence, as "ruddy, and withal of beautiful eyes, and goodly to look upon".[1] Following God's previous statement concerning the discrepancy between human and divine 'seeing', a fine touch of irony appears with the description of the boy David's beautiful eyes. Is it man or God, therefore, who is the one to see into the eyes of the boy destined for leadership? An additional and more profound gap[2] appears later on: "Arise, anoint him", says God to Samuel, who is apparently hesitating "for this is him".

After David has been anointed, for the time being only in the company of his brethren, the divine spirit rests upon him and departs from Saul, and an evil spirit from the Lord terrifies Saul. When a skillful and soothing player is sought, the dramatic projector is again turned upon David, who is now given a further six characteristics in addition to the previous three depicting external beauty: "skillful in playing, and a mighty man of valour, and a man of war, and prudent in affairs and a comely person" – and most importantly – "the lord is with him". When David is brought in to Saul he remains quite passive despite having been sent from place to place, and he plays to the man whom he is supposed to dethrone, "so Saul found relief and it was well with him, and the evil spirit departed from him".

Already at this stage the emotional tension in this complicated plot is well established. The reader is invited to confront the verse "for this is him", stated in the third person by God to Samuel in David's presence, with another, much later important moment in David's biography. After the series of sins committed by David in the Bath-sheba and Uriah affair, a dramatic tension of 'pre-*anagnorisis*' is created between the words of another God-sent prophet and David's own answer. Nathan says "you're the man" when David's moral indignation abates at the end of the play-within-the-play, the fable of the Poor Man's Ewe. David, as the moral indignation of the prophet abates, confesses "I have sinned to God".

Between use of the third person in relating to David at the beginning of his way, and the aggressive second person address to David, now an adult sinner, many years pass; between Nathan's accusation and David's confession – in classical drama the moment of *anagnorisis* – only a short, intensive and highly dramatic moment of time passes; and in between the two, many more characteristics are given of one of the most famous kings in history.

David's character has fed readers' imagination for many generations. Each generation has also interpreted, in a dialogical relationship, the figure of the king according to its own modes, while interpreting itself according to David's ideal traits. According to the following theatrical aspects, the spectator at an ideal theatrical presentation is invited not only to look at the deeds of the beautiful-eyed king by seeing 'into the heart' but also to play David himself and employ the story in a way similar to David's use of the Poor Man's Ewe fable: in order to understand from within what might otherwise remain veiled.

However, it is not only the abundance and variety of characteristics and the contradictions between them, concerning one of the most beloved and thoroughly dealt with biblical characters, that explains the prominence of David in endless works of art; it is also the multi-discrepancy and irony of the biblical poetics itself that demands an active interpretation. Lately, scholars have begun to apply theories by Ingarden and Iser (as well as the old and highly sophisticated hermeneutics of the Talmud) to the Bible, indicating the text's 'absorbancy'. Many of these scholars, like Alter, Fokkelman, Frye and others, and especially Sternberg and Perry's article "An Ironic Look at the King"[3] relate to the term 'dramatic' as a quality of a literary text.

This chapter delineates a basic outline for the treatment of the potential theatricality of biblical drama and attempts to fill in some of the gaps between the well-developed but unpracticed on stage literary theory relating to the 'drama' on the one hand, and the multiple shows, bereft of theory, on the other.[4]

The story of David and Bath-sheba has frequently been found suitable for a theatrical discussion from a number of aspects. It is dramatic in the general sense of tension and anticipation, of a clash of wills and different sorts of justice, of thrilling stories and motifs of sex, power and politics, all of which are a well-tested recipe for theatrical success. Multi-dimensional famous characters participate in the story and arouse public interest in a plot which includes struggle, devious intentions and human 'tragedy' (at least in the simplistic sense) as well as a high degree of emotion. The story functions dramatically by subordinating emotion and mind to a *will*, expressed in *action* in delivering the dramatic facts in an apparently objective way.

This particular story, more specifically, relies on various types of dialogues and on a tight scenic structure which is easily convertible to a play as it stands.[5] In the story of David and Bath-sheba, which also serves as a model for the potential presentability of other bible stories, meticulous attention is given by the authors to elements rightly considered as highly theatrical from the point of view of the uniqueness that an actual presentation may have in a public performance.[6]

In the following, I deal with elements of space, design, movement, entrances and exits, costumes, stage properties and lighting, in an attempt to examine the theatricality of the text. A theatrical analysis of the story may illuminate some aspects of the text that were indeed performed under a certain degree of directorial intuition in biblical shows, albeit without the benefit of theoretical research. Consequently, parts of the Bible need not only be directed according to the information found in the text itself, but can also benefit from a medium-oriented theatrical approach aimed at explicating the text, even if it is not meant for actual presentation. The theatrical approach clarifies the text's potential as a play, as though for the benefit of the theatre, while also deepening the understanding of the text for its own benefit from the point of view of a potential theatrical presentation.

Structure and Characters

The story of David and Bath-sheba extends over Chapters 11 and 12 in the second *Book of Samuel* and can be subdivided in a way similar to any modern or classic well-made play. The following dramatic structure is based on a prologue, five acts and an epilogue; as well as five 'interludes'. This division relies on two dramatic theatrical elements: (a) exits and entrances of particpating characters, whether direct or implied. well-known distinction between *showing* and *telling*, which is appropriate mostly for narrative, can easily be applied to drama as well;[7] and (b) reflecting the needs of this medim-oriented treatment of the text, the division also follows main directorial segments. Since these segments are likely to be perceived as subjective and intuitive criteria used by any director according to his/her understanding and interpretation of the text, the suggested directorial segments here rely mainly on the biblical verb. As an indication of (dramatic) action, the verb, as noted earlier in this book, can be likened to the muscles of the biblical text in which the willful intentions of the characters are expressed. For example, the verb 'to send' (*shalakh*) which appears very often in this text, becomes an evaluative criterion extending far and beyond the quantitative accumulation of its appearances. It becomes a qualitative standard, an image and a major motif. As another example, when David *sees* Bath-sheba, *sends* and *inquires* about her and only then *takes* her and *lies* with her, the mini-scenes and the directorial segments within them follow the verb pattern, each of which justifies a unique dramatic focus.

Prologue – "And it came to pass at the turn of the year . . . but David stayed in Jerusalem" (v. 1).

Act 1	*Characters*	*Verse*
Sc. i David sees Bath-sheba	David, Bath-sheba	2
Sc. ii David asks about Bath-sheba	David, messenger	3
Sc. iii David takes Bath-sheba	David, Bath-sheba, messengers	3–4
Sc. iv Bath-sheba returns home	Bat-sheba	4
Sc. v Bath-sheba announces her pregnancy	Bat-sheba, messenger	5
David (two scenes?)		
Interlude David calls for Uriah	David, messenger, Joab Joab, Uriah	6–7
Act 2		
Sc. i "How the war prospers"	David, Uriah	7–8
Sc. ii Uriah doesn't go home (1)	Uriah, messengers	9–10
Sc. iii "I'll send you tomorrow"	David, Uriah	11–12
Sc. iv Uriah doesn't go home (2)	Uriah	12
Sc. v He made him drunk	David, Uriah	13
Sc. vi Uriah doesn't go home (3)	Uriah (messengers)	
Interlude Uriah's letter	David, Uriah	14–15
Act 3		
Sc. i The war	Joab, Uriah, warriors	16–17
Sc. ii Orders to the messenger	Joab, messenger	18–21
Sc. iii The messenger appears	David, messenger	22–25

Assuming that the structure is metaphoric to the meaning of the 'play', a number of phenomena can be detected. The prologue is retrospectively illuminated by the epilogue, enhancing its ironic aspect, as David has sent all the others off to war, but it is only when Joab sends for him that he finally goes himself to deliver the *coup-de-grâce* to the city of Rabah. Irony is achieved through repetition and the use of deliberate redundancy, such as the detailed list of loot taken from the Amonites. The attitude implicit in the opening and closing sections of the play that provide the framework indicates scorn toward a king who only proves his prowess when it is no longer required. There is also a fine analogue between the conquest of the city and the taking of Bath-sheba. The military and political plot of the war, interrupted by David's illicit love affair, belatedly reoccupies its proper place in the objective scale of importance of the biblical events. Despite the secondary 'value' of David's private affairs, the moral implications of which are also public, it is presented here as the main plot. The framing prologue and epilogue focus on the political plot against which the pseudo-private plot and the moral deterioration of David are evaluated. Both plots compete for the spectators' attention, interlink as the story-line proceeds, and serve dramatically as mutual correctives. In both,

the king is perceived as one whose moral and personal stature is a necessary component of his aura as a leader anointed by a demanding God, for
in an organic world view the king is not only the leader, a symbol of the
entire kingdom, but also a head without whom the whole system
collapses.[8]

David and Bath-sheba's story is presented as a dramatic struggle
between the politically blameworthy inactivity and the initially lascivious
and then murderous affair of love and betrayal. After David's *anagnorisis*
some order is restored, both personally and politically. The tragedy ensues
from the retrospective that David's great days are irretrievably over. His
confession – possible regret, punishment and sorrow – will not suffice to
restore his psychological, religious or even 'professional' status.

The first act presents David's sin in a pseudo-naïve manner (later recognized as pretended naïvete by the biblical author), linking the king's
non-participation in the Rabah siege with his idle stroll on the roof of his
house, where he sees and desires a woman whose precise identity he soon
determines. His political inactivity turns into idleness, then lasciviousness,
and then becomes an explicit sin in knowingly taking Uriah's wife.
David's emotions counter-balance his deeds on two levels. While Joab,
the army and 'all the people' are fighting a war, David finds time for a
much easier prey.

In the second act the three dialogues that take place between David and
Uriah, whose arrival has been well prepared for, lead David on one more
step in his moral deterioration. The tension caused by Uriah's 'knowing'
or not, and David's possible deliberations about Uriah's awareness, add
greatly to the acting and directorial potential in these scenes.

The third act explores the need for 'offstage' events to advance the plot,
namely, the siege of Rabah. Dramatically, this act enhances the motif of
sending and messengers. In traditional plays the protagonists are evaluated according to their deeds and the actions they are expected to perform
or avoid, but for which they must be fully responsible, as actions are a
result of will. Appointing proxies, as David does, creates tactical distor-
tions in the plot and short-circuits communication among the dramatic
personae. While enriching the story line with devious machinations,
sending is implicitly presented as an immoral substitute for *doing*, and
presents David as using and abusing deputies to do his job for him. This
frequently employed motif later sets the background for David's visit to
Bat-sheba. He goes to comfort her but is called by Joab to come and finish
the war himself "lest my name [Joab] will be called on her [the city of
Rabah]". Once David has undergone his moral conversion he accepts
responsibility for both his sins, of deed and omission, and thus the text
underlines the link between true moral considerations and independent

action, despite the almost inavoidability of the protagonist's action.

In the fourth act David confronts his sin and the actual conversion takes place. An external structural and thematic resemblance exists between this act and the second one. In the second act, however, Uriah is given the extra strength generally given to mute characters (an exception is his one speech). Now in the fourth act, the king is mostly silent except for his two words: "I have sinned against God". Crime and punishment are dramatically weighed against each other, and theatrically presented in a spatial mode of talking *down* to both the victim Uriah and the culprit David, as God, through Nathan, treats him. It is here that the full punishment is forecast.

In the final and emotional fifth act, the play concentrates on the protagonist's profound sorrow and soul-searching, elements which have been so far deliberately ignored. While Sternberg and Perry emphasize the irony aimed against David in Chapter 11, the complementary description of his moral recuperation should equally be noted.

The drama includes five interludes. In the first, David calls for Uriah and the text links between the betrayer and the betrayed, connecting the scene with Bath-sheba who has been explicitly identified as Uriah's wife, and the expected dialogues with Uriah himself. In the second interlude, providing one of the most contemptible acts ever committed, David sends Uriah away with his own death sentence in his hands. The gap between "at eventide that David arose from off his bed . . . " and "in the morning . . . David wrote a letter . . . " is particularly striking. The third interlude is dedicated to Bath-sheba's mourning and to the triple emphasis on her position as Uriah's wife. The fourth interlude speaks of the punishment: the baby's sickness and death; whereas in the fifth there is a kind of consolatory 'happy end' since, unlike his dead brother, the new child, who was not conceived in sin, is loved by God. These interludes, concentrated plot-extracts, provide dramatic focii, a five-step ladder in the plot: planning of the sin, the sin, the mourning, the punishment, and the reconciliation.

In each of the acts a different secondary dominant character serves as a dramatic counter-balance to David, but in the last act there is also a scene in which David is alone. It is structurally similar yet thematically reversed insofar as previously David was 'alone' in Jerusalem whereas now he is torn from his introversion within his new family and thrust into a battle in which he has not yet taken part.

Throughout the entire play, and especially in the fourth act, many events from David's rich biography are evoked by Nathan. They serve to illuminate his present insensitivity, immorality and evasion of responsibility in both love and war. Special emphasis is given to his ingratitude to the God who has supported him. Nathan recounts David's many women, his kingdom, and his deliverance from the hands of Saul, encouraging the spectator to examine yet more issues, such as David's battle against Goliath and his eulogy for Jonathan and Saul, in a less favorable and complimentary light. In its emphasis on a rich though not necessarily consistent variety of its heroes' characteristics, the Bible makes them more humanly credible. Chapters 11 and 12 can therefore be regarded as a mid-life crisis that is happening to David, but in which readers and audience alike are invited to participate. Such a biblical crisis occurs through the direct confrontation of human relative psychology with divine, morally absolute demands. Since the drama involves self-awareness and change by the protagonist, it is important to the understanding of the plot to follow how such a conversion happens, not only within David's soul, but also in his relationships with the other characters in the play.

Bath-sheba, originally simply an object of his lust, is presented metaphorically as a strong and active woman in the directions Joab gives to his messenger: "Did not a woman cast an upper millstone upon him from the wall . . . " She is also indicated as being a 'sheep', namely a servile (foolish) victim in Nathan's fable. While the 'real' Bath-sheba may resemble one or both of these images, the text focuses on David rather than on her, and her own attitude to the affair is momentarily, at least, irrelevant. The responsibility lies totally with David, although one may assume that Bath-sheba was not a disinterested figure, as is later revealed by her lobbying for her son Solomon to be king.

While Bath-sheba is constantly called Uriah's wife even after David takes her to his home, after the child's death she is no longer sent to David but he comes to her, and "comforted Bath-sheba his wife". Her relationship with David undergoes a significant change, at least as far as he is concerned.

Joab, who has received foolish and unexpected orders from David, despite David's experience in military strategy, sends in return terse messages which are highly critical. Again with the help of a messenger, David sends Joab pseudo-encouraging war messages, highly cynical in the context. "Let not this thing displease thee, for the sword devoureth in one manner or another. Make thy battle stronger against the city . . . ", etc. In the epilogue David receives a clear message from Joab "gather the rest of the people together and camp against the city . . . ". Joab's obedient and precise cruelty, so different from David's advice "retire ye from him that he may be smitten . . . " is actually what saves David's prestige and enables Joab's harsh words, which do not prove much honor to the king. The psychological and dramatic mechanism of this mutual remote control between David and Joab accurately reflects these two characters' previous relationship as well as their future one. David's demonstrative authority over Joab crashes against the waves of irony that Joab returns him, while the king himself loses respect in the eyes of Joab, who restores the balance between personal and state affairs. A dramatic anticipation of Joab's cool authority over David can already be found in Uriah's words to David 'and my master Joab' instead of, for instance, '*your servant* Joab'.

A further example of the dramatic change of relationships is found in the anonymous group encircling David, including counselors, servants, elders, etc. This group is related to with relative indifference in the beginning, under the title "And *they* told David" that Uriah did not go down to his house. Various characters must have noticed Uriah's wife when providing the necessary housekeeping services to the king and his new beloved. The royal nature of Uriah's rival undoubtedly enhanced the quality of the gossip. However, the lascivious undertone is tactfully missing in the text when this same anonymous group appears later on in the sickness, dying and death scene of the child. Now it is respectful 'elders' who appear, wishing to raise David up from the ground, speaking simple and very human words: "While the child was yet alive we spoke unto him and he harkened not unto our voice; how then shall we tell him that the child is dead, so that he do himself some harm." These words, as a sort of stage *aside*, illuminate David's sorrow as well as his notorious impulsivity. This group is also called 'servants' or 'whisperers' and so retrospectively one may assume that previously they were whispering about matters less tragic. This collective dramatic figure, because David is in the midst of a cathartic process, provides a specific, dialogical and even comforting presence. David undergoes a change toward them too, which is emphasized against his previous background of treating 'others' as inanimate objects, for which Uriah is surely the best example. It is David's sorrow and recognition rather than his hubris that endow even the secondary or tertiary characters of the play with a human image.

David's attitude to Uriah undergoes a three-stage process in the second act. He had already known Uriah before (and certainly after) meeting his wife. Sternberg and Perry develop in detail a number of hypotheses concerning the relationship between these two characters.[9] At least one possibility indicates that Uriah's response had a strong effect on David and may have been the reason why Uriah became the bearer of his own death sentence.

> "The ark, and Israel, and Judah, abide in booths; and my Lord Joab, and the servants of my Lord, are encamped in the open field; shall I go into my house, to eat and to drink, and to lie with my wife? As thou livest, and as thy soul livest, I will not do this thing."

The play reveals a subtle attitude toward a large group of messengers who carry orders and notes from person to person, from house to house, from city to city, and finally, from God to David. Various anonymous characters deliver messages to and from Bath-sheba, to Joab and back; and Nathan, God's messenger, smites David for using messengers at all. The motif of *sending* and the many senders in the play fulfill a role which is not only dramatic but highly theatrical as far as stage movement is concerned. These messengers, and one in particular, are presented as highly aware and cautious with regard to their encounter with David. The text suggests that external participants, readers and spectators, should focus on other messengers' deliberations as well. When David finally becomes his own messenger and goes himself to Bath-sheba, and conquers 'by himself' the city of Rabah, the plot too is given at least a temporary solution. Nathan is clearly presented as a one-way messenger. After David has internalized the prophet's divine indignation, he goes to the House of the Lord and worships, relinquishing Nathan's services as a go-between. David does confess to Nathan, having no alternative, but his attempt to atone is his own, and not only because of the punishment he is about to receive in both the near and more distant future.

"I shall go to him" is a phrase that employs the messenger motif, prominent throughout the entire play, to reflect David's conversion. An uncompromisingly critical view of David might still claim that even this phrase of atonement can be interpreted as an attempt to find grace in the eyes of the Lord, rather than full acceptance of his child's death. He fasts and weeps only as long as there is still a chance to change the Lord's sentence, but *post factum* he gives up. There seem, however, to be better arguments for claiming that David did indeed undergo a genuine conversion of consciousness if one considers the stark and simple phrase "Can I bring him back again? I shall go to him, but he will not return to me."

The relationships between David as the protagonist, the secondary characters, and the 'extras' are designed, until the conversion, as 'I–it' relationships; whereas afterwards, in Buberian terms, they are definitely closer to the 'I–thou' pattern. This occurs despite the marked status differences and perhaps even because of them. All the characters in the play are given expression whether directly or indirectly, even the soldiers besieging Rabah and the Amonites who suffer under David's hard hand.

Stage Design and Movement

In dealing with the theatrical functions of space in the play, a distinction should be made between dramatic space and the potential set-design for the text as implied in the text itself.[10] In the drama of David and Bath-sheba the following physical locations are mentioned:

Semiotically, there are intricate relationships in the text, on various levels of reality, between the theatrical locations mentioned.[11] These locations, like the more dramatic (as genre) elements of the play, also form a sophisticated and deliberate image for the overall meaning of the play. The constant usage of the term *house* obliges the spectator to see 'the house' as the most dominant spatial image in the text. This image extends to become a city, which is also a term functioning not only on the physical and realistic level of the play, but also as a metaphor intrinsic in the text itself.

A house in the sense of a psychologically, socially, nationally and religiously[12] stable, secure structure, is ascribed in this play with a significance that a complete performance can fully reveal. This is achieved by the typical theatrical mechanism of onstage visual realizations of textual metaphors. The text describes the tension between the war raging over the city of Rabah, and David's idle 'sitting' in Jerusalem. The tranquility of Jerusalem is ironically ascribed by David's arising toward evening from his bed after a long rest. Mention of the roof emphasizes David's peace of mind when he seeks the cool breeze of the late afternoon and is suddenly taken aback by the sight of the beautiful woman bathing across the way.

The entrances and exits of the characters from one space to the other serve as a scenaric criterion that characterizes space not only in the geographic, but also in the psychological and moral sense. The mutual penetration of people into houses and the breaking into Rabah not only reflect a historically realistic report, but also constitute deeds expressing the inter-spatial tension of the play. David's superiority over Uriah is revealed in the repeated expression "go down to your house", which is physically understood as the wealthy dwelling in higher places and also in the mental and status-oriented sense, enhanced by David's masterly handling of his high-ranking officer. Uriah's going out of David's house but not down to his own, and going to sleep on the threshold of the king's house, is a superb spatial expression of his mental threshold situation. In this act, space functions as a counterpoint to the text; whereas the space indicates vicious dominance by David, Uriah's text expresses moral superiority. Whether Uriah is naïve or sophisticated, David certainly feels his words about the different 'houses': "Israel and Judah abide in *booths* . . . shall I then go into my *house*?" David tries to play on the social differences and assumes a fake cameraderie by trying to eat, drink and get Uriah drunk, but he cannot avoid the subtextual and contextual ramifications of the clash between city and field, war encampment and king's castle, etc. The spatial image stands for notions of justice. While Uriah takes part in besieging David's enemies, David invades the privacy of Uriah's house.

Whereas David arises from his bed in the evening and takes a stroll on the roof, Uriah goes to sleep with the servants. Between these two locations, as well as indicating time, the Hebrew also uses a verb that derives from the same root – *shachav* (to lie 'with' or 'down') – in relation to David and in the rhetorical question presented by Uriah to David. The answer is significant on many levels. In 11:9 a tense moment is provided after the words "And Uriah lay . . . " when it is made clear that he did not go down to lie with his wife. For the final time in this act the text links the verb with a noun "And he went out in the evening to lie in his lying place . . . " and did not go down to his house. The combination between the movement "and he went out . . . to lie" and the space "in his lying place" parallels a similar combination existing between "his house" and "did not go down". Space is therefore activated by whoever (and *how*ever) occupies it.

The wall, both from a military point of view and as a metaphor for the breaking of a moral and sexual code, is the focus of the next act, in which Joab uses the term *wall* very often. In his own deliberate choice of words and in the allegorical level of the text, the wall is a symbol of punishment from above: "Know ye not that they will shoot from the wall." For the second time Joab emphasizes the connection between a woman and the wall – "Did not a woman cast an upper millstone upon him from the wall that he died . . . " – establishing an indication of David's moral defeat in the hands of Bath-sheba. Finally, Joab puts the words in his messenger's mouth, saying: "Why went ye so nigh the wall?"

In David's relationships with Bath-sheba and Uriah the spatial height differences and the movement between spaces signify the king's dominance and enhance his haughtiness. Joab's words reverse this notion when he mentions the shooting from the wall, implying that there is yet someone higher still than he who thinks himself to be at the top.

David's lying place is subtly equated not only with Uriah's lying place but also with the place in which David "Came, and spent the night and *lay* on the earth" while mourning. As a fascinating axis of stage movement, the verb 'arose' also reveals mental states. There are differences between "And David arose from his bed" in the beginning and "the elders of his house arose to make him arise . . . and he did not want to . . . ". The conjugations of the verb link with the verse related to both space and movement "I will raise up evil against thee out of thine own house". After the death of the child David 'arises' from the earth, ending the cycle of repentance that began with the sin of 'lying'; with 'lying' that was more similar to that of Uriah. (A similar *place* is the place "of valiant men" where Uriah was killed!)

The movement of characters from house to house, as stage entrances and exits, indicates changes in the plot, especially when those characters, headed by David, move themselves rather than send others to act. Appropriating Bath-sheba to David's house is an act of robbery, whereas David's coming to her signifies a shift of mood. External physical changes reflect inner, mental changes, at least with David, who lies down, arises, goes to the house of the Lord (rather than having a stroll on his own roof), returns to his own house, goes to Bath-sheba. His inter-spatial passages as opposed to his previous static sitting are a proof of his attempt to raise himself morally (until he finally *goes* to Rabah to 'conquer' it).

In the spatial syntax of the drama three main locations can be distinguished: the text mentions the city of Rabah many times; the city of Jerusalem; and also two off-stage cities, one of which is Thebez, as a historical military precedent and also as an image of a city saved by a woman,[13] and the other of which is the fictitious "One City" appearing in the fable of "The Poor Man's Ewe". The city is therefore the first main spatial notion.

The second spatial notion is a series of smaller units such as the roof of a house, the 'doorstep', David's mourning place, Uriah's killing place, and the gates of the city of Rabah (and King David's 'doorstep' are the *threshold* locations alloted to be Uriah's nightly and then final resting places . . .). These are the locations for scenes of solitude and introspection, both false and true.

Between the wide public notion of a *city* and the deliberately narrowly focused spatial units which the text illuminates, the main spatial unit is that of the house; of David, Uriah and Bath-sheba, Nathan the prophet, and God's house, as well as the temporary 'houses' of the military encampment in the field before Rabah. David's house is seen from different angles, such as by the elders of his house, from the roof of his house, "he gathered her to his house", etc. When the text mentions Uriah's house, it meticulously emphasizes "he did not go down to his house", once with the stress on *go down* and once on *house*. The house becomes a key word, a self-referential image, when Nathan tells David about his crime and punishment and the house of David gradually turns from a physical structure to a symbol. Nathan moves from "the house of your Lord", reminding David that God gave *him* Saul's dynasty (house), which was not his by right; on to the "house of Israel and Judah", namely an entire and double kingdom. Therefore "the sword shall never depart from thy house . . . and evil shall rise against thee out of thine own house". In a typically biblical educational rationale the sin *itself* is the very source of the punishment, and true recognition of the sin is at least part of the punishment though not always a satisfactory one. If indeed the house can be likened to a human body, the landlord must learn to control it. Lack of moral control over one's own house infers lack of control over the city, over the kingdom and over the entire lineage.

The *movement* between and within the small spatial units is mostly vertical; between the cities it is horizontal; and between the houses the movement begins horizon tally with a slight incline toward the height of David's house, then reverses "and he came to the house of the Lord and bowed down", and ends with a sense of balance within the house of David when Solomon is born. Nathan's house is shown in a pseudo-neutral light "and Nathan went to his house", nevertheless strengthening the motif of the house in general. The play which began on the roof, ends in the iron mines where David enslaves the Amonites before he returns and "goes up" to Jerusalem; this time with all the people with him.

In the same way that the house changes from a physical entity and a lascivious 'place' to being the symbol of the people, so too is the movement gradually refined in David's passage from 'sits', to 'and he arose', 'and took a stroll', 'and sent'; all the way to "came and spent the night and *layed down* . . . and *understood* . . . ". Movement occurs between two stages of David's inactivity. Finally, the verb and movement pattern continues with 'he arose' and from it to "and he washed and he anointed himself and changed his apparel and he came into the house of the Lord and he worshipped", etc. The downward movement becomes an upward one. Whereas the first rising leads to sin, the second is an expression of repentance.

The various theatre 'languages' (or stage instructions) of space and movement are mutually complementary. When juxtaposed with the dialogical text, they also deliver independent information not found in the dialogue itself. Space and movement supply subtext and context not delivered by the dialogue text. The synthesis and interpretation of all these languages are expected to occur through the active participation of readers and *audiences* alike.

Stage Lighting, Properties and Costumes

Lighting

The sophistication and technical ability of modern theatre lighting systems may serve as an excellent tool for a subtle interpretation of the staged-events.[14] A lighting plan for Chapters 11 and 12 can be based on the passing of time in the play, as well as on the atmosphere implicit in the scenes; e.g., if 'the return of the year' means spring time, the general illumination of the show can move, at least in the first two acts, from the moderate to the harsh Jerusalem summer light. The lighting, if based on the text, can be 'realistic', psychological and even self-referential; in creating a self-conscious interpretation, emphasizing the difference between the objects lit and the lighting itself. It can establish in and outdoor locations as well as time of day, for which the opening of Act I – 'towards evening' is a hint. David's room is likely to be shadowy, whereas the roof is still lit by the last rays of the setting sun, bathing Bath-sheba's beautiful body. David lay with her 'in secret', probably in darkness, and part of his punishment will be that Absalom will do the same, but on the roof (!), and 'to the eyes of the sun' while all the people of Israel will be looking (II *Sam.* 16:22). David's encounters with Uriah could take place at any time of the day, probably indoors. Extra emphasis is given to Uriah going to bed in the evening, and on the following *morning* when David writes the letter. The lighting may enhance the tension between deeds of the evening and deeds of the morning – by both Uriah and David.

A realistic light-set could differentiate between Rabah and Jerusalem. While David's talks with Uriah may occur any time, his talks with Joab's messenger are likely to occur in the same place but under a different light, in order to stress the delivery of a death message. Spotlights could be used for personal emphasis. Following the triple emphasis of Uriah and Bath-sheba's intimate, mutual, conjugal relationships, especially in the 'light' of his death, a narrow 'spot' could serve as a 'personal' light when she mourns for him. On the other hand, Bath-sheba could also be presented on this occasion as overly exposed under some very bright light, indicating the possible discrepancy between her social need to mourn and her true feelings.

For Nathan's fable yet another set of lighting cues could be used. The word *sun* appears here twice and, as noted, could justifiably be used as a realization of a metaphor.

David's mourning scene could be kept in heavy shadow. The changes between the scenes with the elders could shift focus to partly lit people or sections of bodies. Whoever still does not subscribe to David's sincerity, even here, could light the scene with a higher degree of discrepancy between the characters and objects lit, on the one hand, and angle, color and intensity of the light itself on the other. Similar treatment could be applied to the second meeting between David and Bath-sheba, when Bath-sheba's lighting could be toned down.

Special lighting cues could be kept for the epilogue. Quite obviously, the text focuses on the golden crown set with a precious stone that is now 'on David's head', a perfect metaphor best presented with a unique stage light. David returns to Jerusalem, perhaps under the same evening light with which the prologue began the play. A slow fade could come in handy here.

Props

The narrative text includes a number of objects that, in a theatrical context, ought to be perceived as potential stage instructions for 'props'. David send Uriah a gift. Food and drinks are brought to a party. David writes a letter to Joab. Around such props a consistent theatrical syntax is created, weaving the overall meaning into a language of objects.

The *washing* motif, for instance, can easily concentrate on various aspects of personal hygiene. Bath-sheba is first seen bathing; (or purifies herself from her uncleanliness, as some have – wrongly suggested) yet plunges into a morally impure affair. David sends Uriah to wash his feet, whereas Uriah in his answer seems careful *not* to mention washing while explicitly mentioning eating, drinking and lying with his wife. It is an indirect refusal to physically purify himself from moral and emotional dirt. In a physical, psychological and ritual act of purification, David washes, anoints himself and changes his clothes after hearing that the child has died.

Dealing with the human body through clothing, nudity and washing on stage is not only intensively theatrical, due to the self-indulgence involved in such acts when performed in public; it also draws attention to complex relationships between the initially unattainable mental and spiritual *interior* of the characters and the required exterior with which they express themselves theatrically. Bath-sheba washes (naked as expected), David changes his clothes.[15] Clothing (a more external layer than the human skin) and washing indicate an inner change.

Another step toward the (physical) interior is made through ingesting food. The food motif appears between David and Uriah, again in the fable of the slaughtered sheep, where the ewe eats from its master's bread and drinks from his cup, and is itself eaten, later. In fact, both Uriah and Bath-sheba can be seen as sheep in this context! David thus avoids food by fasting, as well as avoiding excesses on many levels, as Nathan forces him to understand.

Other props also appear, on different levels of literary, dramatic and theatrical reality. The upper millstone is an historical allusion to a military precedent, yet also an image of how a woman defeated a man. In an interesting metamorphosis this upper millstone becomes the Amonite king's heavy crown, described in minute detail, gathering metaphoric weight.

Though a real sword is never presented, the weapon is well-known in David's biography. He had 'no sword' in his hands when he killed

Goliath, but used a sword in his eulogy "Saul's sword will not return empty", to quote but two of many examples. The sword is not only a weapon, but an image for the ability to make distinctive partitions and to *cut* in the proper places. The sword becomes a sharp metaphor, turned and returned to David. With the same educational justification that "evil will come from your house", Nathan reminds David of his "sword waving" speech, "Thus and thus devoureth the sword" when he says – "the sword will not go away from thy house", since "you have killed him [Uriah] with the sword of the Amonites".

In great detail the various implements of torture of the conquered Amonites are also described.

Using minimum props (a common approach in modern theatre), each prop has several uses and is employed by more than one character, endowing the inanimate, perhaps imaginary, object with a personal touch. The props shift from concrete matter, to image, to symbol. Most of them are used by David and revolve around him, changing in accordance with his relationships to people. In the end, the abundance of loot plundered in Rabah counterbalances the emotionally exhausted David.

A Play Within a Play

Intertextual connections link the various parts of the play as far as space, movement, props etc. are concerned, with the text and the dramatic structure, characters and other genre-oriented elements. The text also includes three units that can be regarded as internal analogies,[16] relating self-reflexively to the main developments.

The story of Thebez, theatrically observed, is the first of the two 'plays-within-a-play', and readily lends itself to a live stage presentation (should a director choose to do so with the help of a maquette, slides, a sand-table, etc.). Joab prepares the messenger for his encounter with David, 'staging' a future scene between the king and the messenger, using a quote-within-a-quote to parallel this play-within-a-play. This 'directed' report of the war furnishes a semi cover-up story for the battle itself (also 'staged', but with many real victims), in order to change, yet still carry out, David's orders to kill Uriah. The other soldiers serve as a collective mask to hide David and Joab's 'non-theatrical' intentions. The ramifications of this cynical event lead the audience to the inevitable conclusion that other wars too have been fought, with many more lives lost, for equally irrelevant motives. The Thebezian trap is meant to turn the gaze of the morally and politically blind David inwards, while using the technique of 'distancing the evidence' to other times and places. Defending himself in advance from David's expected wrath, Joab may not be aware of the analogy between the Thebez affair and the present one, but the author certainly is, as Sternberg and Perry noted.

The second, and most theatrical analogy is the Poor Man's Ewe fable, relating neither to a distant past nor to a real but remote city, nor to the future of Jerusalem, but evoking 'one city' in the present tense of the plot, with masked dramatis personae.

With his transparent story of the Poor Man's Ewe, Nathan (and the author) manages to create a classical production of dramatic irony where everybody except the protagonist recognizes the face behind the mask. As soon as David realizes the truth, and more importantly – that it is *his* truth – the seemingly offstage nature of the rich man's sin becomes a profound internal, first-person singular matter. This Ewe-trap is a wildly humorous depiction of characters, situations and emotional charges of David's affairs with Bath-sheba and Uriah. The ewe is portrayed here as small, bought by the poor man who "returned her to life", and raised her together with his sons. Up to this point the audience may still go along with the overt sentimentality, but from here on the verisimilitude of this pseudo-report diminishes – since sheep do not usually share the bread and cups of their owners. When the text adds – "and lies in his lap", some ears may prick up at the suggestion of bestial sex, but the prophet immediately calms his audience – "and she was to him like a daughter".

To his camouflage mechanism, Nathan adds an anonymous traveler, a mute participant, a seemingly superfluous character, who in fact helps to focus attention on David's own hospitality in inviting Uriah to a feast. Nathan emphasizes this element through thrice repeating the verb 'to come'. Just as criminals can often be sentimental, David too reacts strongly to this rather overstated story. Moving elegantly from the third person to "You are the Man", following David's indignation as well as impulsive sentence, Nathan needs only to tie up a few more loose ends and supply the precise explication. He details the discrepancy between all that God has *given* David and what David *took* for himself. Thus the sheep connects with "the women of thy lord/master in thy lap", whereas here David is presented as Uriah's master. Bath-sheba was previously an almost sexual image who lay in her master's lap, and now – in David's. The age-old connection between food and sexual consumption is quite explicit.

The third analogy – Nathan's prophecy – now makes its appearance. It is addressed to the future, rather than the past, forecasting grim prospects in David's life. The status of 'play-within-a-play' in this section is less clear-cut, but the prophecy does serve as dramatic anticipation. The future will soon be concretized outside the structural framework of this particular play and will involve a much larger parade of characters and events, of which this play too forms a major section. Certain acts bear consequences for many generations. Furthermore, Nathan's prophecy realizes the fable told previously, and explicitly establishes the internal/external metaphor. The motifs of *house* and *sword*, the women 'in your lap', the double murder of Uriah – physically and morally, the punishment of not only killing the child, but of David's sufferering beforehand – all these explicit issues have been implied in David's sins. Nathan draws the punishment from the sin itself, by killing the child, the flesh and blood fruit of the sin.

Joab's analogy was subtle but too premature to lead to David's conversion. Nathan's play-within-a-play is fairly simple (but in no way simplistic), funny and efficient. The trap encourages the assumption that David's was a *crime passionnel* rather than a Machiavellian plot; since it is based on the king's notorious impulsiveness as well as his moral reflex. Nathan activates a moral lever on an uncorrupted facet in David's character. He breaks through his blindness and insensitivity with an ethical tactic. Now the light dawns on the sinner, who admits – "I have sinned to God". One could ask – why 'sinned to *God*' rather than to Uriah; but the answer to this question has already been given, when David explains his severe punishment planned for the imaginary rich man – "because he had no *pity*".

Offstage, Human Consciousness and Divine Presence

The play of David and Bath-sheba reveals the dominance of a divine value-system which hovers above the text, sometimes explicit in it and always implied: "The thing that David did was evil in the eyes of God", and Nathan's wrath is poured upon David in the name of God. David prays to God and says "I shall go to him". God then bestows his love and acceptance upon the second child born.

God's role in the Bible, and in this piece in particular, certainly needs no further explanation in this context. God's presence entails an absolute moral standard, an ultimate demand for conversion to belief in Him and His laws and, on a different level, an interesting relativization of human behavior. The text sends out many feelers to the God beyond it, and one must therefore examine the limits of Divine unattainability, as well as the divine sparks of the human psyche, in dramatic and theatrical terms.

Because theatre is an immediate, live and present medium, using many 'languages', its *indeterminacies* should also be dealt with in medium-oriented terms. The theatrical equivalent of a literary indeterminacy is *offstage*. *Offstage* can be described as the dark halo uniquely encircling each and every performance, dependent on the particular activation of all the theatrical elements, which are *never* quite the same, audience included.[17] It is from and to offstage that characters, sets, events – and especially 'messages' – come and go. The stage is activated from 'there' and intensely communicates its own *here and now* with the offstage correctives of *then and there*. Offstage in the David and Bath-sheba play is designed, predominantly, as the 'dwelling' of God, perhaps even in the heart of the hero.

Nevertheless, offstage is also well established here in 'technically' theatrical terms. The prologue first concentrates on the area that will retroactively influence how the main events, dramatically perceived, will take place. The fervent offstage war activity is juxtaposed with the onstage tranquility. Closing in on David in his house, Jerusalem slides into offstage, as does David's house itself when Bath-sheba is in focus. A similar fading of stage location takes place when David lies in mourning. However, there is no dramatic penetration *into* Bath-sheba's house, neither by David nor by Uriah. Unlike Rabah, it remains throughout an offstage location, uninvaded.

The intensive movement of messengers draws attention to the offstage spaces between the dramatic locations. The messengers seem to fade out on the physical/metaphoric verge of stage/offstage and further activate the spectators' imagination to direct the *mise-en-scène* to which the messengers have lead them in their own heads and hearts. In an actual performance the decision must be made whether – and how – to show (or sound) other places than David's house – Jerusalem, etc. It is always in the light of the *other* that the staged location is evaluated. A hierarchy of spaces is thus created under the ultimate dominance of God, in and out of His House. Judged according to textual borders, there is a difference between Nathan, for example, who goes to his house but vanishes on the threshold, and David, who goes to God's house to worship. David is followed *into* the house which is presented as an *on* stage location.

The most important offstage *characters* are the two infants. Children are stage favorites and sometimes even more so in their absence. These two children, conceived and born within the time frame of the plot, are the object of many possible projections by author, characters and audience. It may be assumed that whereas God loved Solomon Yedidya (= friend of God), David favored the first but dead child. Babies, in their practical but mainly conceptually justified absence, create an immense theatrical gap, yearning to be filled by the audience, who thus become more involved and more committed to the play.

Another manifestation of offstage is detectable in the allusions to

Thebez and "One City". These offstage locations, once properly under-stood by the protagonist, do not really happen 'out there' but, rather, 'in here', in David's soul. Offstage hence addresses itself to the human consciousness and conscience as its authentic target.

One amazing verbal offstage notion is the word *davar* (a thing; linked also with the Hebrew word for *dibur* [talking]). The dramatic shift occurs when David internalizes (God's creative, performative, word or *thing*). The word appears in Uriah's speech and in Joab's; David encourages the messenger by saying "let not this thing . . . ", and God finds the 'thing' David did as evil. David, in his reaction to the Ewe fable uses the word; and so does Nathan, a number of times, in his scathing sermon to David. The elders in David's house ask him about 'this thing' he did.

'This thing' is used to express many possible interpretations: as David's sin which is tactfully avoided and circumscribed in words; as an expression of hubris; as lying with a woman; and as a major, national and perhaps universal sin as well as punishment in Nathan's speech.[18]

David learns a hard lesson, compatible with the gravity of his sins. He is shown at his physical and mental peak, from which no further material advancement or external achievements can be made, and indeed the plot leads David to blindness and to a severe moral fall, later to be followed by a spiritual opening of the eyes and a more profound insight. It offers a superb example of the gap between the seeing of the eyes and the seeing of the heart. When he says "I shall go to him, and he will not return to me", David recognizes the final phase of offstage. The deeper he delves into his own consciousness, the more he succeeds in internalizing offstage, as the present 'form' of God's will. He learns from within himself that (this) *stage*, metaphorically speaking, is only a short and painful section of a much larger span of times, spaces and events. This enables him to do the one and only truly humane act in the play – to go and comfort the woman who only now, when he has returned to his true self, becomes his wife.

"The bible works as an anti-myth . . . and deals with one thing only: the status of man in front of God . . . and you can teach bible only according to its own elementary principles."[19] In the biblical text about King David this basic assumption is clearly seen in the relationship between the 'staged' events and the offstage presence that really matters. A certain frail and short-lived human solution is achieved only when 'this thing' is fully understood.

Notes

Introduction

1 Yair Hoffman, *Aspects of Modern Biblical Criticism*, Broadcast University, Israel, 1998, p. 39.
2 Uriel Simon, *The Status of the Bible in Israeli Society*, Tel Aviv: Orna Hess, 1999.
3 Yeshayahu Leibowitz, 'Between Job and Sophocles', *Mahanayim* (1967): 112.
4 Baruch Kurtzweil, *In Combat with Jewish Values*, Tel Aviv and Jerusalem: Schocken, 1970, pp. 3–26.
5 Shimon Levy, *The Altar and the Stage*, Tel Aviv: Or'Am,1992, p. 8.
6 E. R. Dodds, *The Greeks and the Irrational*, Berkeley: University of California Press,1966, pp. 1–27.
7 Karl Jaspers, *Ueber das Tragische*, Muenchen: Piper, 1958, p. 16.
8 John Barton (ed.), *Companion to Biblical Interpretation*, Cambridge: Cambridge University Press, 1998, p. 1.
9 Clifford Geertz, 'Deep Plays: Notes on the Balinese Cockfight', in *Interpretation of Cultures*, New York: Basic Books, 1973, pp. 412–53.
10 Victor Turner, *From Ritual to Theatre*, *Performing Arts Journal* (New York, 1982): 89–10.
11 Richard Schechner, *Environmental Theater*, New York: Hawthorn Books, 1973.
12 David Cole, *The Theatrical Event*, Middletown, Conn.: Wesleyan University Press, 1975.
13 Christopher Innes, *Holy Theatre*, Cambridge: Cambridge University Press, 1984.
14 Eli Rozik, 'Mythical Thought: From Holy Scriptures to Drama', *Assaph* 12 (1996): 82.
15 Peter Brook, *The Empty Space*, New York: Discus Books/Avon, 1969, p. 38.
16 Erika Fischer-Lichte, 'Returning the Gaze', in *The Shadow and the Gaze of Theatre*, Iowa: University of Iowa Press, 1997, pp. 221ff.
17 Marvin Carlson, *Performance*, London and New York: Routledge, 1996, p. 188??.
18 Meir Sternberg, *The Poetics of Biblical Narrative*, Bloomington: Indiana University Press, 1987.
19 Robert Alter, *The Art of Biblical Narrative*, New York: Basic Books, 1981; and Robert Alter, *The World of Biblical Literature*, New York: Basic Books, 1992.

20 Uriel Simon, *Reading Prophetic Narratives*, Jerusalem: The Biblical Encyclopedia Library and Bialik Institute, 1997.

21 Nisan Ararat, *Drama in the Bible*, Jerusalem: World Centre for Bible, 1997, p. 2.

22 Mieke Bal, "Dealing/With/Women; Daughters in the Book of Judges", in Alice Bach (ed.), *Women in the Hebrew Bible*, New York and London: Routledge, 1999, p. 317.

23 Jack Miles, *God: A Biography*, New York: Vintage Books, 1996, p. 395.

24 Alice Bach (ed.), *Women in the Hebrew Bible*, New York and London: Routledge, 1999.

25 One of the first Israeli anthologies is Israel Zmora (ed.), *Women in the Bible*, Tel Aviv: Mahbarot Le'Sifrut, 1964, including a useful concordance.

Part I *Samuel's Initiation: On the Possibility of Biblical Theatre*

1 Lord Raglan, *The Hero, A Study in Tradition, Myth, and Drama*, New York: Vintage Books, 1956, pp. 141ff. See also Joseph Campbell, *The Hero with a Thousand Faces*, in Bollingen Series XVII, New Jersey: Princeton University Press, 1973, pp. 30ff.

2 A thorough and insightful literary analysis of Samuel's 'initiation' can be found in Uriel Simon, *Reading Prophetic Narratives*, in *The Biblical Encyclopedia Library*, Jerusalem and Ramat Gan: The Bialik Institue and Bar-Ilan University, 1997, pp. 1–56.

3 This is one of the reasons why Samuel's stature was compared to Moses's. See Moshe Garsiel, *The First Book of Samuel, A Literary Study of Comparative Structures, Analogies and Parallels*, Ramat Gan: Revivim, 1983, pp. 46–7.

4 Some of the notions of 'Dramatic Times' used here follow Itamar Even-Zohar, 'Correlative Positive and Correlative Negative Time in Strindberg's The Father and Dream Play', *Hasifrut* I (1968–9): 3–4, 538–68.

5 Ibid., 543.

6 Following some of the distinctions of Michael Issacharoff, 'Space and Reference in Drama', *Poetics Today* 2, no. 3 (1987): 212 ff., regarding architectonic, dramatic and designed spaces.

7 Gaston Bachelard, *The Poetics of Space*, Boston: Beacon Press, 1964.

8 Meir Sternberg, 'Language, World and Perspective in Biblical Narrative Art: Free Indirect Discourse and Models of Covert Penetration', *Hasifrut* 32 (1983): 88–131.

9 Gloria Sheintuch and Uziel Mali, 'Towards an Illocutionary Analysis of Dialogue in the Bible', *Hasifrut* 30–1 (1981): 70–5.

10 Keir Elam, *The Semiotics of Theatre and Drama*, London and New York: Methuen, 1980, pp. 156 ff.

11 Joshua Trachtenberg, *Jewish Magic and Superstition*, New York: Atheneum, 1974, pp. 117 ff.

12 John Archibald Wheeler, 'Creation and Observation', *Mahshavot* 44, (August 1976): 80–8.

13 See Shimon Levy, *Samuel Beckett's Self-referential Drama, The Three I's*, London: Macmillan, 1990, pp. 48–57.

Part II Female Presentations, Oppressed and Liberated

1 The Concubine in Gibea

1. J. Cheryl Exum, 'Plotted, Shot and Painted', Sheffield Academic Press, *Journal for the Study of the Old Testament, Supplement Series* 215 (1996): 9.
2. Compare with Alice Bach, 'Rereading the Body Politics', Alice Basch (ed.), in *Women in the Hebrew Bible*, New York and London: Routledge, 1999, pp. 389–401. (With an excellent bibliography.)
3. Mieke Bal indulges in a lengthy explanation of the verse, then of the entire story in *Death and Dissymmetry*, Chicago and London: The University of Chicago Press, 1988, pp. 80–93.
4. Compare with Athalya Brenner, *The Israelite Woman (Social role and literary type in biblical narrative)*, Sheffield: Sheffield Academic Press, 1994.
5. Bal discusses 'cutting speech-acts' in this context, See Mieke Bal, *Death and Dussymmetry*, Chicago and London: The University of Chicago Press, 1988, pp. 231–4.
6. Meir Sternberg, *The Poetics of Biblical Narrative*, Bloomington: Indiana University Press, 1987, p. 238.

2 Deborah: Anti-feminism in Text and Stage Directions

1. Frank Polak, *Biblical Narrative (Aspects of Art and Design)*, Jerusalem and Ramat Gan: The Biblical Encyclopedia Library, Bialik Institute and Bar Ilan University, p. 123.
2. Robert Alter, *The World of Biblical Literature*, New York: Basic Books, 1991, p. 43.
3. Meir Sternberg, *The Poetics of Biblical Narrative*, Bloomington: Indiana University Press, 1987, p. 283.
4. Shamai Gelander, *Art and Idea in Biblical Narrative*, Tel Aviv: Hakibbutz Hameuchad, 1997, p. 56.
5. Compare with Susan Niditch, 'Eroticism and Death in the Tale of Jael', in Alice Bach, *Women in the Hebrew Bible*, New York and London: Routledge, 1999, pp. 305–13.
6. Adin Steinsaltz, *Women in the Bible*, Tel Aviv: Broadcast University, Ministry of Defense, 1983.

3 Tamar: Acting out a Role Imposed

1. An extensive analysis, with about 700 biblical and post-biblical references to the Tamar story can be found in Avigdor Shinan and Yair Zakovitz, *The Story of Judah and Tamar*, Jerusalem: The Hebrew University, 1992.
2. Bloom maintains that his feminine J has a particular soft spot for Tamar. See Harold Bloom, *The Book of J*, New York: Grove and Weidenfeld, 1990, p. 32.
3. Mieke Bal, *Lethal Love* (Feminist Literary Readings of Biblical Love Stories), Bloomington and Indianapolis: Indiana University Press, 1987, pp. 95–6.
4. Robert Alter, *The Art of Biblical Narrative*, New York: Basic Books, 1981, p. 4.

5   Compare with Phyllis Bird, 'The Harlot as Heroine', Alice Bach (ed.), *Women in the Hebrew Bible*, New York and London: Routledge, 1999, p. 102.

4 Ruth: the Shrew-ing of the Tame

1   About 25 different playscipts are available, 10 of them by some leading literary figures. See Avraham Yaari, *The Hebrew Play* (A Bibliography), Jerusalem: Ha'Noar veHehalutz, 1956, p. 169.
2   A thorough textual analysis and a different, literary division is offered in Yair Zakovitz, *Ruth, Introduction and Commentary*, Tel Aviv and Jerusalem: Am Oved and Magnes Prees, 1990, p. 4. See also Athalya Brenner, *Ruth and Naomi (Literary, Stylistic and Linguistic Studies in the Book of Ruth)*, Haifa: Haifa University, Sifriat Poalim and Hakibbutz Hameuchad, 1988.
3   I beg to differ with Frank Polak, *Biblical Narrative, Aspects of Art and Design, The Biblical Encyclopedia Library*, Jerusalem: Bialik Institute, 1994, pp. 133–5.
4   Biblical speech-acts have been given a lot of attention. See for example Mieke Bal, *Death and Dissymmetry*, Chicago and London: The University of Chicago Press, 1988, p. 233.
5   Danna Nolan Fewell and David M. Gunn, '"A Son Is born to Naomi!" Literary Allusions and Interpretation in the Book of Ruth', in Alice Bach, *Women in the Bible*, New York and London: Routledge, 1999, p. 233.
6   Northrop Frye, *The Great Code*, Toronto: Academic Press Canada, 1982, p. 155.
7   For laws concerning the 'redeemer', see, for example Number 25:25–9.
8   Ilana Pardes, *Countertraditions in the Bible: A Feminist Approach*, Tel Aviv: Hakibbutz Hameuchad, 1996, pp. 35–50.

5 Esther and the Head of the Sceptre

1   Mordechai, as a dramatic figure who dwells mostly in offstage, receives a fine dramatic description: "shrouded in darkness beyond the gate of the palace while the feasting goes on within, a feasting to which he is totally indifferent and from which he is totally cut off." Harold Fisch, *Poetry with a Purpose: Biblical Poetics and Interpretation*, Bloomington: Indiana University Press, 1988, p. 12.
2   Compare with Robert Alter, *The World of Biblical Literature*, New York: Basic Books, 1992, p. 32.
3   Nisan Ararat sees the *Book of Esther* indeed as a genre rejected from the Old Testament: A satire. *Drama in the Bible*, Jerusalem: World Bible Centre, 1997, p. 382.
4   Compare the present approach with Esther Fuchs, 'Status and Role of Female Heroines in the Biblical Narrative', Alice Bach, *Women in the Hebrew Bible*, New York and London: Routledge, 1999, p. 81.

Part III *Women and Men, Physics and Metaphysics*

6 "The Voice of my Beloved Knocketh"

1   *Part I:*
    (a) eyes – like doves
         hair – like a flock of goats
         teeth – like a flock of ewes
         lips – like a threat of scarlet
         temples – like a piece of pomegranate
         neck – like David's tower
         jewels – shields of mighty men
         breasts – two fawns
         in v. 6 – until the day be cool and the shadows flee
         mountain of myrrh
         hill of frankincense
    (b) mountain tops (Lebanon, Amana, etc.)   (c) thine ointments
         lions' dens   lips – as honeycomb
         mountains of the leopards   tongue – milk + honey
         thou has ravished my heart   garment – Lebanon
    (d) a locked garden
         a locked spring (or wave)
         a sealed fountain
         thy shoots – an orchard
         fruit
         spikenard
         spikenard and saffron   "with all
         calamus   the chief
         cinnamon   spices"
         trees of frankincense
         myrrh
         aloes
         a fountain of gardens/a well of living waters/flowing from Lebanon

    Part 2:
    (a) blow upon my garden
         its spices may flow out
         let my beloved come into his garden
         he will eat his precious fruits.
    (b) I am come into my garden
         I have gathered my myrrh with my spice
         I have eaten my honeycomb with my honey
         I have drunk my wine with my milk
    (c) (Eat, O friends, drink, yea, drink to intoxication, O lover)
         [Perhaps not an image]

    Part 3:
    (a) the voice of my beloved knocketh
         my dove
         my head is filled with dew | Are these indeed
         my locks with the drops of night | images?

And my heart was moved
My hands dropped with myrrh
Myrrh passed through my fingers
My soul left me
(b) and (c) The images are conspicuous by their absence!
(d)   most prominent among ten thousand
    his head is as most fine gold
    his locks black as raven
    his body as polished ivory set with sapphired
    his thighs as pillars of marble set upon gold
    his aspect like Lebanon
    excellent as the cedar
    eyes, like doves
    cheeks, as banks of sweet herbs
    lips, lilies dropping liquid myrrh
    his hands, rods of gold set with beryl

2 IV 1   thou art fair
    (hinekh yafa)

    2   all are paired   ve   sh,k,l
                          and all of her *(sheh'*
                          kulam mat'eemot
                          vesha'kulah)

    3   thy mouth/thy
                                             temple thy tresses
                                           (midbarekh/
                                           rakatekh
                                         tsamatekh)

    4   tower . . . thousand bucklers   l
                          hang all the shields *(migdal . . .*
                          letalpiot elef . . . talui kol
                          shiltei)

    5   thy two breasts like two
                          . . . lilies *(shnei shadayikh*
                          kishnei shoshanim)   sh

    6   the shadowns flee, I will get
                          me to *(hatslalim elekh li el)*   l

    8   with me from   from Lebanon, my bride from l
       Lebanon   Lebanon *(mi Levanon kalah*
       (itee mi   *mi Levanon)*
       Leivanon)

                          look from the top . . .   r,sh
                          (tashuri mirosh . . .)
                          lions from loepards   r

mountains *(arayot mehararei nemerim)*

9   thou has ravished
with one *(libavtini b'ekhad)*
      thine eyes
thy neck
*(eynayikh
tzavaronayikh)*

10 how fair how much
better *(mah yafooh mah
tavooh)*

11   thy lips, O my bride
drop as the honeycomb,
honey and milk are
under thy tongue   n,p,t
*(nofet titofnah siftotayikh
 kala . . . khalav takhat
leshoneikh)*

and the smell of thy
 garments is as the smell
of Lebanon   kh,l
*(vereyakh simlotayikh
kereyakh
Levanon)*

12   a garden shut up is
my sister, my bride   ve   n,l,m
a spring shut up,
a fountain sealed
*(gan na'ul akhott
kala gan na'ul ma'yan
khatum)*

13   si   p,r   orchard pome
granates
precious fruits
spikenard
and saffron
*(pardess rimonim
im pri*

*megadim/kefarim
im neradim)*

14   calamus and   k,n
cinnamon
(kaneh ve'kinamon)

15   a fountain of gardens m,n
      a well of living waters
      and flowing streams
      from Lebanon
      (ma'yan ganim be'er mayim khayim
      ve'nozlim min Levanon)

16   ... O north wind and come
       ... blow ... that the spices may
      flow out ... and eat his
      precious fruits
      (... tsafon uvo'ee ... vesamav;
      yavoh ... ve'yokhal ... me'gadav)

V 1   I am come into my garden my
      sister, my bride
      I have gathered myrrh with my spice;
      I have eaten my honeycomb with my
      honey;
      I have drunk my wine with my milk.
      Eat, O friends; drink, yea drink
      to intoxication, O beloved si
      (bati le'gani akhoti kala ariti
      mori im besami akhalti ya'ari im
      divshee shatiti yeyni im khalavee
      ikhlu re'im she'tu
      ve'shikru dodim

  2   my beloved knocketh ... d,t
      "open ... my sister, my
      love, my dove,
      my pure one"
      dodi dofek ...
      pitkhi ... akhoti, ra'ayati yonati
      tamati

  3 how *(ekhakha)* I have put off my coat ... t
      (pashateti kutanti ...)

  5 myrrh
    (mor)   h I sought him/
                I could not
                find him
                (bikashtitu/
                lo metsa'tihu)

  7   found me,
                smote me
                wounded me
                metsa'uni,

hikuni
petsa'uni)

9	what is thy beloved more than another beloved *(ma dodekh mi'dod)*			
12		washed with milk *(rokhetset b'khalav)*	kh	
13		his lips . . . drop liquid myrrh *(siftotav . . . notfot mor over)*	t r	his hands are *(yadav zahav)*
14		beryl . . . ivory *(tarshish . . . eshet shen)*	sh	
15		thighs . . . marble *(shokav . . . shesh)*		
16	this is my beloved this is my friend *(zeh dodi, zeh re'I)*			sweet/lovely *(mamtakim/ makhmadim)*

3 Meir Sternberg, 'Structure of Repetition in Biblical Narrative', *Hasifrut* 25, Tel Aviv (1977): 109–38.
4 Athalya Brenner, *The Israelite Woman* (Social Role and Literary Type in Biblical Narrative), Sheffield: Sheffield Academic Press, 1994, pp. 46–50.
5 Paul Ricoeur, 'Biblical Hermeneutics', *Semeia* 4, Scholars Press, Missoula MT (1975): 35 ff.
6 J. L. Austin, *How To Do Things with Words*.
7 Mieke Bal, *Death and Dissymmetry*, Chicago and London: The University of Chicago Press, 1988, p. 132.

7 The Educational Theatre of Proverbs

1 Carol A. Newsom, 'Woman and the Discourse of Patriarchal Wisdom', Alice Bach, *Women in the Hebrew* Bible, New York and London: Routledge, 1999, p. 95.
2 Adin Steinsaltz, for one, argues that Proverbs does not treat women as mere 'toys'. Chapter 7, at least, proves that the text indeed does much worse. See *Women in the Bible*, Tel Aviv: Broadcast University and Ministry of Defence, 1983, p. 96.

Part IV *Prophets as Performers*

8 Elisha: Religion, Sex and Miracles

1   Alexander Rofe, *The Prophetic Stories*, Jerusalem: Magnes Press, 1983, p. 48.
2   For a comprehensive and profound literary analysis of this story see Uriel Simon, *Reading Prophetic Narrativs*, The Biblical Encyclopedia Library, Jerusalem and Ramat Gan: Bialik Institute and Bar Ilan University,1997, pp. 97–316.
3   Meir Sternberg, *The Poetics of Biblical Narrative*, Bloomington: Indiana University Press, 1987, p. 310.
4   Shimon Bar Efrat notes on the deviation from accepted style, in the Shunamite's answer to Elish. *The Art of Narration in the Bible*, Tel Aviv: Sifriat Poalim, 1984, p. 91.

9 Jonah: a Quest Play

1   Amos Funkenstein, 'A Prophet Who is No Prophet', *Haaretz* (no date).
2   Israel David, 'Purpose and Genre in the Book of Jonah: Basic Considerations' and Dov Noy, 'International Motifs in the Jonah Story' – two papers given at Ben-Gurion University at the Jonah Day Conference, 25 April 1996.
3   Nisan Ararat, *Drama in the Bible*, Jerusalem: World Bible Centre, 1997, pp. 367–85.
4   Meir Sternberg, *The Poetics of Biblical Narrative*, Bloomington: Indiana University Press, 1987, pp. 318–20.
5   Robert Alter, *The Art of Biblical Narrative*, New York: Basic Books, 1981, p. 33.
6   Norman Simms, 'Belly Laughs: A Look at the Wit and Wisdom of Jonah', *Mentalities* 12 (1997): 1–2.

10 Ezkiel: the Holy Actor

1   S. R. Driver, *An Introduction to the Literature of the Old Testament*, Cleveland and New York: Meridian Books, 1967, p. 513.
2   Dunbar H. Ogden (ed.), *The Play of Daniel: Critical Essays*, Michigan: Western Michigan University, Kalamazoo, 1996, pp. 11ff.
3   Alan Reid, *Theatre and Everyday Life, An Ethics of Performance*, London and New York: Routledge, 1993, p. 194.
4   Bruce Wilshire, *Role Playing and Identity (The Limits of Theatre as Metaphor)*, Bloomington and Indianapolis: Indiana University Press, 1991, p. 245.
5   Jacques Derrida, *Writing and Difference*, Chicago: Chicago University Press, 1978, p. 325, fn. 14.

Part V *Leaders: A Theatrical Gaze*

11 Moses in Flesh and Spirit

1   Sarah Halperin, 'The Tragic Aspect in Moses's Life', *Bamah* 86 (1981): 12–23.

2 Yeshayahu Leibovitz, *Judaism, The Jewish People and the State of Israel*, Jerusalem and Tel Aviv: Schocken, 1975, pp. 182ff.

12 Jehu's Bloody Show

1 Polak sees in the two intertwined series of events a perfect example of combining two 'sequences' in biblical narrative. See Frank Polak, *Biblical Narrative, Aspects of Art And Design*, in *The Biblical Encyclopedia*, Jerusalem and Ramar Gan: Bialik Institue and Bar Ilan University, 1994, p. 164.
2 Adin Steinsaltz, *Figures in the Bible*, Tel Aviv: Broadcast University and Ministry of Defense, 1984, p. 94.
3 Meir Sternberg, *The Poetics of Biblical Narrative*, Bloomington: Indiana University Press, 1987, p. 38.

13 The (Unabridged) Play of David and Batsheba

1 Yair Zakovitz, *David: From Shepard to Messiah* (A Biography), Jerusalem: Yad Ben-Zvi, 1995.
2 This article has been inspired by Sternberg and Perry's article 'The King Through Ironic Eyes' in *Hasifrut*, vol. 1, no. 2, (summer 1968): 263–92. An English version can be found in Meir Sterberg, *The Poetics of Biblical Narrative*, Bloomington: Indiana University Press, 1987, pp. 190–221.
3 Ibid.
4 Bjorn Krondorfer (ed.), *Body and Bible*, Philadelphia: Trinity Press International, 1992, p. 4.
5 In winter 1987 I directed a theatre workshop in Kibbutz Giv'at Brenner, where some 70 actors, musicians, playwrights and designers finally mounted the entire 'play', verbatim.
6 In Hebrew drama alone there are about 25 versions-adaptations to this and other biblical David stories, among them Cohen, *King of Israel*; Ring, *David and Joab*; Eliraz, *The Bear*; Galai, *Uriah's Story*; Shabtai, *A Crown on The Head*. See also Avraham Yaari, *The Hebrew Play* (Bibliography), Jerusalem, 1956, p. 155.
7 Sternberg and Perry, The King . . . , p. 226 (note).
8 Comparisons in many respects mentioned here can be made with characters in world drama such as King Lear, Hamlet, Oedipus, Agamemnon. See also Arthur Lovejoy, *The Great Chain of Being*, Boston: Harvard University Press, 1933.
9 The King . . . , pp. 275ff.
10 Michael Issacharoff, 'Space and Reference in Drama', *Poetics Today*, vol. 2, no. 3, (spring 1981): 212.
11 J. P. Fokkelman notices the spatial specifications of the story in his *Narrative Art and Poetry in the Books of Samuel* (vol. 1), Assen: Van Gorcum, 1981, pp. 51ff.
12 Gaston Bachelard, *The Poetics of Space*, Boston: Beacon Press, 1969.
13 For the sake of precision, it ought to be mentioned that Thebez had been conquered and only one "tower" was in it, defended by a woman (*Judges* 9).
14 Herta Schmid, *Strukturalistische Dramentheorie*, Kronberg TS, 1973.
15 See I *Sam.* 18:4 where David changes his full attire with Jonathan.

16 The King . . . , p. 283.
17 Shimon Levy, *Samuel Beckett's Self-referential Drama, The Three I's*, London: Macmillan, 1990, pp. 48–57.
18 Absence is 'presentified' also with the world 'halo' (= is it not that . . .), implying a rhetorical question, assuming the partner is supposed to know the answer, like "is it not Bath-sheba"; "Don't you come from a long way . . . "; "don't you know that they shoot from the top of the wall?" etc.
19 From an interview with Prof. Yeshayahn Leibowitz, *Zomet Hasharon*, 28 September 1990, p. 41.

Index